'A thoughtful and entertaining journey into the world of diplomacy. A must-read for anyone interested in how it really works or aspiring to work as a diplomat.'
Baroness Cathy Ashton, *former High Representative of the EU*

'A vital guide. Diplomacy is sometimes glamorous, often painstakingly slow, but Nick Westcott reminds us that it is the vital hinge that keeps doors and windows open between countries. And that's never been more important than now as a generation of politicians try to slam doors shut.'
Lord Mark Malloch-Brown, *former UN Deputy Secretary-General*

'Nick Westcott deftly exhibits the mechanics of diplomacy. His eye is acute and original, and, valuably, he can draw on the experience of both professional diplomat and seasoned academic: a must-read for anyone who wants to understand the world today.'
Zeinab Badawi, *Journalist, filmmaker, writer and President of SOAS*

'This book provides a precious insight into what diplomacy is today, in real life, with accurate and sharp descriptions, thoughtful analysis, and a style that makes it a pleasure to read. Nick shares stories, lessons learned and wisdom that are bringing us to the heart of an exceptional practitioner's experience: that of serving for decades one of the best national diplomatic services, and the European Union's unique "external action service", in years of turbulent transitions. A must-read for all those interested in how diplomacy works in real life!'
Federica Mogherini, *Rector of College of Europe, Bruges and former EU High Representative for Foreign Affairs (2015–20) and Italian Foreign Minister*

'Anyone working in international relations needs to understand how it gets done in practice, and this book is a practical, readable and wonderfully witty guide to the diplomatic arts, illustrated with the kind of observations that can only come from deep experience of the whole range of diplomatic activities.'
Bronwen Maddox, *Director and Chief Executive of Chatham House*

How to be a Diplomat

With the international system entering a period of extreme flux, diplomacy has never been more important, and how to do it successfully more relevant. This book considers what diplomacy is, its purpose, rules, structures, how it is done, what it involves, the skills required, the impact of technological and societal changes, and how diplomats ensure success. In short, it is about handling people and problems, particularly in other countries, without coming to blows. Drawing on the author's extensive personal experience, this readable volume focuses on the practical problems diplomats regularly face, such as negotiating an agreement, working with a hostile government, dealing with dual nationals imprisoned for political reasons, looking after local staff, engaging with civil society, responding to humanitarian crises, and knowing what to do if a war breaks out on your doorstep. This is an invaluable training resource for anyone working at the coal face of international relations and a guide to how to navigate, operate, behave, negotiate and survive diplomatic life. Such diplomatic skills will be of wider relevance in many walks of life – international, commercial, bureaucratic, even family.

Nicholas Westcott is Professor of Practice in Diplomacy at SOAS University of London and a Visiting Fellow of the Oxford Martin School, University of Oxford. He worked previously as a British diplomat for the Foreign Office and the European Union.

How to be a Diplomat

Nicholas Westcott

R Routledge
Taylor & Francis Group

LONDON AND NEW YORK

Designed cover image: Getty Images

First published 2026
by Routledge
4 Park Square, Milton Park, Abingdon, Oxon OX14 4RN

and by Routledge
605 Third Avenue, New York, NY 10158

Routledge is an imprint of the Taylor & Francis Group, an informa business

British Library Cataloguing-in-Publication Data
A catalogue record for this book is available from the British Library

ISBN: 978-1-032-83617-1 (hbk)
ISBN: 978-1-032-87584-2 (pbk)
ISBN: 978-1-003-53343-6 (ebk)

DOI: 10.4324/9781003533436

Typeset in Times New Roman
by Apex CoVantage, LLC

For Anna and Finn, and in memory of Miriam, who accompanied me, and for Birgitte who accompanies still

Contents

Preface and acknowledgements

When I retired as a diplomat in 2018, I started giving a couple of lectures to the SOAS Masters course on Global Diplomacy about what it meant to be a diplomat in practice: what does a diplomat actually do all day, and why? When I retired for the second time (from the Royal African Society) in 2023 it grew to a four-lecture series. Looking for books to recommend to the students I found precious few: plenty on diplomacy written by academics; the weighty tome of Sir Ernest Satow's *Diplomatic Practice*; and (way too) many memoirs by eminent diplomats, some more readable than others, from each of which a few nuggets might be gleaned. But no single, readable volume I could offer them to say, 'There, that's what a diplomat is and what they do.' Hence this book.

I need to make two caveats. Though it draws on my own experience, it is *not* a memoir in disguise. I cite examples I was personally involved with where they are relevant to the point, but draw evidence more widely from the literature and the experience of others. It is written from a British and European perspective because I have been a British and European diplomat, but it endeavours to be of relevance and use to those working in international affairs from every continent. If I dwell as much on the challenges as on the excitements of diplomatic life, it is because that is when you need guidance and preparation. It is better to know in advance than run into the problems when you are not expecting them.

Secondly, it is not a disquisition on the nature of diplomacy. There are plenty of more detailed and learned accounts of the history and the theory; my priority is the practice of diplomacy in the world as we find it today. Nevertheless, as it is what diplomats do, it is important to have some understanding of what diplomacy is. I therefore set out my own views on this in Chapter 2, reflecting practical experience as much as theoretical reading. I have tried to avoid getting entangled in academic debates on, for example, what is or is not 'old', 'new' or 'modern diplomacy', 'digital diplomacy' or even 'diffused diplomacy'. The *forms* of diplomacy are constantly evolving, as is the international context within which it takes place. But the *substance* and the core *skills* required remain largely the same.

The Foreign Office I joined in 1982 is very accurately portrayed in Geoffrey Moorhouse's entertaining book *The Diplomats: The Foreign Office Today* (1977). But it reads now like ancient history. Some things, like human nature and the way hierarchies behave, remain the same. But so much else has changed dramatically.

This book therefore has an ulterior purpose. Diplomacy has existed since humans first developed collective societies; but it has, like those societies themselves, evolved constantly ever since. The diplomat therefore needs to be aware of and able to respond to the social, political, organisational, technological and climatic changes that are shaping global society. If anything, the diplomat needs to adapt faster than others, to anticipate what is coming down the track and be prepared to deal with it. In theory, politicians do the same, but in practice – as we see at the time of this book going to print – many are as happy looking backwards as forward, and turning a blind eye to inconvenient truths. The diplomat cannot afford to do that, even if challenging the powers-that-be makes life, and the job, uncomfortable at times. The truth is that you never know what will happen next: the best you can do is be honest about the risks and be prepared to respond swiftly.

The growing turbulence in world affairs, the weakening of multilateral institutions that countries have used to mediate their disagreements, and the spread of conflict rather than consensus over how to deal with the world's problems, as well as the accelerating rate of change, are all making more work rather than less for diplomats. Diplomacy is more needed than ever, even if it is ever more challenging to do. So more, and better, diplomats will be needed if we are to avoid young people being drafted into the military, and young children and the elderly suffering all the consequences of war that we see currently in parts of eastern Europe, the Middle East and Africa. Diplomats will also increasingly be needed not just in foreign ministries, but in every walk of life from business to religion. So I hope this book will prove useful to everyone.

* * *

In the course of 35 years as a diplomat and six years of teaching about diplomacy, I have acquired many debts.

To all my former colleagues in the Foreign Office (then the FCO, now the FCDO) and other ministries across Whitehall I want to express my thanks for their friendship, companionship and cooperation, and my admiration for the job they do. Public service has not always received the respect or recognition that it deserves – certainly not from the media, patchily from politicians, and only occasionally from the public itself. But I have found almost everyone I have worked with over the years public-spirited, collaborative, cheerful, helpful, intelligent and determined to do the best job they can in the public interest. Thank you. The same goes for diplomatic colleagues I have worked with throughout the world, especially in Africa, the Middle East, Asia and the United States, and particularly in the European Union where I laboured, in one form or another, for 12 of those 35 years. Despite the inevitable disagreements on some issues, there was always an underlying mutual respect and solidarity in carrying out the diplomatic work we were all called upon to do.

I am genuinely grateful to the FCO for giving me jobs I was not always expecting but which turned out far more interesting than I could have imagined; and I owe

xii *Preface and acknowledgements*

a particular debt of gratitude to Cathy Ashton and Federica Mogherini for giving me exactly the jobs I did want in the EEAS.

I am equally grateful to many colleagues in academia. It is a very different world, at least in the UK, but I applaud and support the continuing efforts to bring it into closer connection with government. There is great benefit to both from closer collaboration. Colleagues in SOAS have made me very welcome, and I have benefited greatly from the intellectual stimulation and encouragement received from them and friends, teachers and colleagues in Cambridge, Oxford, London, Birmingham, Warwick and Edinburgh. My warmest thanks to everyone.

In writing this book, I am most grateful to Routledge for agreeing to publish it and Robert Soresby as a most supportive and understanding editor. I am particularly grateful for advice, comments, help and inspiration received (wittingly or unwittingly, over the years) from Michael Arthur, Piritta Asunmaa, Zeinab Badawi, Anthony Barker, Jerome Bonnafont, Steve Browning, Robert Cooper, Stefan Dercon, Comfort Ero, Ehab Fawzi, Jo Gauld, Ann Grant, Anji Hunter, Andrew Hyde, Mohamed Ibn Chambas, Michael Jay, Nick Kay, John Kerr, David Lidington, Fiona Lunny, Mark Lyall Grant, Bronwen Maddox, Mark Malloch-Brown, Simon McDonald, David Miliband, Rami Mortada, Chantal Moser, Sayasat Nurbeck, Jonathan Powell, Alex Rondos, Matthew Rycroft, John Sawers, Helga Schmid, Ricardo de Oliveira Soares, Hanna Tetteh, Pierre Vimont, Roger Westbrook and Myles Wickstead.

Finally, my children, Anna and Finn, have been a constant support and inspiration, and my late wife Miriam (who appears occasionally in these pages) contributed more than I can ever express. Above all, I owe a special debt to Birgitte Markussen who has supported me throughout the writing with kindness, food, ideas and much more.

List of illustrations

List of abbreviations

ACP	African, Caribbean and Pacific group
ADB	Asian Development Bank
AfCFTA	African Continental Free Trade Area
AfDB	African Development Bank
AGOA	African Growth and Opportunity Act
AI	Artificial Intelligence
AMISOM	African Union Military Mission in Somalia
APEC	Asia-Pacific Economic Cooperation
ASEAN	Association of South-East Asian States
AU	African Union
BA	British Airways
BAES	British Aerospace Systems
BBC	British Broadcasting Corporation
BRI	Belt and Road Initiative
BRICS	Group of Brazil, Russia, India, China, South Africa
BRICS+	Group of BRICS plus a growing number of other countries
CIO	Chief Information Officer
COP	Conference of the Parties
COREPER	Committee of Permanent Representatives to the EU
CPATPP	Comprehensive and Progressive Agreement on Trans-Pacific Partnership
DFID	Department for International Development
DRC	Democratic Republic of Congo
DUP	Democratic Unionist Party
E3	European Three (France, Germany, United Kingdom)
EAC	East African Community
ECCAS	Economic Community of Central African States
ECHR	European Convention on Human Rights
ECJ	European Court of Justice
ECOWAS	Economic Community of West African States
ECtHR	European Court of Human Rights
EEAS	European External Action Service
EPA	Economic Partnership Agreement

EU	European Union
FAA	Federal Aviation Authority (US)
FAC	Foreign Affairs Council (EU)
FAO	Food and Agriculture Organisation
FCO	Foreign and Commonwealth Office
FCDO	Foreign, Commonwealth and Development Office (from 2020)
G7	Group of Seven
G8	Group of Seven plus Russia
G20	Group of Twenty
G77	Group of Seventy-Seven
GATT	General Agreement on Tariffs and Trade
GCC	Gulf Cooperation Council
HIPC	Highly-Indebted Poor Countries
HRVP	High Representative and Vice-President of the EU for Foreign Policy
IAEA	International Atomic Energy Authority
ICC	International Criminal Court
ICJ	International Court of Justice
ICRC	International Committee of the Red Cross
IFI	International financial institution
IGAD	Intergovernmental Association for Development
ILO	International Labour Organisation
IMF	International Monetary Fund
IMO	International Maritime Organisation
IOM	International Organisation for Migration
IRA	Irish Republican Army
IRGC	Iranian Revolutionary Guard Corps
ISIS	Islamic State in Iraq and Syria
IT	Information technology
ITU	International Telecommunications Union
JFK	John F. Kennedy Airport, New York
LDC	Least developed country
MINUSMA	United Nations Military Mission in Mali
MONUSCO	United Nations Military Mission in Congo
MSF	Médecins Sans Frontières
NAFTA	North American Free Trade Area
NAM	Non-Aligned Movement
NAO	National Audit Office
NATO	North Atlantic Treaty Organisation
NGO	Non-governmental organisation
NYPD	New York Police Department
OECD	Organisation of Economic Cooperation and Development
OIC	Organisation of Islamic States
OSCE	Organisation for Security and Cooperation in Europe
OSF	Open Society Foundations
P5	Five Permanent Members of the Security Council

PA	Palestinian Authority
PLO	Palestine Liberation Organisation
PM	Prime Minister
PUS	Permanent Under-Secretary
PWD	Public Works Department
R2P	Responsibility to Protect
RAS	Royal African Society
RSF	Rapid Support Force
SADC	Southern African Development Community
SAF	Sudan Armed Forces
SCR	Security Council Resolution
SOAS	School of Oriental and African Studies
SRSG	Special Representative of the (UN) Secretary-General
UAE	United Arab Emirates
UN	United Nations
UNDP	United Nations Development Programme
UNEP	United Nations Environmental Programme
UNESCO	United National Educational, Scientific and Cultural Organisation
UNGA	United Nations General Assembly
UNHCR	United Nations High Commissioner for Refugees
UNHRC	United Nations Human Rights Commissioner
UNICEF	United National International Children's Emergency Fund
UNIFIL	United Nations Interim Force in Lebanon
UNMISS	United Nations Mission in South Sudan
UNOCI	United Nations Operation in Cote d'Ivoire
UNRWA	United Nations Relief and Welfare Agency
UNSOM	United Nations Mission to Somalia
US	United States
USMCA	United States-Mexico-Canada Agreement
USTR	United States Trade Representative
VPN	Virtual Private Network
WB	World Bank
WHO	World Health Organisation
WTO	World Trade Organisation

1   What is a diplomat?

Diplomats have always been exotic figures, at least in the popular imagination. They appear to be involved in the highest matters of state, in the most public and the most secret international affairs, and in negotiations on which hang the fate of nations, questions of war and peace, and potentially the lives of thousands. Diplomacy is seen, with reason, as a fascinating, rewarding and even enviable career. No foreign ministry has ever been short of aspiring recruits.

But to be a good diplomat, in whatever field, to make the kind of difference you may aspire to, is not easy. The challenges and obstacles are substantial, the skills required many and various, and the necessary character traits a diverse mixture of solidity and flexibility, knowledge and invention, stoicism and humour, infinite patience and, when necessary, great speed.

This book aims to provide a straightforward guide to what a diplomat does in practice, how to do it well, and how to handle the kinds of challenges that most diplomats face sooner or later. It is intended for all kinds of diplomats, not just for those who want to work for a foreign ministry or an international organisation, but for all those who need to deploy a range of diplomatic skills, whether as businessmen, politicians, soldiers, lobbyists, experts, academics or humanitarians.

Over the past hundred years, physical and virtual improvements in communications have vastly increased the interaction between people and businesses as well as governments around the world. The number of those involved in some form of diplomacy has increased exponentially. The decades ahead will see this trend continue, not because globalisation is an irreversible trend, but because the challenges the world faces will force us to interact more, and the more divided and contested the world becomes, the greater the need for diplomats.

This book has a theme: the practice of diplomacy is not one of immutable norms, customs and practices, nor does it take place within an unchanging institutional structure. It is constantly evolving. True, some aspects of it have remained unchanged since time immemorial because they reflect human nature. But the balance of global power, the institutions that are built around this, the technology we use to run our lives and businesses, the very norms of human society – all are constantly changing. They all impact on how diplomacy is done. So the diplomat too must constantly evolve in response. This book is therefore shooting at a moving target, and tries to identify the skills that *will* be needed as much as those needed in the past.

DOI: 10.4324/9781003533436-1

So what exactly does a diplomat do? To say a diplomat does diplomacy may be true, but not helpful: diplomacy itself is a many-splendoured thing, as we discuss in the next chapter. It might therefore be helpful for a start to distinguish more clearly between the image and the reality of a diplomat's life.

The image

There are many definitions of a diplomat. The dictionary definition specifies (a) an official who represents one country in another and usually works in an embassy, and (b) a person who is skilled at dealing with difficult situations in a way that does not offend people (Cambridge Dictionary, 2024).

Many people have tried to encapsulate it more elegantly. With that characteristic English weakness for puns, the great Elizabethan envoy Sir Henry Wotton described a diplomat as 'an honest man sent to lie abroad for the good of his country', in the sense of 'to lie' being to rest or stay in one place as much as to tell an untruth. More recently, a diplomat has been described as 'someone who tells you to go to Hell with such charm and persuasion that you will look forward to making the trip' (or 'even ask for directions'), attributed to both Winston Churchill and US humorist Caskie Stinnett but probably predating both (Quote Investigator, 2018). It certainly bears out the common use of the term 'to be diplomatic' as implying a quality of persuasion and pacification, whether official or not. In 1984, a BBC documentary on the Foreign Office described British diplomats as like 'members of an antique and mysterious freemasonry' (Jenkins and Sloman, 1985, 22), and more recently Carne Ross condemned it as 'an unaccountable elite' (Ross, 2017). The Bible at least is more charitable: 'Blessed are the peacemakers, for they shall be called the sons of God' (according to Matthew, 5:9).

Since then, sadly, diplomats have had a more mixed reputation. Jokes about them abound: the diplomat is 'a man who thinks twice before saying nothing', 'someone who will lay down your life for his country', or 'someone who puts his cards on the table, but still has some up each sleeve' (Rolland-Piegue, 2018). For George Lichtheim, 'the ideal diplomat is the man who, told that the world is coming to an end, replies that he will draft a report on the matter' (Lichtheim, 1964). Diplomacy itself is often described as the art of 'letting the other side have your own way'. In ancient Greece, envoys were traditionally placed under the protection of the god Hermes, Zeus' herald, who symbolised the qualities of charm, cunning and trickery (Nicolson, 1939, 19). For Stalin, 'a diplomat's words have no relation to actions – otherwise what kind of diplomacy is it? Sincere diplomacy is no more possible than dry water or wooden iron' (Marshall, 1997, 7) – a dictum still respected by some Russian diplomats.

I treasure an old postcard found in a second-hand shop and given me many years ago. Titled 'Le Diplomate', the cartoon depicts a suave diplomat of the old school, elegantly suited and hatted, smoking a cigar and carrying a small attaché case, arriving at a grand house amidst the popping flashbulbs of the waiting press, which he greets with a nonchalant wave of the hand. The same image is encapsulated in W.H. Auden's poem, 'The Embassy', its diplomats floating in ornate surroundings disposing of the lives and fortunes of men through the words they conjure (Auden, 1938, quoted in Fletcher, 2016). This is the diplomat carrying the fate of nations in their hands (or briefcases), privy to the secrets of state and the close adviser of presidents and prime ministers.

Figure 1.1 'Le Diplomate', postcard by Roland Genestre.

Source: in author's possession

This glamorous image was exemplified by the infamous Ferrero-Rocher TV commercial where, amidst an embassy's crystal glasses and chandeliers, a platter of Ferrero Rocher chocolates is passed around by a bow-tied butler: 'Oh Ambassador,' gushes a svelte young guest standing a little too close to her host, 'you really spoil us . . .' It is this supposedly privileged and opulent lifestyle that has turned parts of the press, at least in Britain, against the profession: 'We are as a matter of editorial policy hostile to diplomats', the then political editor of the *Daily Express* told Christopher Meyer when he started his job as the FCO's spokesman in 1984 (Meyer, 2009, 7). This attitude is shared to this day by a number of British tabloids, which never miss the chance to dig up a story of extravagance or scandal among the nation's diplomats.

On the other hand, diplomats have an equally common reputation as devious, duplicitous, untrustworthy and willing to abandon any principle for the sake of striking a dodgy deal, condemning foreign communities to oppression or oblivion if it so suits their national interest for commercial or political gain. Machiavelli, a diplomat himself, wrote about it, Talleyrand epitomised it, and Henry Kissinger, according to his obituaries in 2023, manifested all aspects of diplomatic skill, cynicism and deviousness.

In fiction, diplomats have made far less of a splash than spies: books, films and TV series about the latter outnumber the former by at least ten-to-one. The most common portrayals show diplomats as incompetent, comic or just plain dull. Lawrence Durrell, who knew of what he wrote having served in a mission in the Balkans, satirised the profession mercilessly in *Esprit de Corps* (1957). Graham Greene's *The Honorary Consul* (1973) was both drunk and incapable. John Le Carré's *The Constant Gardener* (2001) describes a British mission in Nairobi in hock to dodgy business interests. The 1940s British film *Carlton-Browne of the FO* caricatured the bumbling idiocy of the Foreign Office's backroom bureaucrats, while the BBC's *An Englishman Abroad* (1983) has a painfully convincing portrait of the casual superciliousness and misogyny of the diplomats in Britain's Moscow Embassy when the actress Carole Browne decided to visit the disgraced spy Guy Burgess in the 1960s. The more recent (and equally excellent) French film *Quai d'Orsay* (2013), based on a comic book of the same name, provides a similarly satirical view of French diplomacy based on an up close and personal observation of the real thing. Most recently, the Netflix series *The Diplomat* (2023), about a US Ambassador to London and her adventures, has a tenuous connection to reality, even if it has successfully raised the profile of the profession. The locations are perfect but the action, particularly its speed, is fanciful – this is fiction after all.

The reality

In short, diplomats have not always had a good press. But despite attracting this odd combination of envy, abuse and ridicule, most diplomats are dedicated to their work, find it both challenging and rewarding, and often stay in it for life. What keeps them going is that they aspire – and in many cases actually manage – to make a difference.

There are not so many jobs in the world where, in the space of a few short months, you can meet or entertain Presidents George W. Bush and John Atta-Mills, musicians and campaigners Bono and Bob Geldof, the super-model Christy Turlington, Archbishops Desmond Tutu and John Sentamu, former UN Secretary-General Kofi Annan, Nobel prize-winner Wole Soyinka, Chelsea midfielder Michael Essien, Lord Mark Malloch-Brown (as minister for Africa) and a then relatively unknown Keir Starmer. But they all passed through Accra in 2009–10 and in many cases through the British High Commissioner's Residence (which was my home at the time). Between these glamorous visits, though, we were also dealing with the tragic death of a young British volunteer, swept out to sea and drowned during a midnight swim, innumerable visa problems for Ghanaians seeking to visit the UK, a growing drug-trafficking problem on flights to London, two elderly British citizens robbed of all their savings by online scammers who persuaded them to bring it in cash to Ghana for (they thought) a local charity, and a visit of British ophthalmologists from the Moorfields Clinic in London to do a lightning set of eye operations at the main Accra hospital in their summer holidays.

This was not all in a day, but every day brought something interesting, challenging or unusual, and looking back it is extraordinary how much we actually did. In the mix, though often moving quite slowly, were bigger issues – negotiations on a double taxation treaty that would make life easier for businesses and encourage more investment in Ghana; discussions with the government over their position on climate change, or their attitude to the upcoming elections and the resumed civil war in neighbouring Côte d'Ivoire; what message President Atta-Mills would bring on his first official visit to the UK, whom he would meet (which royal in particular), and where he would visit.

Overseas postings, of course, are the exotic bit. In fact, around half of most diplomatic careers are spent at home, not abroad. You are always asked 'So where have you served?' not 'So which departments have you worked in?' The life may be less exotic and the work less adventurous (a daily commute on London's District Line has to be endured, where the drive to work at dawn alongside the Indian Ocean in Dar es Salaam uplifted and inspired), but these days the opportunities to make a difference, to shift policy in productive directions, or to make the right response to an unexpected crisis, are far greater when working at the heart of government, alongside ministers, than in an embassy overseas. The transformation in communication in the last twenty years has blurred the distinction between embassies abroad and ministries at home: audio-visual meetings and conference calls can bring in colleagues from around the world, and while this has reduced the autonomy of embassies, it has increased the policy input they can make and allowed teams at headquarters to include remote workers from overseas. Of course, it also makes a difference that when overseas you receive the additional allowances that in many cases make the career an affordable option. So many diplomats still prefer to be overseas than at home.

Whether at home or abroad, the diplomat finds themselves working most of the time in four broad areas: political, representational, commercial/economic and consular/visa work. Inevitably, along with this goes a fair degree of administrative and management work. But for now we will focus on those four.

Diplomatic duties

Since the dawn of human society diplomats have been involved in maintaining peaceful relations between states. But over time diplomats have found themselves engaged in many less exalted activities, ranging from the humdrum and tedious to the frustrating and exhausting.

Political and policy work is the most obviously connected to the original purpose. In a mission abroad it involves understanding the political dynamics of the host country or organisation so that one's bosses back home can build productive partnerships, navigate and neutralise problems that arise, or prepare for troubles to come. It means knowing whom to contact to influence decisions and to get things done (not always the same people at all), and how to avoid the traps that await the politically unwary. And it means understanding the *ideas* that motivate both the leaders and the public. Those diplomats who really understood the public mood or the leader's mind knew that Brexit was more than likely to happen, and that Putin was bound to invade Ukraine. Those working on the politics of foreign policy always need to remember that ideas matter at least as much as interests, and that ideas influence the public as much as the political elite. That is why deliberate disinformation can be so damaging, and why undertaking public diplomacy, building links between people and exercising soft power remain crucial elements of successful political work. Political work also involves managing the fallout and picking up the pieces when conflict has broken out, from alliance building to peace-making and peace-keeping, work that has waxed rather than waned in recent years.

Security is a distinct, but closely integrated, element of political work, central to keeping one's country safe. Many embassies will have a defence attaché, and some will have a 'station', a branch of the intelligence services. Back home, foreign and defence ministries are closely joined-up, though more at the head than the hip, and there are close (but discreet) links with intelligence agencies – at least in the UK: others may and do work differently. 'Security' is now defined more widely: in recent decades, both transnational crime and environmental issues have become major areas of diplomatic activity, from the response to money laundering and criminal trafficking of drugs, guns and people, to managing the response to climate change, through the annual COP conferences, for example.

Secondly, the aim of representational work is to give as positive an impression as possible of one's own country or organisation to as wide a range of the local population, business, youth, government and media as you can and, when necessary, to explain and deliver clear public messages about your own policies, positions or values. It means getting everywhere and being seen by all the constituencies and interest groups that impact, directly or indirectly, on foreign relations. It also means being visible and available to the community of one's fellow citizens – difficult when they may number in their tens of thousands. But it is expected, and needs to be done. While personal interactions on television, radio, and public and private meetings remain central, the relentless rise and influence of social media has added a new dimension to this work, making it easier to reach a wider audience, but harder to influence the closed echo chambers or the tide of disinformation that now impact so many. Promoting cultural and educational exchange is an essential part of this effort to influence perceptions and build links between people.

Thirdly, economic, commercial and development work has grown enormously in the past century. In the 19th century, Britain fought the Opium Wars to force open the Chinese market to British merchants. Methods of opening markets and support-ing national businesses are (usually) more scrupulous these days, but the diplo-matic competition for major business opportunities – for oil and mineral contracts, infrastructure projects, telecom operations, aircraft orders and especially military supplies – is intense and ruthless. Without serious political and diplomatic backing, businesses will easily find themself out-manoeuvred or outgunned in securing such business. Smaller companies seeking investment or export opportunities also need help navigating unfamiliar markets, and the commercial sections of embassies are regularly called on to brief visiting businessmen or help arrange meetings for them with the ministers and officials concerned. Where the state runs many of the sec-tors concerned, diplomatic support is essential. For the international businessman, negotiating deals with a foreign company requires many of the skills that diplomats bring to their job.

Wider economic work has also expanded. As transnational flows of goods, infor-mation and money grow, more and more sectors have become subject to national and international regulation, requiring close engagement with other countries and authorities to harmonise rules or negotiate differences if trade and the global exchange of information and technology are to continue to flow freely. The increas-ingly frequent application of sanctions has made it important for governments to understand the economic and financial structures of other countries, coordinate with like-minded countries, and be aware of how imposing sanctions on others may impact their own economies at home. Similarly trade deals, whether negotiated in the World Trade Organisation or bilaterally, need the full range of diplomatic skills to be landed successfully; and the growing risk of trade disputes turning into trade wars will require more active diplomatic involvement if they are to avoid turning into real wars, as they risk doing between the US and China.

'Development' has become an industry of its own since the Second World War, and one that has been a key (and contested) element in diplomatic relations between donor and recipient nations, as well as an issue in the restructuring of the relevant international institutions. Development experts need to be diplomats too, whether they are trying to reduce poverty, accelerate private sector growth, expand health and education services, reform agriculture, or – especially – meet the ever-growing demand for humanitarian support to people displaced or made destitute by disasters, natural or human. Those working with multilateral, humanitarian or advocacy organisations often find themselves in conflict-afflicted areas amidst political minefields every bit as complex as anything that regular diplomats do and requiring diplomatic skills of the highest order, even more so if they do not have the benefits of diplomatic status.

Finally, consular and visa work has grown exponentially as the global population on the move has multiplied, for work or leisure, temporarily or permanently. Looking after your citizens abroad is one of the principal tasks of any embassy or diplomatic mission. Tourism now covers every corner of the globe: from the highest point (Everest) to the lowest (viewing the Titanic), at both of which some tourists manage to die and need to be repatriated or at least commemorated; from the coldest point to the hottest where, in the Sahara, tourist hostage-taking became for a while a major source of revenue for rebel movements – until the tourists stopped coming. So consular work has increased. It also invariably attracts media and political attention when nationals feel they have been ill-served by their diplomatic representatives abroad and complain vociferously to anyone who will listen. Visa work too has increased massively to become both more important and more contentious. Except during a pandemic (which brings its own diplomatic challenges), the numbers travelling around the world continue to multiply, and the political sensitivity of immigration policy means that those issuing visas or managing asylum cases have to tread with ever greater care, requiring more rather than less political and diplomatic finesse. But it is the service with which most foreigners have most contact, and is therefore vitally important to get right to preserve your country's good name and reputation.

There is obviously a domestic side to all this diplomatic work. To be a good diplomat, you need to master the political dynamics at home or headquarters as much as abroad, understand what your own political masters (or senior management) want and what the limits of their political and financial flexibility are, and be able to negotiate the sometimes byzantine structures of political and civil service power in your own government, or the balance of management power in your organisation. Understanding this internal context is just as important for doing an effective job as understanding the external situation. In each area, it is essential to build a network of trusted contacts in home ministries or departments – the finance or interior ministries, or those dealing with trade, industry, environment, agriculture and development (if or when there is one). The fact that you are all nominally working for the same government in no way diminishes the potential divergences of view or the need to negotiate a policy line that reflects your department's priorities as much as theirs.

Those working for international organisations, non-governmental organisations (NGOs) or corporations are also involved in some of these areas but tend to be more focused. Businesses need to make money, from investments or trade. Advocacy groups need to get their message out and build coalitions to support their cause. Humanitarians need to get access to the people often desperately waiting for help, sometimes with government cooperation, sometimes without, and occasionally with the acquiescence of rebel groups controlling access. The humanitarian, the aid official, the businessman doing an international deal, even the internet warrior hunched over a laptop posting inflammatory or corrective social media posts – all are engaged in diplomacy of one form or another.

All these areas are explored in more detail in the following chapters. But if so much of the work involves so many problems, it is worth asking: why do people do it?

Motivation

Robert Cooper's book *The Ambassadors* (2021) tracks the lives and impact of historic figures famed for their diplomacy, from Machiavelli, through Richelieu and Talleyrand, to Kennan, Kissinger, Monnet and Brandt. He includes, however, two chapters on lesser known diplomats – Finnish, Danish, British and Japanese – who in their own personal way changed the fate of individuals and nations for the better, navigating imperfectly but ultimately effectively in times of war dangerous diplomatic waters that threatened to drown them all. That is the kind of work that, each in their own modest way, most diplomats and international workers aspire to do: what good they can in the circumstances they find themselves in, helping those who have need, and supporting their nation's way forward in the world.

'Making a difference' sounds rather pretentious. But it is what many of us want to do in our lives; diplomats just want to do it in the international sphere.

I was an accidental diplomat myself. It was certainly not a lifetime ambition, though I was always curious to know how the world worked, what other places looked like, how other people lived, and how things could be made better, particularly in Africa which was the focus of my studies. Trained as a historian for eight years, including a year doing research in Tanzania, I was attracted to work in academia or development. But when I emerged, blinking into the light of day after completing a PhD, there were no available jobs in either, so *faut de mieux* I took the civil service exams. I was, rather to my surprise, offered a job in Her Majesty's Diplomatic Service, which seemed at least worth trying in case it suited me. It did. In fact, each job I was thrown into – only rarely the one I'd asked for – turned out to be even more interesting than the one before. So I stayed, for 36 years in the end, the last seven working on secondment at the European Union (back in the day . . .). It is a rare career in which every three, four or five years you find yourself doing something so utterly different from your previous job that you might almost have changed career completely, though always in the context of an institution where your cumulative, if diverse, experience and wisdom would become more and more useful – if you are lucky. But in all these jobs, from cultural relations to IT, from Washington DC to the Middle East, I did feel I was doing something to try and make the world a better place. Not always succeeding, it has to be said, but always trying.

In some ways, the work of the diplomat is like the labour of Sisyphus. In the Greek legend, Sisyphus, the king of Corinth, displeased the gods who condemned him for eternity to push a boulder up a mountain. Each time he neared the summit, the boulder would slip from his grasp and roll back down to the bottom, where he would have to begin again, pushing it once more up the mountain. For the diplomat, the summit would be a wholly peaceful world. Sadly we are still far from that. But the diplomat is always trying to get there. There are plenty of summits along the way, just never the final one. The consolation is that as long as you are pushing the boulder uphill, things are getting better, the view is improving, and you are stopping it rolling back down to the bottom. So be happy – and keep pushing. The more hands to help the better. For if it does roll down again, you will find that the bottom of the mountain is a very dark place indeed.

Qualities

Fundamentally, diplomacy has three essential characteristics.

Firstly, the diplomat is a representative of a government or an international organisation, so represents the policies set by others. You can influence those policies and there is plenty of scope for individual initiative within the limits set; but you are representing someone else, not yourself. That is integral to the job. You are a public servant and it therefore requires loyalty to your government or your headquarters, and to your colleagues.

Secondly, a diplomat's work involves above all dealing with people who are *different from you*. People who live in a different country, often speaking a different language, have a different culture, different diet, different history and often a different view of the world, coming at it from their own very different direction. Of course, some are more different than others, though it is a big mistake to think that just because people speak the same language they think the same way. I was not the only Briton living in the US who, the longer I lived there, felt increasingly strongly that I had more in common with my European colleagues than with many Americans I met, especially when you ventured out of the Washington or New York bubbles. A land awash with guns, religious fundamentalists, believers in capital punishment and 'pro-life' activists felt at times quite alien. The opposite was also true: travelling across China or through rural Africa, I was often struck how similar all people are and how deeply rooted in all cultures are traditions of hospitality, kindness and respect towards strangers, even if there were wide differences in customs and assumptions. But unless you understand how and why countries or people are different, and learn to speak their language – metaphorically as well as literally – you will never be able to understand it or make yourself understood, and therefore to deal with the issues you have to raise. To be successful, you become in effect an interpreter between two governments and two cultures, explaining one to the other so that they can get business done and avoid coming into conflict.

This is essential because the third characteristic of diplomacy is that you are dealing with *differences*, with problems and with potential or actual conflicts. The diplomat is most required when people *don't* agree. The work can often involve challenging other people's ideas or interests, looking for areas of agreement where they are scarce, trying to build consensus where it does not exist, and offering or seeking compromises in order to achieve that. It is therefore inherently difficult work and requires a good deal of physical and mental agility and resilience.

In particular, the most essential pre-requisite for dealing with these differences is to build *trust*, a diplomat's most valuable asset, hard to build and easy to lose. And to be trusted by people, you have to be honest, and seen to be honest.

There is also a schizophrenic element to the job. A good diplomat needs to be a personal optimist – things can be done – and a professional pessimist – but these are the problems that need to be overcome and the risks that might arise if you take that course of action. Politicians tend not to like the second part, but it has saved them from many disasters in the past and ignoring it has proven costly.

In some ways the ideal training for a diplomat is to be a social anthropologist (Engelke, 2017). The discipline is about how people live in groups and interact with others. You are trained to listen, to observe and to understand other people's way of thinking. You become an expert in rituals – and rituals still play an important part in diplomatic life, for reasons I will explain. The only trouble is that social anthropologists are trained to observe and analyse rather than act, and taking action, or at least creating a pro-active dialogue to exercise influence, is an essential part of what diplomats do. So the ideal diplomat should be a mixture of social anthropologist, psychologist, linguist, lawyer, historian, actor and engineer – to make things work – as well as being a kind of intellectual entrepreneur, creating ideas that might help shift the dial on some intractable problem.

In practice a good diplomat can come from any kind of background, from nuclear scientist to theologian, linguist to lawyer (I have known excellent diplomats with each of these backgrounds). Of the twenty people I joined the Foreign Office with in 1982, only one had studied international relations. It is not what you study, but who you are that makes the difference between a good diplomat and a great one. One of the best I know, Sir Nick Kay, spent fourteen years as a schoolteacher before he decided to try something different and joined the FCO at the grand old age of 35. Of course, not every head of recruitment in every foreign ministry shares this approach, and a good knowledge of international relations will often be essential to secure the job you want, and help you do it well. But it alone is not enough.

So what are the qualities that make a good diplomat?

Obviously to be interested and open to other cultures; to have empathy and an ability to get on with people of all backgrounds and gain their trust; the analytical skills to master the detail of a complex subject such as climate science, artificial intelligence or human rights law, often at short notice, and deliver a simple, concise summary of the issues comprehensible to a non-expert (which includes most ministers and the public); an ability to operate under pressure and stress while keeping a clear head and remaining unfazed by disagreement; stamina, to work often long hours in the office during the day and then attend the obligatory social events in the evening, or sit up all night at a conference until the text is finally agreed; patience, to attend interminable official events, and wait for the opportune moment in a negotiation; and, especially, good judgement of people and situations. As one former diplomat summed it up: 'It requires a quick mind, a hard head, a strong stomach, a warm smile and a cold eye' (Meyer, 2009, 260).

But underlying all these are the most important qualities of all: intelligence, honesty and curiosity.

Diplomacy has not always been open to all people with these qualities. For many years, centuries even, diplomacy was considered an elite activity and was the almost exclusive preserve of the male Establishment, especially aristocrats, with the occasional intellectual and eccentric thrown in. Until 1918, recruits to the British diplomatic service had not only to be recommended by an existing member of the service, but to have a guaranteed *private* income of at least £400 a year (equivalent to £20,000 in 2024). Only in 1920 did the Foreign Office revise salaries to provide a living wage so that junior staff (and ambassadors) no longer needed a private income to sustain themselves; but they still recruited candidates almost exclusively from Oxford or Cambridge universities by taking them on a country house weekend to judge their suitability for the role (Nicolson, 1939; Moorhouse, 1977). This was true even in the US where the State Department in the early 20th century was known as the 'Pretty Good Club' for graduates of Harvard and Yale (Larson, 2011). Things have changed, democratised like politics itself, and foreign ministries now look for a rather wider skill set and more diverse background. This is a good thing, as one requirement for an effective diplomat is to represent their nation or their organisation in its full diversity.

It is only in the last 50 years that women have come to play a central role in many diplomatic services (though still not all), becoming not only more numerous but more equal in status, rank and pay to male staff. In Britain, women were first admitted to the service in the 1940s, but it was not until 1976 that the first was appointed as an ambassador – Dame Anne Warburton, as Ambassador to Denmark. Until 1970 it was also a requirement that women who got married should retire from the service, so it was only in 1986 – four years after I joined – that the first married woman, Veronica Sutherland, reached ambassadorial rank. In my intake of 20, only four were women, though a more radical (female) head of recruitment ensured that the following year the intake was 50:50. Still, it was only in 2021, thanks to the determined efforts of the then Permanent Under-Secretary, that for the first time women simultaneously filled 18 of the top 26 ambassadorial posts overseas, and constituted 35% of all senior management positions (Marks, 2021; McDonald, 2022). Most are married and many have children, taking maternity leave when needed. One head of mission post (in Zambia) has even been filled by a husband and wife team as a job-share. It is not just in the UK: in Finland's diplomatic service, women now outnumber men.

Given that women possess the qualities needed for diplomacy in equal (if not greater) measure than men, it is not surprising, now that society has provided the opportunity for them, that the last 40 years have seen the emergence of a number of outstanding women diplomats. Among many, the most prominent in my time have been Madeleine Albright (US), Mary Robinson (Ireland), Christine Lagarde

(France), Ursula von der Leyen (Germany), Margot Wallstrom (Sweden), Cathy Ashton (UK), Ngozi Okonjo-Iweala (Nigeria) and Hanna Tetteh (Ghana), with many more following in their footsteps. Many of these came from politics into diplomatic or international leadership roles, but that is equally true of many outstanding male diplomats.

Equality of opportunity in diplomacy for ethnic minorities remains more challenging in many countries. European diplomatic services tend to be whiter than their societies, at least in comparison to the US foreign service, but measures are now being taken to redress this. Quite a number of diplomatic services around the world remain the preserve of elites, particularly where educational opportunities are less than equal, or traditional career paths are deeply entrenched. Not just in the US, there is also a tradition of political appointments to senior diplomatic posts, which can either diversify or limit the gene pool. Ambassadors with strong political links to their president, king or government can be invaluable in providing both sending and receiving countries with access to top level thinking. But it also has its problems if they are, for example, rich but unskilled or inexperienced in diplomatic ways, or take too overtly a political or passionate stance on an issue requiring dispassion and equilibrium.

Recruitment

How then should you go about becoming a diplomat? You may wish to finish this book before deciding whether it is really the career you want, and even then it may not be the career you get. But there are avenues.

Most diplomatic services and international organisations now recruit by competitive examination, with processes that can last from weeks to years. The details of how to apply and what to expect can be found on their websites, and the criteria used for selection may differ substantially from the qualities identified above. Certainly, a knowledge of international affairs, languages and experience of working abroad will be no drawback. Many now also look for working experience, rather than recruiting candidates direct from university. This points to looking for job opportunities that give you a chance to experience international work of some kind, from internships to journalism, from multilateral agencies to NGOs. The European Commission *stage* (internship) programme, which I joined in 1984 and which is also open to some non-EU nationals, has proved its value over many years as a way to build not only experience but a network of contacts that often last a lifetime. In my case, it was how I met my wife.

It is important to remember that diplomacy is not something exclusive to diplomats. Many of those who have had the greatest influence on international affairs have never worked for a government. So you can do diplomacy in many different ways. Most of these will be challenging in one way or another, as the differences and imperfections of the world are some of the things that make it endlessly fascinating. To play even a small part in pushing that diplomatic boulder up the hill is a rewarding life for those that choose it.

* * *

I remember walking back home one night at about 4 am from an EU Budget Council meeting at which we had finally agreed a financial package for the next five years. The Brussels streets were damp, dark and deserted. As I passed a park, a blackbird was singing its heart out in the darkness. It made me think what on earth was I doing heading home at that time for a very few hours' sleep having spent the best part of 48 hours cooped up in windowless meeting rooms arguing over numbers. And the answer was that we had reached agreement: the deal was done, the budget had provided for those that needed it, and we could stop arguing about it for a few years. We had made a difference. And that was something worth singing about.

2   What is diplomacy?

The primary purpose of diplomacy is the avoidance of war.

Diplomats do other things too, as we have seen, and diplomacy carries on even when war does break out. Nevertheless, like the cleaner at NASA asked by President Kennedy what he was doing who replied 'Helping put a man on the moon, Mr President', the diplomat might answer that it all helps keep the peace. This does not exclude some countries' use of diplomacy to foment wars, especially proxy wars, usually as an assertion of power against a rival. But in most cases, underneath all the diverse diplomatic activity is the objective of stopping states trying to settle their disputes or achieve their ends by force rather than discussion.

Origins

All human societies, since time immemorial, have had political processes for ensuring people's security and agreeing how resources should be distributed. Initially these societies were small scale and geographically scattered, living together as families, clans or villages. As production became more sophisticated and trade and exchange grew, societies became larger and more complex (Wilson and Wilson, 1945). About 6,000 years ago, states emerged, but only in some geographically favoured areas and without many of the trappings, processes or borders that we now associate with the term. Most were what we would consider 'city states', with a ruler based in an urban centre from which control radiated out. In fact, while population was relatively sparse, controlling the allegiance of people was often more important than controlling the land. Where land is plentiful and borders loose, people who did not like their ruler or the rules could simply move elsewhere. Many did. But people within reach of a powerful ruler were expected to offer allegiance and pay tribute in return for being left in peace – or suffer the consequences. Thus kings and empires were born (Harrison, 2009).

Nevertheless, even these early communities and states had relations with each other and had to find ways of settling disputes. War has never been the automatic resort for settling arguments – yet in the earliest available records, such as those from Mesopotamia and Egypt, it was evidently common, even if something that rulers nevertheless went to some lengths to avoid (Cohen and Westbrook, 2002; Hamilton and Langhorne, 2011). Strangers could be perceived as a threat, or

DOI: 10.4324/9781003533436-2

neighbours as rivals for the control of resources or the allegiance of people living in between two centres of power. But then, as now, war was expensive, risky and destructive, even if a sought-after source of glory, wealth and honour. While to the victor the spoils, to the loser, often enough, subservience or death. Most communities therefore preferred to avoid it if they could. Many were equally aware that there could be mutual benefit from exchange rather than conflict, in the form of trade in goods, exchange of skills and sharing of knowledge. So ways were found to open relations with neighbours, to discuss problems before they gave rise to conflicts or before the stronger decided to assert their superiority over the weaker by force. The ruler, or the community, would choose someone they trusted to visit the neighbour to discuss the problem, with authority to settle it, but on condition that they were not killed in the process. These were envoys, emissaries or, in practice, the earliest diplomats.

To simplify, 'politics' might be defined as the process for settling disputes *within* self-governing communities and 'diplomacy' as the art of settling disputes *between* those communities (Bailey, 1969). In effect diplomacy is the politics of relations between distinct communities or states, where there is no ruler or ultimate authority able to impose rules and adjudicate disputes. Hence international politics took place in what one scholar called an 'anarchical society', one without an ultimate authority (Bull, 1977; see also Jönsson and Hall, 2005, for stimulating views on this).

The critical point is that for most of history (and I would argue actually all of it) diplomacy involves dealing with entities that you do not control, and may not agree with. Within a community or state, the ruler has authority based on some form of legitimacy. The authority might be limited, it might be contested; but it exists. People accept the ruler's authority either because they have chosen them (or recognise an acceptable process to choose them), God has chosen them (through the 'divine right of kings'), or because they have no choice: the rule is imposed by force. In international society, relations are between free-standing entities that owe no automatic allegiance to the other.

There is a vast literature on the origins of international relations, debating and defining when 'international relations' began: how the modern state system emerged from the ruins of the Roman Empire and the residual authority of the Popes and the Holy Roman Emperor; how empires gradually became states (of a long list, I suggest Hinsley, 1963; Kissinger, 1994; Reus-Smit and Snidal, 2008). As has been pointed out (Buzan and Lawson, 2015; Zarakol, 2022), this is a particularly western approach to international affairs which overlooked how people and empires related to each other during several thousand years and across the whole globe before 1648 and the Treaty of Westphalia – even if that approach explains the assumptions on which the global system has run for some time since.

So the existence and arts of diplomacy long predate the modern state. It is sometimes described as the second oldest profession in the world, with something of the unsavoury reputation of the oldest profession itself. As legend and Herodotus recount, the war between the Greeks and Trojans began with a succession of women-stealing expeditions followed by diplomatic demands for return or reparations. Only when these were rebuffed was war engaged (Herodotus, Book 1). The first surviving diplomatic correspondence from Mesopotamia dates back to around 2,500 BCE, and the first treaty of which a record survives is that between the Egyptian Pharoah Ramesses II and the Hittites in 1,300 BCE (Cohen and Westbrook, 2002).

From the outset, therefore, diplomacy is the art of dealing with 'others': those who are different from 'us' in our village, group, community, territory or state, and who do not come under the same authority.

This implies a number of things. It means being able to communicate with the others, by speaking their language for example (the first treaty was written in neither Egyptian nor Hittite but Akkadian, a language of Babylonian origin that became the first diplomatic *lingua franca*). It also means being *allowed* to communicate with them: in other words being given access to those in authority, being granted audience and listened to, and not being simply ignored, rebuffed, expelled or executed. It also implies being recognised as speaking with the authority of the sender, and it implies reciprocity: if you give my envoys safe passage, I do the same for you. But most important, as I explained in the previous chapter, it requires understanding of where the 'other' is coming from, not just physically, socially, historically or politically, but psychologically.

Given that diplomacy is also about dealing with differences, and particularly with difficulties and disagreements, it requires some agreement on rules and procedures to allow differing points of view to be ventilated, disagreements to be expressed, and alternative solutions to be explored first, before people take up arms and come to blows. These rules of diplomacy are discussed in more detail in the following chapters. Firstly, though, we need to look at the underlying forces that condition the conduct of diplomacy, and how these have affected the historical evolution of the rules.

Diplomacy, politics and power

International society is as unequal as any. Some countries are big and rich, some are small and poor, but most are somewhere in between. Although under the principles of the United Nations all sovereign states have equal status, the reality of diplomacy is that it involves relations between unequals. 'Sovereignty' is a slippery concept (Krasner, 1988; Marshall, 1997), as the UK found during Brexit, and, like all things, turns out to be relative. 'Defending national sovereignty' can be one of the purposes of diplomacy, but it makes a difference whether you do this as the United States, North Korea or Luxembourg: each takes a totally different approach.

International politics therefore reflects the distribution of power between the participants – which makes it essential for the diplomat, or any international actor, to understand what power is, where it comes from and how it is used.

Power comes from three things: economic strength, military might, and having friends, for example through alliances or treaties (see Nye in Cooper et al., 2013, ch. 30). The combination of these can vary.

In the contemporary world, some countries are wealthy but not powerful in the conventional sense. Germany and Japan are economic superpowers but weak in military terms, depending (until 2025) on their alliance with the US to protect themselves against powerful and threatening neighbours. Denmark is a small, rich country, whose power comes primarily through its alliances: with NATO, with other members of the EU, and with its Scandinavian neighbours. Other small countries, like Israel or Rwanda, have exerted far more power than their size or wealth would suggest, by having exceptionally effective militaries and powerful international friends (though enemies as well). Switzerland is an exception as a small country with influence but few alliances: its immediate neighbours have long accepted that it poses no physical threat to themselves (though it maintains a strong citizens' army for self-defence), that it serves a purpose more useful than disruptive through its role as a financial broker, and its tradition of maintaining strict neutrality has allowed it to play the role of honest diplomatic broker in others' disputes, if requested. A few large countries have both economic strength and military might: the US and China above all. While the US retains a military edge for now, the main difference between them is largely the extent of their alliances, the US having a significantly wider network than China – a point President Trump appears not to have registered, but which President Xi Jinping certainly has. One country, Russia, remains a military superpower, but – for all its natural resources – it is economically weak and, being currently short of allies, increasingly dependent (in 2025) on China, Iran, North Korea and a few others. This has not, however, prevented it seeking to impose its will on its neighbours, on the premise, it seems, that if they won't join you, beat them.

So even now political independence needs to be backed up by force if it is to last. The potential use of force therefore effectively continues to underpin all diplomacy. If push comes to shove, does a country have the means or the friends to defend its independence and its interests? However legitimate a democracy, without the means to defend itself it will not long remain one. At the time of writing, these issues are very current in eastern Europe, East Asia and the Middle East.

A classic statement of this reality is provided in Thucydides' history of the Peloponnesian War. The Melian Dialogue is an essential text for all diplomats or students of diplomacy, and should be read in full. It is the only part of the history that is set out explicitly as a dialogue, though it is not known whether this reflected a first-hand account that Thucydides received, that he was present himself, or that it was simply his way of representing the arguments that were used to justify each position in the negotiation. This is the story it tells.

The island of Melos had been colonised by settlers from Athens' rival, Sparta, but insisted it was neutral in the war between the two states and should be left in peace. The Athenians saw this as a threat to their maritime dominance of the Aegean Sea and their fleet arrived at Melos in force. Before taking any action, they sent representatives to negotiate with the Melians, who allowed them to meet the city council but not speak before the public assembly. The Athenians began by proposing to avoid specious arguments of principle and focus only on practicalities. The Melians complained that the Athenians appeared to have come simply to kill them or enslave them. The Athenians responded: 'when these matters are discussed by practical people, the standard of justice depends on the equality of power to compel, and that in fact the strong do what they have the power to do and the weak accept what they have to accept' (sometimes translated more succinctly as 'the strong do what they can and the weak suffer what they must'). The Melians pointed out that there is still a concept of fair play, from which the Athenians would benefit if they ever suffered a defeat themselves; and to destroy one neutral state would encourage the other neutrals to band together to resist Athens. So it was in Athens' self-interest to let them be. The Athenians disagreed: they were more at risk from being seen by other parts of their empire as weak if they allowed Melos to remain neutral, and this would encourage resistance. So it was strongly in Athens' self-interest to make Melos join their empire, by persuasion if possible or by force if not. Only the strong could remain independent: all others had to join one side or the other – and since Athens dominated the seas and was by far the stronger, for the islanders there was little choice. It was not a question of fairness, but of whether the Melians wanted to save their lives. The debate continued, but in the end the Melians refused to give up their liberty, sent the Athenian delegation away and prepared for a siege. This continued for many months but the Spartans never came to the rescue of their colony, the city was eventually betrayed from within, and when the Athenians took it, true to their word, they slaughtered the men and sold the women and children into slavery. They then brought their own colonists out from Athens to populate the island.

The Melian dialogue is a fine example of a failed diplomatic negotiation. War and disaster (at least for the Melians) followed. It illustrates that effective diplomats need not only to use the best arguments, but to be conscious of the balance of power between the negotiating partners, and of the wider political context.

Many things have changed since the fifth century BCE. Above all, one explicit purpose of the post-war political settlement of 1945, including the creation of the United Nations (UN), was to make a world safe for small states, so that self-determination became possible for small nations as well as large.

In 1945, European empires still existed in Africa and parts of Asia – though not for long – and a *de facto* Soviet empire was emerging in eastern Europe, extending the former Russian empire even further west. But the structure for international politics established then has enabled a proliferation of states, large and small, to achieve and retain independence since. How long this will last is uncertain: nothing lasts for ever and there are a number of states which seem to believe their self-interest lies in undermining this order and asserting their control over neighbours or clients. We may be heading towards a more multipolar world where rival great powers seek more explicitly to encourage, cajole or force smaller states into alliance with them. This will create more, if rather different, work for diplomats. The next section discusses in more detail how the system of diplomatic rules has developed, how it might evolve further, and how this will impact on the way diplomacy is conducted.

Of the three sources of power, economic and military strength are quantifiable; alliances and informal influence are less easily measured.

Having friends matters in diplomacy, so joining clubs is popular. Most countries belong to many: the UN and its agencies, obviously (though the US has been in and out of UNESCO and the WHO more than once); local regional organisations (unless in a fit of populist pique they decide to exit); international financial or economic institutions that provide support (IMF, WB, ADB, AfDB) or set rules (ITU, IMO, WTO); and then the selective groups that choose their membership – G7, G20, G77, NATO, BRICS, the Commonwealth, Francophonie, etc. The media are often sceptical, regarding some as little more than talking shops that issue long and tedious declarations which nobody reads and which don't change the price of fish (unless of course it is the EU's Fisheries Council). But they have relevance and value in demonstrating who your friends are. Despite its imperial origins, the Commonwealth provides an opportunity for anglophone countries from every continent, large and small, rich and poor, to get together and talk about common problems and meet each other bilaterally in the margins. The shrinking of the G8 to G7 in 2014 mattered, in signalling that Russia was no longer considered a democracy that respected others after its invasion of Crimea. The recent expansion of the BRICS in 2023 to become BRICS+ reflected the growing enthusiasm of other countries to become friends with China and share a platform with its leader. The BRICS+ are not (yet) a decision-making or rule-making body, but the grouping has clear symbolic, and therefore geopolitical, significance. Joining and attending such groups is a political decision, demonstrating priorities in a country's foreign policy, as China did in joining the WTO in 2001. Leaving such groups also sends important signals: the UK's decision to exit from the EU in 2016 significantly weakened its economy and its international reputation, reduced its links with the other EU member states and, as a result, reduced its power. But it also weakened the EU itself. The accession of Sweden and Finland to NATO in 2023–4 strengthened the alliance in response to concerns about the risk of Russian aggression.

Power is not confined to states. There are many non-state actors that have power in one form or another, which some of them choose to use in the international arena. Large multinational corporations – oil majors, mining companies, internet or tech giants, trading conglomerates – have a market value far greater than the GDP of many countries and tremendous latent economic power which they occasionally exercise, sometimes working in alliance with their host state to further their economic and financial interests, sometimes independently. The recent regulatory tussles between the US and EU and internet companies like Amazon, Alphabet and Meta reveal the extent of their economic and social influence. But they are not themselves states, have no sovereignty, and are very rarely able to deploy force (if you exclude mercenary groups like Wagner). Terrorist groups, on the other hand, deliberately have military means and often create international alliances with other such groups or sympathetic states, to mobilise financial resources or secure a safe haven from which to operate. Using force for political ends is their *raison d'être*. Sometimes they try to create a state, as the Islamic State (known locally as Da'esh) did in Iraq, or take over an existing one as the Taliban did in Afghanistan and Al-Shabab in Somalia; they thereby become state actors, and pose a problem for the international system which has to decide whether to recognise or do business with them, or treat them as pariahs. Other non-state actors have neither military means nor economic power but exercise international influence through their alliances, often also with state governments. Many operate in the fields of human rights (e.g. Amnesty), humanitarian affairs (MSF), development (Oxfam), corruption (Transparency International) and the environment (Greenpeace); some operate in the media (BBC, Al-Jazeera, France 24, Fox News) and some even in the political arena (OSF, the Carter Center and the various German *Stiftungs*). Global religious movements too, especially the more organised like the Roman Catholic church or American evangelical Christians, can deploy spiritual and sometimes temporal influence, particularly if in alliance with secular actors. Through mobilising public opinion and influencing governments these non-governmental organisations have become significant diplomatic actors in their own right on a number of international issues. Coordinating with, or contesting, them has become an important job for diplomats.

Besides power, the second thing it is essential for any diplomat or international actor to understand is the politics that lies behind any country's foreign policy. That is why accurate and insightful political reporting remains an indispensable function for diplomatic missions. It is a myth long since demolished that foreign policy or the 'national interest' can exist in an apolitical realm divorced from the day-to-day domestic political preoccupations of a government, and yet many media commentators are still held by it. It therefore bears repeating. All governments, however authoritarian or democratic, are primarily interested in their own survival – in short, with staying in power. It is a rare politician who leaves power voluntarily: some do retire gracefully at the end of their term of office but most are either voted out (in democracies) or thrown out (in autocracies) or die in harness. This affects a government's foreign policy as much as its domestic policy. It has often been acknowledged that foreign adventures or xenophobic nationalism can be deliberately used to distract attention from difficulties at home, from economic hardship or political unpopularity. But it goes much more widely than that.

This is one reason that foreign policy decisions tend to float to the top of government, to become a major preoccupation for the heads of government themselves, because they want to ensure that foreign policy contributes to, and does not undermine, their political survival. The second reason is that, as indicated above, diplomatic relations are between at least nominal equals. With no adjudicator to settle differences, when these become serious they can *only* be settled by interaction between the leaders on both sides. Diplomats can take it only so far: it is the head of government who will take the life or death decisions affecting their regime and their country. So foreign policy *always* drifts into the office of the president or prime minister. And yet this still comes as a surprise to so many, and is sometimes falsely ascribed to political leaders 'preferring to grandstand on the world stage' because it is easier or more glamorous than dealing with domestic problems, or 'usurping the role of the foreign ministry'. This is wrong: they do it because they need to, and if they are not present at international meetings, their position will go by default and their government will suffer. There are ancillary benefits for sure: being seen alongside respected leaders of other nations rarely harmed any politician's reputation (or their ego). At the same time, too much absence abroad can also harm a regime's chances of survival (as President Ruto of Kenya nearly found in 2024). So a balance is needed. But any leader who ignores foreign affairs these days is riding for a fall.

For the diplomat therefore, as I mentioned in the last chapter, it is just as important to understand the politics of your own country as the politics of the country where you are working. For one thing, your hosts may ask you to explain it to them – sometimes not easy, as many British diplomats found during Brexit. But it is just as important to enable you to send advice that is compatible with, or framed sensitively to respond to, a leader or government's domestic political concerns. There is no point proposing a more liberal visa regime for country X if the government at home has set its face against any increase in immigration: the diplomat will simply lose credibility, and therefore any influence on policy. But it is likewise important for your own government to understand, for example, that without a concession on visas, country X will not contemplate the free trade deal they seek, as recently in the case of Britain's negotiations with India. It's the diplomat's job to explain that, to ensure the government understands the consequences of its policies, and to suggest practical ways of achieving their objectives.

To understand the political dynamics of the country where you are working is more obvious, whether employed as a diplomat or in any other capacity. The potential to influence that government's policy, help settle disputes, or persuade them to support global policies of mutual benefit – on curbing carbon emissions to combat climate change, or admit refugees from a neighbouring country in crisis, for example – depends on being able to put the arguments in a way that responds to domestic political pressures on the host government. This is why a good diplomat always gets out of the capital city when they can. All politics is local, as US Speaker Tip O'Neill was wont to say, and understanding the dynamics of what is going on locally will give a better insight into a government's preoccupations than many a speech on foreign policy itself. It is equally important to know whether a government has become divorced from local opinion as this can spell trouble – and pose problems for delivering diplomatic outcomes. It is especially difficult where an authoritarian regime allows no free media and little free movement for diplomats.

It is important to realise that the purpose of diplomacy for many governments is to ensure their regime's survival, rather than to pursue some idealised notion of 'the national interest' or 'a peaceful and prosperous world', or even in some cases their country's integrity. Understanding how this will affect their decision-making is vital. The 19th-century British Prime Minister Lord Palmerston is famed for his remark: 'We have no eternal allies and we have no perpetual enemies. Our interests are eternal and perpetual, and those interests it is our duty to follow' (Brown, 2010). To which one might say, 'Up to a point, Lord Palmerston.'

The evolution of rules

The current network of international organisations, rules and practices has evolved over centuries, but has developed particularly significantly in the last hundred years.

For most of human history the basic arts of diplomacy would have been more familiar to the Athenians than those currently deployed by many contemporary diplomats, closeted for example in the negotiating rooms of the UN in New York, pouring over interminable texts, or providing consular support to improvident tourists.

The evolution of the international system is a vast subject on which much has already been written (Reus-Smit and Snidal, 2008, and Cooper et al., 2013, include useful guides to the literature). But it is helpful in understanding how diplomacy works today to give a brief summary, if only to illustrate how some aspects of diplomacy have scarcely changed while others have been transformed.

Until the 16th century, relations between the different parts of the world were relatively distant and discreet. In many places trade and diplomatic contact existed, but broadly – to simplify grossly – by 1500 the emperor of China managed relations with his immediate neighbours, the emperor of India likewise, the Ottoman empire dominated the Middle and Near East, the Aztec and Inca empires flourished within their arcs of influence, and the kingdom of Kongo and the Songhai empire held sway in their respective parts of Africa (Frankopan, 2015; Badawi, 2024). Despite the existence of a so-called Holy Roman Empire, however, Europe was effectively a mess of small warring states.

Traditionally, the Treaty of Westphalia of 1648, bringing to an end the Thirty Years War, is seen as a turning point in European history and the beginning of an era defined by the relations between states that pursued primarily their national interest, not a universal global order based on the Roman Empire or on a single religion (Kissinger, 1994, 65). It was not, naturally, so clear cut, for the state was still fundamentally defined by the ruler to whom people paid allegiance: hence the Westphalian principle that whoever rules defines the state's religion (Croxton, 2013). This also meant that people could still shift their allegiance from one ruler to another while remaining exactly where they were: lands and the people in them could be exchanged between rulers by force, by marriage or by inheritance. In diplomatic terms there was no significant shift from the tradition that a diplomat represented the ruler, not the people. In this, Europe remained much like the rest of the world, with envoys of one monarch visiting the courts of other monarchs or rulers elsewhere to conduct their business. The legacy of this remains: British diplomats are still appointed by the monarch to His Majesty's Diplomatic Service (something I always found rather comforting when elected governments pursued their party political interest more than the national one in foreign affairs). Foreign ambassadors to Britain are still accredited to the Court of St James, not to the government or prime minister of the day.

It also meant that conflicts were still largely dynastic, with a number of wars in the 18th century fought over the question of succession (the war of Spanish succession, 1701–14; the war of Austrian succession, 1740–8; the war of Bavarian succession, 1778–9) because that dictated who had control over what lands. England, France and Russia were exceptional in the national nature of their aggrandisement (Blanning, 2007).

This changed with the French Revolution and the ensuing Napoleonic wars. The revolution explicitly made the focus of people's loyalty the country, not the ruler. The English had experimented with this in the 17th century by cutting off their king's head and not anointing another. But the experiment was not a success, and after ten years they restored a monarch, even if he was expected to be a good deal more accountable to his subjects than his predecessors (Schama, 2001). In France, the abruptness of the change brought by the revolution and the ensuing chaos allowed Napoleon to emerge as a ruler in practice more absolute than the monarchy that was overthrown. His apparent ambition to unite all Europe in a single empire, with himself as emperor and the whole firmly under French control, united other European powers – England, Prussia, Austria, Russia – in opposition. A further 15 years of war was required to defeat his ambitions. It was followed by one of the landmark diplomatic negotiations in history: the Congress of Vienna in 1815 (Meyer, 2009; Cooper, 2021; Blanning, 2007, 670–2). This re-set the diplomatic map of Europe and established a system based on a balance of power between the major states ('great powers') of Europe that effectively lasted for the next hundred years.

The 19th century was certainly not peaceful, but much of the instability in Europe was within countries rather than between them, as economic change and popular pressure led to the emergence of a growing number of nation states whose rulers became increasingly accountable to their citizens. It also saw the expansion and consolidation of European empires in the rest of the world, except in the Americas, where first England and then Spain lost colonies following wars of independence, though the continent was already remoulded along European lines. The 19th century has come to be seen by some as a golden age for European diplomacy. Rules existed, but they were for the globally privileged: if diplomatic manoeuvres contributed to the maintenance of the balance of power in Europe and avoided a wider war there, their purpose was achieved. Beyond Europe, exploiting their economic, technological and transportational dominance, European powers felt they could propose and dispose of the fate of other parts of the world as they saw fit in their own national interest. The Congress of Berlin in 1884 which carved up Africa was only one example. Russia's expansion to the east and south, the acquisition of colonies in south and south-east Asia – all spread a euro-centric view of the world and integrated so-called 'peripheral' areas into a global economy that brought the world's wealth to Europe's shores (Bayly, 2004). Only China, Japan, Thailand and Ethiopia successfully resisted European control, but at a price. Traditional diplomacy took place overwhelmingly in Europe. In other parts of the world, 'diplomacy' tended all too often to take the form of an imposition of control through the gunboat and the Gatling gun – an approach that would have been familiar enough to the Athenians.

The balance of power nevertheless became increasingly precarious, not least through the rise and unification of Germany (Taylor, 1954). In 1914 the balancing act failed, and the ensuing mass slaughter in the First World War led the peacemakers of Paris in 1919 to look at alternative ways of managing relations between the countries of the world (MacMillan, 2001). The diplomats at the Paris peace conference no longer represented rulers but the elected governments of nation states that sought self-determination and the defence of what they saw as their national interest. Representatives from across the world were present, from the Middle East, Asia and Latin America as well as Europe. But most had little input to the eventual outcome which was effectively negotiated between the victorious powers: France, Britain and the US. The Wilsonian principle of self-determination led to the creation of a number of new, small nation states out of the ruins of the Austro-Hungarian and Ottoman empires – though those in the Middle East were effectively subordinated to the British and French spheres of influence, carved out to support their existing empires (Gallagher, 1982; Frankopan, 2015).

In contrast to the Congress of Vienna in 1815, the Treaty of Paris in 1919 reflected the evolution of the nation state in the intervening century. Borders had become a defining feature and the paraphernalia of citizenship – passports, visas, consular responsibilities – became ever more elaborate. The role of the diplomat changed accordingly. He (and it was still almost universally a male occupation in 1919) no longer represented primarily a ruler, but a state with citizens and businesses. Consular and commercial work, followed by media and public relations, became in the 20th century integral parts of daily diplomatic labour (Nicolson, 1939; Hamilton and Langhorne, 2011).

But Paris also recognised the limitation of purely bilateral relations between nation states, or rival alliances of states. At the instigation of US President Woodrow Wilson, the Peace Agreement provided for the setting up of a League of Nations to bring together on a regular basis the nations of the world and head off potential future conflicts – or 'abolish war' as one of its proponents put it (Lord Robert Cecil, quoted in MacMillan, 2001, 93). It was well-intentioned and marked a major shift in global diplomatic thinking by introducing the principle of permanent multilateral bodies to help manage matters of global concern, accompanied as it was by the foundation of the International Labour Organisation. But the League suffered a number of fatal flaws. Although it was Wilson's brainchild, on his return to the US he was unable to get the isolationist majority in Congress to approve the treaty or join the League; a racial equality clause vigorously pressed by the Japanese was rejected, primarily by the British for imperial reasons; almost all voting had to be done by unanimity; and efforts to give the League teeth to intervene in disputes were all rejected (Macmillan, 2001, 94–106).

As a consequence, it didn't work. It didn't work not only because of the League's in-built weaknesses, but because a number of countries – Italy, Spain, Japan and Germany – fell under the control of leaders who wanted to destroy it, as they wished to be free to assert physical control over weaker neighbours, and other members of the League were not sufficiently united or committed to stop them until it was too late. The result was that a second world war, starting in Europe and dragging the rest of the world in, followed only twenty years after the first. In the aftermath of that catastrophe a more serious and effective effort was made to establish a solid and lasting basis for managing international affairs through the agency of multilateral organisations. The cornerstone was the United Nations, but it included the plethora of agencies created under its umbrella in the following years (from the FAO to UNESCO and the WHO – see Roberts, 2017, chs.16–19), and the global economic institutions designed at the Bretton Woods conference in 1944 to avoid a recurrence of the Great Depression of the 1930s: the international financial institutions (IMF and World Bank) and the General Agreement on Tariffs and Trade (GATT) which became in due course the World Trade Organisation (WTO). It also gave rise to the brainchild of Monnet and Schuman – the European Coal and Steel Community which evolved over time into the European Union, and which has been by far the most effective organisation in the world in resolving economic and political disputes between its member states without recourse to force. It became the prototype for other regional organisations throughout the world that sought to build local free markets (see Chapter 3).

This constituted the most significant evolution of global diplomacy since the emergence of the nation state (Cooper, 2003). The UN was based on two principles: that every country or people had the right to self-determination, and that the rights of all nations should be protected by international law and multilateral institutions. As stated above, it was designed to make the world safe for small countries, to allow self-determination without subordination to bigger neighbours. But it also took a more realist approach to power than the principled but impractical League of Nations. The creation of the Security Council with its *directoire* of five permanent members (effectively the victors of the Second World War) was designed to recognise that power politics would continue to have a place in the world. Only those five had the power to veto resolutions, which were otherwise adopted by majority vote. Its existence helped avoid the Cold War turning into a hot one, and helped force Britain and France to accept the process of decolonisation that multiplied the UN's membership from its initial 51 to the current 193 members (United Nations, 2024).

Prospects

Most diplomatic guides, memoirs and studies in international relations take for granted the continuation of these global institutions and of the multilateral diplomacy they allow. But they are not a given. What is called the 'rules-based international order' which in theory provides the superstructure for the relations between states is a very recent creation. It has been underwritten since 1946 by the support, power and restraint of the United States. As things evolve, as other powers, like China, grow to become rivals or, like Russia, fight their decline by ignoring the rules, or as a number of 'middle powers' such as Turkey, Iran, India and the Gulf states assert their autonomy, and as the US itself threatens to retreat once more into an isolationist huddle, the question arises whether this is another temporary phase of world affairs, now in retreat, or whether the multilateral system will survive – or even be strengthened in response to current challenges. Its appropriateness, representativeness and effectiveness are all being questioned. Its weaknesses have been exposed by recent crises in the Middle East (in Iraq, Syria and Gaza), Africa (in the Sahel and Sudan) and eastern Europe (in Ukraine), and both disillusion and the aspiration for reform have been widely expressed. There is a strong case for reform that would take it further in the direction of representing people, not just power, of giving smaller, poorer but populous nations a greater say. Events, however, seem to be heading in the opposite direction, with those who possess power looking for ways to exert influence more directly over weaker states, and more governments seeking to free themselves from the constraints of existing international rules. Under economic, political, demographic and climatic pressures, some weaker states in Africa and the Middle East are in effect already disintegrating, and the multilateral system is proving unable to support them. How these debates develop will be at the heart of global diplomacy for the next few decades and are likely to pose diplomats with ever more delicate and difficult problems as both the rules and the structures of international relations evolve.

But other factors will also influence it. Recent developments have brought a growing number of actors into the field of international relations, part of what some have called a shift from 'club' diplomacy, with a small number of powerful actors, to 'network' diplomacy, with a larger, more diffuse and more diverse number of participants (Cooper et al., 2013, ch. 2). At the same time, the world is faced by a growing number of challenges besides the maintenance of peace and expansion of prosperity that demand a collective response. Three in particular will influence what and how diplomacy is done.

Climate change is the greatest of these, because it is the most inexorable and existential, the one impacting the most people, and the one that most requires a collective response if it is to have any chance of being dealt with. Countries have wrestled with this diplomatically since the 1980s, creating a UN process at the Rio conference in 1992 (Brenton, 1994; Bulkeley and Newell, 2023). The challenge is that the global common good runs expressly counter to the short-term national interests or regime survival of many UN member states, and without a collective response that imposes some disciplines on all members, national policies will revert to a *sauve qui peut* approach that risks national and personal survival trumping collective action, and bringing escalating conflict in its wake. The difficulty of making the global compromises necessary, however, has stimulated a denialism in some quarters that will simply compound the problem and multiply the world's diplomatic challenges. In short, if we don't deal with climate diplomatically, we will need more diplomats to deal with the ensuing wars anyway.

Since the Black Death in the 13th century, health has also been a vector of global change that even the development of modern medicine has not been able to abolish, as the Covid pandemic demonstrated. Here, too, collective action is likely to be the only form that can genuinely protect humanity as a whole from future threats to its existence.

Technological change has had a profound impact on global relations, and hence on diplomacy, ever since sailing ships began to circumnavigate the globe, though not necessarily in the way anticipated. In the 1950s people expected that mankind would move outwards to conquer space, but up to now the transformation wrought by technology has been primarily on the terrestrial economy and societies: transport has not fundamentally changed in the last 50 years, but the communication of information and the global economy itself has been transformed by the internet. This has raised a whole new set of challenges that need a multilateral response, from regulating the global corporations that dominate the internet to managing the whole new level of information warfare that it has enabled. It has also had a profound impact on how diplomacy itself is conducted – as discussed in the following chapters – even if it has not changed the underlying substance of international relations (Fletcher, 2016).

In consequence, the multilateral system is unlikely to disappear. But it could easily fall into disrepair, its institutions going through the motions of managing global affairs, from technology and trade to health and security, while having little real influence on events on the ground or decisions in capitals. Bilateral diplomacy may become once more the dominant order and the trend from 'club' to 'network' diplomacy posited by some commentators go into reverse. But we will all be the poorer and more vulnerable for it. It would greatly increase the risks of war, or of natural events whether pandemics, famines or flood, overwhelming mankind's ability to manage them. But preserving the *effectiveness* of multilateral institutions requires a critical mass of member states to be willing to support them and respect their rules.

A globalised economy, through the ever-expanding flows of people, money, information and goods over the past 70 years, has brought an unprecedented era of economic growth, population growth, technological advancement and poverty reduction. But it has also brought a new range of challenges that existing international institutions are struggling to adapt to, let alone manage. Freer capital flows brought badly needed investment to emerging economies, but also brought unsustainable debt, stock market bubbles and busts, and greater inequality both within and between countries. Companies are having to navigate more complex and diverse regulatory environments in foreign markets. The freer movement of people, despite its evident economic benefits, also brought a political backlash that has dominated politics in many countries. The internet itself, engine of the globalisation of information, now supercharged by the development of Artificial Intelligence (AI), has created a whole set of new regulatory challenges as well diplomatic opportunities and political risks. Many of the ensuing problems from these developments are falling into the lap of diplomats, who have never needed to be more economically or technically literate, as well as skilled in the traditional arts of diplomacy (Bjola and Manor, 2024). And many people outside the formal diplomatic structures are having to learn diplomatic skills to navigate a more complex and contested world. If the old global structures are no longer adequate to the task, urgent reform is needed before the creaking structures break down entirely.

In short, diplomacy has never been more important than now: as the former diplomat Lord Strang commented already in the 1960s, 'diplomacy is everybody's business' (Hamilton and Langhorne, 2011, 1). Understanding how it is done in practice, and done well, also therefore matters more than ever. And that is what the rest of this book is about.

3 The varieties of diplomacy

As we have seen, the traditional image of diplomacy is focused very much on the bilateral relations between states and the policy work undertaken in foreign ministries. The reality is that more and more diplomatic activity takes place in a multilateral space or outside foreign ministries, involving a far wider range of institutions and actors. There is a big overlap in the skills needed by the diplomat operating in either context, but also significant differences. This chapter looks first at bilateral diplomacy, including the importance and challenges of dealing with economic, commercial, consular and visa work; then at multilateral diplomacy and how that differs; thirdly, at the role, deployment and limitations of soft power; fourthly at the changes that digital diplomacy is bringing to the way we work; and finally at how the diplomat needs also to be a master of handling their own government or headquarters at home as well as those abroad.

Bilateral diplomacy

The Chinese have a way with words. At every Chinese National Day I have attended, the Ambassador's speech always ends with the local variant of the phrase, 'Long live China-Ghana friendship! Ten thousand years!!' This neatly encapsulates the ambition of bilateral diplomacy – perpetual friendship, mutual respect, fruitful economic relations, and positive political exchanges. If only this was always the case.

The role of a bilateral diplomatic mission is to foster harmonious and beneficial relations between your own country and the host nation, and avoid any disagreements becoming so severe that they lead to a breach or, at worst, to a conflict. The aim is to do this through as high and wide a range of contacts in the host country as possible, by sending honest, insightful and timely analyses of the situation to your own government, managing inward visits from senior, famous or useful visitors from your own country, and encouraging visits to your capital by host government representatives. In addition, the mission has responsibility for its national citizens resident in or visiting the country, for offering advice to your national businesses operating in or looking for contracts there, and delivering an aid programme where that exists. It also (usually) provides visas for visitors to its own country.

In many posts there will be a security relationship, often pursued directly service-to-service in allied countries, or through a defence attaché in the embassy,

DOI: 10.4324/9781003533436-3

and occasionally clandestinely where relations may be more hostile. An ambassador would nevertheless normally expect to be kept informed of such links, even if they are maintained independently of the diplomatic mission, as it is essential for them to have an overview of the full breadth of relations between the two countries. Often, though, other members of the mission will be unaware of this. For the UK, the security relationship with the US and other members of the 'Five Eyes' partnership (Canada, Australia and New Zealand) dating back to the Second World War has been especially important, but so too are the long-standing relationships with France, Cyprus, Kenya and some of the Gulf states. Foreign officers training at Sandhurst or the Royal College of Defence Studies have built lasting relationships that are crucial to Britain's bilateral relations, and other countries – especially the US, China, Russia and France – do the same with their own military training institutions. Security diplomacy is equally important in the multilateral sphere, and, as we have seen in Chapter 2, the intimate relationship between war, the threat of war and diplomacy makes it hard to disentangle the two. So I treat the security element as integral throughout the book.

Within the Commonwealth, tradition dictates that governments exchange not ambassadors but high commissioners, reflecting the original view that they are not really 'foreign' countries at all, but part of the same family. Though the role is identical, in the UK at least high commissioners take precedence over ambassadors, which on ceremonial occasions leads to the interesting sight of the High Commissioner of Kiribati taking precedence over the US, Chinese or French Ambassadors. For simplicity, wherever I refer to an embassy or ambassador it can be taken to apply equally to a high commission or commissioner.

Not every country is represented in every other. Only the US and China currently have more or less universal diplomatic relations with and representation in every country. Britain (163 embassies), France (160), Japan (156), Germany (153), Russia (146), and India (123) are also represented in the bulk of countries (information from Embassy Pages, 2024). For most countries, however, many ambassadors are multi-hatted.

When I was appointed British High Commissioner to Ghana (2008–11), I was simultaneously accredited as Ambassador to four neighbouring countries – Côte d'Ivoire, Burkina Faso, Niger and Togo, which were covered from the mission in Accra. It took nearly a year before I had presented my credentials to all five heads of state, taking the best part of a week to travel to Niamey, capital of Niger, and back for that purpose. My New Zealand colleague covered the whole of western and central Africa, over 20 countries in all, and had scarcely finished presenting credentials before his four-year tour was completed and his successor had to start all over again – rather like painting the Forth Road Bridge. In Abidjan, the British Embassy to Côte d'Ivoire had been closed and our staff withdrawn in 2003 when a full-blown civil war broke out. A lone British diplomat, political officer Jo Gauld, now lived in the British Ambassador's former residence and worked with three Ivorian local staff (a driver, a gardener-cum-butler and a fixer). In the other capitals I depended on an Honorary Consul in Ouagadougou, a local Nigerien political officer in Niamey working part-time from the back of the French Embassy, and no one at all in Lomé, perhaps because the Togolese capital was in principle only three hours' drive from Accra, depending on the state of the road and the length of the border check. This multiple accreditation meant that there was usually a crisis of some sort in at least one of the countries at any one time (including a coup, a civil war, several elections and a few hostage-takings during my three years). Multi-hatting is increasingly common as diplomatic services are retrenched. But it is a fact that you cannot give the same level of attention to a country where you are not resident, and the four Presidents would regularly ask me when Britain would set up full diplomatic relations and open an embassy in their capital. This has now happened in Côte d'Ivoire and Niger, but Togo and Burkina Faso are still waiting, despite Togo's accession to the Commonwealth in 2023.

At that time, the British High Commission in Accra employed over 300 people, including large aid and visa sections, many local staff and a force of 50 security guards. It has since shrunk as the visa section was moved to Pretoria and the security contract was outsourced. But diplomatic missions can vary enormously in size from a single person to over 1,000 (in the US mission in Baghdad in 2022). Often the number of diplomatic staff sent from capitals will be outnumbered by local staff (of either nationality) recruited on the spot. Local staff are often cheaper than diplomatic staff, as they do not benefit from expatriation allowances, and stay longer than diplomats, providing more continuity, so have become indispensable to the functioning of most missions. But they do not have diplomatic status and often lack the security clearance to undertake more sensitive diplomatic tasks, so are often employed in administrative and management work or in the consular and commercial sections where less sensitive work is undertaken. In a few countries, where relations are difficult or local intelligence agencies aggressively target employees at foreign missions, it is not feasible to employ local staff except for the most routine tasks. Elsewhere, as for me in Niger, a member of local staff can be the sole presence. When the British withdrew their diplomats from Afghanistan in 1989, they left the Embassy compound in the hands of two local caretakers. Though it was transferred to Pakistan in 1994, who abandoned it after an attack the following year, when British diplomats finally returned in 2001 they found that the Ambassador's Wilton china service, crystal glasses and silver tea-pots, as well as the full-length portrait of King George VI, had been meticulously packed up, hidden in the loft and guarded throughout the years of civil war and Taliban rule by the embassy's two remaining local staff. They were rightly rewarded and honoured for their exceptional service (Harding, 2002).

Whatever the size of mission, and whatever level you are working at, to be effective in bilateral diplomacy requires five skills.

Firstly, you need to build good relations with the government, and particularly with the foreign ministry whose job it is, even in hostile countries, to talk to you when necessary. The bulk of diplomatic work will involve them. Some countries still insist that calls on any minister in the government are formally requested through a traditional written Note Verbale (the official means of communication from an embassy to its host government) sent to the foreign ministry. No contact was allowed until the official reply was received. Some also insist that diplomats seek formal permission before leaving the capital. At the same time, the diplomat is normally expected to build links and relations with the political opposition (if there is one), with civil society and lobby groups, and with all those who have political, social or economic influence, including religious groups and leaders. In Ghana it was important wherever I went to call on the traditional chiefs. Though strictly excluded from politics since independence, they were still much respected and retained considerable moral authority and social and economic influence. It is important to recognise that 'civil society' goes way beyond the familiar non-governmental organisations beloved of diplomats. Trade unions, cooperatives, youth groups, churches, charities, professional organisations or sports clubs – all can help you understand the wider social context within which politics is taking place.

Secondly, it is essential, where you can, to travel outside the capital, for work as well as leisure. I had a French colleague in Tanzania who liked nothing better at a weekend than to head out of Dar es Salaam in his Land Cruiser to some obscure historic location, giving lifts to people along the way and chatting to them in Swahili about their life, jobs, crops, families and politics. He was always the best-informed diplomat in town and an invaluable source on Tanzanian public opinion, rarely reflected in the official media. Getting out of town is just as vital in developed as in developing countries, and nowhere more so than in the US where opinions in Iowa, Ohio or Texas can bear little resemblance to those in Washington DC. Notifying a local parliamentarian or congressman that you are visiting their district always produced a positive response and introductions to local notables, and often provided a chance to talk to politicians informally, away from government eyes and ears, about what was really going on. Talking to elites and officials in the capital is often comfortable and easy. But in countries as vast as India, China or Brazil, or as diverse as Germany, Italy, Nigeria or Indonesia, you risk missing local political developments that will be just as influential as official views in shaping the country's foreign policy – if not more so.

Thirdly, always maintain fruitful relations with the media. They are an important source of information for the diplomat, being well-plugged in to political trends, and are the people you need in order to get your own message out, whether on a bilateral issue, a new initiative, a misunderstanding or a forthcoming visit. There is a balance to be struck between being visible and accessible, and maintaining sufficient distance to avoid getting dragged into controversy. Treading the narrow path can be tricky, as I discuss in Chapter 5.

Fourthly, the ceremonial side of the job matters too – attending national days, state occasions, the opening of parliament, royal weddings and political funerals, official banquets and receptions. Normally this falls to the ambassador or the deputy, but at some stage any staff in a mission may be required to attend. In Ghana, each event provided opportunities to network or meet ministers or senior officials who are rarely accessible in their offices. That is not to say that some events are not interminable and dull: forced to be seated an hour or more before the event begins, then listening to long speeches of sometimes spectacular dullness. Until the smartphone arrived, allowing perpetual connection and the ability to work anywhere, any time, these events could seem a frustrating waste of time. But they are always an opportunity to network, and the act of presence is often diplomatically vital: absence is noted, and retribution may follow.

Fifthly, entertainment is a key instrument of diplomacy. Customs vary. In some countries, contacts are more willing to be entertained in a restaurant than at home, and for many junior diplomats their accommodation is too modest to be used for formal entertainment. But most ambassadors are provided with a residence that is traditionally designed for hosting dinners, receptions and events so that valued contacts can be wined and dined, and visiting VIPs introduced socially to those they have to do business with. The problem is often finding the money to do it, but if it can be found entertainment is (almost) always money well spent. Inviting people into your home builds social relations that are rewarded with influence and impact when business needed to be done. One Foreign Office colleague, more musically gifted than I, would regularly end dinner parties with a sing-along around the piano which made him a popular man – especially in Ireland. But you need to know your audience and adjust your forms of entertaining to match.

Two additional skills will make a huge difference: learn the language, and read the literature.

The ubiquity of English rather than French since 1945 as the dominant diplomatic language makes it tempting for diplomats to rely on just that. But being able to make yourself understood to local officials and the local public in their own language makes a vast difference to your impact. Even an imperfect knowledge is often appreciated, as it demonstrates respect for the local people and their culture. The FCDO still places great value on language learning, particularly for French, Spanish, Portuguese, German, Arabic, Chinese, Russian, Japanese, Turkish, Urdu and Hindi, and devotes considerable resources to enabling staff to become skilled in the language before a posting. I spent many hours being tutored in Swahili at the Africa Centre in Covent Garden before my posting to Tanzania, and learnt invaluable lessons from Saidi, my tutor, about Tanzanian life and politics. Once learnt, a hard language can become a 'career-anchor' with the opportunity to serve in the relevant countries more than once. When I joined, it was assumed that all British diplomats would also speak French to an advanced standard, but I fear this standard has dropped. It is difficult to promote your country's interests in the local media or at public events if you cannot speak the language. Certainly in Tanzania, I got a richer and more subtle understanding of the politics and the culture from read-ing the Swahili press and listening to politicians talking to each other in their own language rather than that imported by the colonial power.

The same with literature. Wherever I was posted, I would ask those I met to recommend one book – of any kind: literature, history, poetry, politics, fiction or journalism – that they thought I should read to get a clearer idea about their country. This produced a fascinating reading list, including the Swahili poetry of Shaaban Robert in Tanzania, Stephen Ambrose's book *Undaunted Courage* about the Lewis and Clark expedition in the US, *The Beautyful Ones Are Not Yet Born* by Ayi Kwei Armah for Ghana, and *The Yakoubian Building* by Alaa Al Aswany for Egypt. Time spent reading these was never wasted. (My reciprocal recommenda-tion for Britain was George Dangerfield's *The Strange Death of Liberal England*: old but still resonant.)

There are many ways to keep relations peaceful, friendly and fruitful, but it is not always possible. Differences will arise. To formally lobby on some issue, like a vote in the UN, or to lodge a protest, for example about the arrest of a British citizen or a case of gross human rights abuse, one can deliver a *démarche* to

Figure 3.1 Blending in on a visit to Agadez, Niger, September 2015.

Source: author's photograph

the foreign ministry, usually by Note Verbale, if necessary requesting a formal response from the host. If on the other hand the host government wishes to show its displeasure to some act or opinion expressed by you or your country, the ambassador may be summoned to meet the foreign minister or the secretary-general of the ministry – the degree of displeasure being signalled by the length of time you are made to wait, whether any refreshment is offered and, in extremis, having a standing meeting where the ambassador is not even invited to sit down. If things deteriorate further, either government can withdraw its ambassador from the other, usually 'for consultations', leaving a *chargé d'affaires* to keep things ticking over. The complete withdrawal of an embassy and all its staff is usually only in response to a threat of imminent danger to the life of the diplomats, or a serious political rupture resulting in the formal breaking of all diplomatic relations. A host government may also choose to declare an ambassador or some member(s) of the diplomatic staff *persona non grata* giving them a limited time, from 24 hours to a few days, to leave the country (Chapter 6 describes my own experience). This extreme step can also be used if a diplomat has committed some gross indiscretion or crime, or undertaken 'activities incompatible with their status' – the usual euphemism for spying. The latter can often result in tit-for-tat expulsions, a way of signalling that 'we also know who your spies are'. This is discussed further in Chapter 6.

Trade and commercial diplomacy

For some, including ministers, this is an increasingly important diplomatic function – helping your country prosper. Leaders increasingly frequently travel to bilateral meetings with an entourage of senior businessmen, ready to cut deals with the host. British prime minister David Cameron took 120 with him to China in 2013 (Berridge, 2015, 193).

For some embassies it can even become the main function. In the 1980s, the British Embassy in Riyadh devoted years, and a number of prime ministerial visits, to helping British Aerospace (now BAES) land the *Al Yamamah* arms deal with the Saudi Arabian government, worth an estimated £43 billion over 20 years (Perlo-Freeman, 2017). Selling arms to foreign governments is a particularly political, as well as lucrative, business and concluding a deal will invariably involve a great deal of diplomatic advice and lobbying – assuming it is above board and clean. Embassies may well be called upon to advise whether a particular deal will pass the sniff-test: will the arms be used purely for defence, or is there a risk they might be used for external aggression or internal repression? And is any bribery involved in the deal which may come back to haunt the seller? Exports of arms from the UK have for years required an elaborate certification process that is closely policed by the law officers and parliament. Advice, however confidential, may at some stage be made public and exposed to legal scrutiny, so great care is needed in crafting it. Some other governments are less scrupulous and the global arms trade is second only to drugs in its murkiness.

Similar considerations apply to major deals by mining and oil companies, which are often long term, involve eye-watering sums of money, and may hang on government decisions that involve political as much as commercial considerations. Diplomatic advice in these circumstances can make all the difference between success and failure – one reason perhaps that so many of the oil and mining majors employ former diplomats in their government relations departments.

While I was in Ghana, Vodafone were negotiating to buy Ghana Telecom, the bankrupt national phone company. The decision ultimately rested with the president, but getting access to his key advisers for the company was something the High Commission could help with given the excellent relations we had built up over years. There was plenty of internal and external lobbying against the deal by a variety of parties (rival bidders, local vested interests, unions fearing lay-offs, security agencies) even though it brought $1.5 billion in external investment into the country. But in the end it went through. The High Commission also helped provide contacts with the opposition party, who had claimed the deal was a bad one and won the election only a few months later. In the event, Vodafone persuaded them not to unpick it.

Along the coast in Guinea, the British mining company Rio Tinto were granted exploration rights in 1997 for Simandou, a mountain in the inaccessible east of the country containing an estimated two billion tons of iron ore. Subsequent efforts by the government to reallocate some of the rights to other companies were mired in controversy and alleged corruption – an intriguing tale too long to tell here. In 2023, agreements were finally signed between the Guinean government, Rio Tinto and its Chinese partner, Chinalco, to begin development. The small British Embassy in Conakry exists largely because of this contract. Without a physical presence on the ground, the UK would have less idea what was going on in Guinea's turbulent politics (with two coups and four different Presidents since the initial rights were granted), and would lack the necessary access to the Guinean government to support such a major British investment (Ashcroft, 2024). The British Embassies in Angola and Senegal similarly support BP with their major investment in offshore oil and gas, and cases could be multiplied around the world.

Of course, when Elon Musk goes to China, he does not need the US embassy to arrange his meetings with the leadership, and many multinationals will use strategic advisory firms to help them gain access rather than (or as well as) the embassy. Sometimes companies want to keep the embassy well away from their business. But you still need to know what is going on.

Even where such major investments do not exist, most British missions overseas maintain a commercial section to promote British exports and encourage investment in both directions, providing advice on how to access the local investment promotion authorities, participate in trade fairs, navigate the regulatory and tax environment, or secure the necessary permits to do business. Where they exist, the embassy will liaise closely with the local British Chamber of Commerce. The same goes for other countries. Companies from all major economies now compete energetically for business throughout the world, and will regularly seek a briefing on the state of the local economy or the prospects for political stability, or ask for help in making political or official contacts. It is also worth keeping in regular contact with firms already well-established in the market. They don't need advice on how to do business, but in West Africa companies like Unilever, Standard Chartered, Tullow Oil or Vodafone often had a better idea of what was happening in the local economy than the press or even the Finance Ministry because their customers and suppliers provided them with a day-by-day insight into how much money they had, what they were buying, whether infrastructure was working well, or how robust local businesses and contactors were. All this was invaluable to our economic reporting. I would therefore meet regularly, once every few months, with the Rotary Club in Dar es Salaam, representatives of British businesses in Accra, or with BABA, the British-American Business Association in Washington DC.

Dealing with commercial issues in the US, as I did from 1999 to 2002, was very different from Africa. British companies had operated in the US for decades and needed little support from the embassy – except when there was trouble. This could arise from regulatory, trade or Congressional problems: new rules from the Food and Drugs Administration or the Federal Communications Commission; the regular tussle over landing slots at major airports (JFK in New York being the most sought after), where two British companies, British Airways and Virgin Atlantic, were competing against each other; or court cases against BP following the Deepwater Horizon blow-out. On the day of 9/11 in 2001, all US airspace was immediately closed, and every aircraft flying over the country grounded at the nearest available airport. Those heading towards the US were diverted, many from the UK ending up at a small airfield in Nova Scotia. This affected over 100 British-owned or operated aircraft. As the Embassy's point person for liaison with the Federal Aviation Authority, my phone was ringing off the hook with calls from British airlines wanting to know how long the close-down would last, how long they would have to accommodate passengers, and when they could get their aircraft in the air again. Every day cost them millions. When I finally got through to my contact at the FAA, he admitted he had no idea. Everything was in chaos. In the end it was a week of daily lobbying before flights were allowed to take off again and normal service began to resume. On that occasion, British airlines were in the same boat as everyone else. In other cases, new rules appeared to be introduced with deliberately discriminatory or protectionist intent. The endless litigation between Boeing and Airbus (parts of which are made in the UK) over who received illegal subsidies, or the rules governing aero-engines which affected Rolls-Royce's ability to compete with Pratt & Whitney, were intensely political as well as commercially critical, and required constant lobbying of the relevant authorities and congressmen to try to ensure a level playing field.

But the biggest problem was bananas. Since it fell on my plate, as it were, I was the Embassy's 'Mr Bananas'. When Britain's Caribbean colonies achieved independence, they were given the right to export bananas into the UK duty-free. This was grandfathered into the UK's accession agreement when it joined the European Economic Community (later the EU) in 1973, and became part of the Lomé trade agreement between the EU and the Africa, Caribbean and Pacific (ACP) group of former British, French and Portuguese colonies. This helped Caribbean banana growers, many of them small-scale farmers, keep market share and a reasonable price. The United Fruit Company, owners of the Chiquita brand, produced cheaper (but, I was assured, far less tasty) bananas on their vast estates in central America and were keen to break into the European market. They accused the EU of protectionist tariffs in favour of ACP producers and mobilised both the US Trade Representative (USTR) and Congress, through Trent Lott, the senator for Mississippi, where Chiquita landed their bananas in the US, to put pressure on the EU. As Lott was also Senate majority leader, he had a lot of leverage. Knowing that the UK was a key defender of the Caribbean producers, the US threatened to introduce 100% retaliatory tariffs targeted, among other things, on Scottish cashmere exports. The cashmere weavers (dear to the Labour government's Scottish Chancellor of the Exchequer Gordon Brown and Foreign Secretary Robin Cook) were outraged, and demanded that the EU – and the British Embassy in Washington DC – take action. The Ambassador, Sir Christopher Meyer, and I devoted many hours to negotiating a settlement with Gene Sperling, the President's chief economic adviser, and Condi Rice the National Security Adviser, who then sold it to Senator Lott – and in parallel negotiated with the European Commission delegation, which led on trade policy. A deal was eventually cut that provided limited additional EU access for 'dollar bananas', in return for the lifting of the threat against the Scottish cashmere industry (Meyer, 2005). But it illustrates just how politically sensitive and contentious trade issues could be.

Negotiating concessional access for foreign goods is always going to be delicate when there is domestic competition. To help poorer countries develop their export industries, the EU and US have offered duty-free, quota-free access to a limited number of countries for a limited number of products under the Economic Partnership Agreements (EPAs) and the US African Growth and Opportunity Act (AGOA). But both measures faced parliamentary or congressional opposition for being too generous, and criticism from the beneficiaries for not being generous enough. The WTO also negotiated duty-free access to all developed markets for almost all exports from least-developed countries (LDCs) under the 'Everything

But Arms' agreement, designed to encourage investment in export industries in these countries. It has had some success, but other constraints exist, for example from phyto-sanitary controls designed to prevent the spread of plant and animal diseases. These often restrict access to developed markets, imposing protectionism by other means. So these too can become the subject of heated negotiation.

If the world moves away from negotiating its trade relations through the WTO and begins to engage in competitive protectionist tariff-raising, as President Trump has done, bilateral trade diplomacy is going to become core business for many governments, and smaller economies will need to be very nimble – and their trade diplomats very good – to preserve their market access.

Commercial work can be contentious in three other areas. Some of the companies may not be wholly transparent about the business they are doing or seeking. Whether it is pharmaceutical companies doing product testing, finance companies offering generous but high-priced loans or carbon-trading deals, multinationals seeking to offshore business to low tax jurisdictions, or construction companies looking for contracts with the help of generous 'commissions', it is wise for the diplomat doing commercial work to do a minimum of due diligence on the companies they are dealing with. Though such cases may be rare (if not as rare as they should be), ministers will not thank you if the media expose the fact that an embassy's commercial section have helped one of your country's businesses land a dodgy deal. Similarly, some investors may be less scrupulous about human rights of workers, which can rebound on the government as well as the companies involved.

Finally, the regulation of technology has become a critical source of competition and friction, in terms of internet and social media content and advertising, the use and abuse of artificial intelligence, trade in hi-tech products, and the foreign ownership of technology companies. Today's tech giants – Alphabet, Amazon, Apple, Meta and Microsoft as well as Huawei and Samsung – are the multinational titans of our time and their technical and investment decisions have global as well as national impact. Regulating them will be a diplomatic as well as economic issue.

Economic and development diplomacy

In the past century, the global economy and, more recently, development issues have become a core part of diplomatic activity. In a globalised world economy what happens in one economy can have a profound impact on all the others, as witnessed in the Depression. This led, as we saw in the last chapter and explore more below, to the evolution of a growing number of multilateral institutions to help manage the global economy. But these issues involve bilateral missions too, and require diplomats to have some economic awareness and finance officials to acquire some diplomatic skills (Cooper et al., 2013, ch. 21). The British Treasury seconds officials to a number of embassies overseas (Washington, Berlin, Paris, Brussels and Tokyo, for example) to liaise directly with the local finance ministry on local and global economic policy.

Development assistance programmes, on the other hand, have a major impact on bilateral relations and an embassy's work. By and large, providing help to reduce poverty, accelerate growth or relieve those in humanitarian need is a good news story, a classic win-win for both parties. But successful development projects require close cooperation with the host government and communities, a good deal of experience and expertise, rigorous monitoring and scrupulous accounting. The media in both the donor and recipient countries will seize on anything that looks like extravagant waste of taxpayers' money or corrupt diversion of funds; inappropriate or insensitive projects that harm communities; or support to some groups or causes (human rights or LGBTQ+ activists, women's education, police forces, peacekeeping missions or even refugees) which might be controversial with some groups in the host country. So careful handling is always needed. Well-planned and well-prepared aid projects are usually warmly welcomed by the communities they help and by their governments, so they reap diplomatic rewards as well as developmental benefits from the closer relationship with both politicians and the public, and by demonstrating one's own country's commitment. Many books have been written on the pros and cons of aid programmes (e.g. Moyo, 2009; Mills, 2021; Dercon, 2022). But where they exist, they should be as beneficial to the communities concerned as possible.

A great deal of aid is delivered entirely independently of official government, UN or World Bank programmes. In West Africa these varied from major projects run or funded by Care, Concern, Save the Children, the Bill and Melinda Gates Foundation and other international NGOs, to small private initiatives, sometime funded by one family or church group or community in the UK, dedicated to helping one village, or a home for street children, or a rural clinic. There were too many to follow all of them, but they formed invaluable links between people in the UK and Ghana, were often efficiently run, and made a real difference to individual lives. I tried to visit such projects whenever travelling outside Accra as they were just as important a link between our countries as some of the larger, more costly government-to-government projects.

How development assistance is treated in organisational terms varies enormously from country to country. From 1997 to 2020 the UK managed its aid programme through the Department for International Development (DFID) and some other countries still manage development through a separate department or agency, such as AFD (France), GIZ (Germany) or USAID (US, until 2025). These agencies are sometimes housed separately from the diplomatic mission overseas and report directly back to their own headquarters rather than through the ambassador – a matter of friction in some posts, though my personal experience was of seamless and fruitful cooperation. DFID has now been re-integrated into the foreign ministry, which in 2020 became the Foreign, Commonwealth and Development Office (FCDO), and local development sections report through, rather than around, the ambassador. The effects of this re-merger are still being absorbed, but it means that more diplomats need to be more versed in development issues, and development experts more attuned to the geopolitical context – not necessarily a bad thing (though see

Lowcock and Dissanayake, 2024). For the recipient, however, it *ought* to make the aid more effective.

* * *

One particular instrument of economic diplomacy has been used increasingly frequently: the imposition of sanctions.

These are designed to damage or punish a state, company or individual for contravening international laws, norms, trade rules, or for committing acts of aggression against another state or for supporting terrorism. The effectiveness of these is much debated (e.g. Harding and Landsman, 2023), but they are popular as a 'peaceful' way of exerting pressure on states and individuals to abide by the rules, or to impede support to criminal or terrorist organisations. The diplomat is often called upon in advance to advise how effective they will be, to explain the justification to their host country, and after imposition to monitor their impact on the target country or entity, and report back. Many are of some technical complexity, with very specific targets, and need to be imposed by a group of countries to be effective, for example the EU (with the UK and others in tow) or the G7. They are usually coordinated by experts from trade and finance ministries and central banks. Obviously, they tend not to improve relations with the targeted country, which may impose reciprocal sanctions; but it is rare that they lead to a rupture in diplomatic relations. Sanctions imposed on South Africa by the opponents of apartheid in the 1980s are credited with having helped force its democratic transition (Crawford and Klotz, 1999) and those on Iran on the 2000s to have paved the way for the Iran nuclear deal in 2015 (Bajoghli et al., 2024). Western sanctions against Russia following its invasion of Ukraine in 2022 have been the most extensive and elaborate yet, but, though clearly a nuisance, have (so far) tended to divert business and trade through other channels rather than stopped it. Their impact therefore depends very much on the specific circumstances, but they will remain a key element of economic and diplomatic pressure before or during conflict.

Consular and visa diplomacy

Consular matters have been at the core of diplomatic work for over a century, as states accepted a degree of responsibility for their citizens overseas. The amount of work this involves, however, can vary dramatically. I cite mainly British cases here as those are the ones I know, but most countries have similar issues relating to their own citizens abroad.

It is estimated that around 5.5 million British nationals live overseas (Smith, 2020; Migration Watch UK, 2016). These tend to be concentrated largely in a few places – the US (700,000), the EU (1.2 million in 2016, mainly in Spain, Ireland, France and Germany), Australia (1.3 million) and Canada (600,000) – where the main service to resident Britons is renewing their passports, now done mainly online. But there are a few British citizens living in almost every country in the world, many of them dual citizens, but to whom consular services are due all the same. In Sudan, for example, when civil war broke out in 2023, the UK helped evacuate 2,450 British citizens still living there (FCDO, 2023, 54). Growing numbers of people hold dual citizenship, which can complicate things. But if you have the passport, you have the right to at least some consular support.

That may not be as much as you would like. Migration has always brought people from one place to another, but in most cases migrants have looked to their new country as home, and not sought support from their old one. By the early 20th century, most embassies had a consular officer who could provide passports when they expired and help stranded nationals in an emergency. Consular work was transformed, however, by the age of mass tourism and global travel, beginning in the 1960s with package tours and cheap flights anywhere in the world. Suddenly, thousands of people would travel to foreign countries for a week or two; some would inevitably get into trouble, ending up in hospital or prison; regular as clockwork, others would lose their passports or have all their possessions stolen; and a few would die and their remains need to be evacuated home for the funeral. Some would also stay for months or years, get married, find a job, have children and want to have them registered as British citizens at the embassy. Consular work quadrupled. So it became important to define more tightly what was and was not provided. A surprising number of travellers would turn up at an embassy having run out of money or luck and ask to be repatriated at public expense to the UK. They got short shrift.

Nevertheless, consular issues can also have a disproportionate political impact. In countries with robust democracies and an active media, there is a perpetual risk that the misfortunes of citizens overseas will become a political issue at home. Certainly in the UK, MPs will regularly raise the plight of their constituents overseas either with the FCDO or directly to ministers through Parliamentary questions. Some parts of the media love nothing better than to splash a story about privileged diplomats ignoring the suffering of ordinary Brits abroad, abandoning them to penury or injustice while they sip their gin and tonic by the pool. Social media has also made it possible for local problems to be communicated instantly to a worldwide audience. Ministers are invariably sensitive to the charge of leaving citizens in the lurch, so consular work has assumed a priority that has attracted more and more resources, and ambassadors ignore it at their peril.

There are four broadly distinct areas which consular work deals with: visiting nationals, resident nationals, imprisoned nationals, and emergency planning.

Firstly, there is dealing with the misfortunes of travellers and tourists. Though very occasionally this can indeed go wrong, it is now the most routine, if time-consuming, part of the job. The British Embassy in Greece, for example, gets an annual reinforcement of consular officers to cope with the influx of British tourists during the summer months. The volume of emergency travel documents issued, to allow those whose passports have been lost, stolen or strayed to get home again, has increased in line with tourist numbers travelling overseas. By and large, though, the insistence that embassies will not deal with anything that should normally be covered by travel insurance, limits their liability and the risks of dealing with the drunk or destitute.

Dealing with the dead, however, can still be serious and sensitive. It is almost invariably unexpected; there may or may not be relatives present, though if not they will often fly in, and the local bureaucratic procedures for death certificates and the repatriation of remains are often the last thing they want to deal with. Again, the more remote the country, and the more unusual the circumstances, the more likely the embassy will get involved, particularly if the death was suspicious or violent and the local police take an interest. In Ghana we dealt with 2–3 deaths a year, and our local consular officer was exemplary in dealing with grieving relatives, helping them wherever we could. Knowledge of local procedures and contacts with local undertakers can be essential to help support the family. Occasionally a staff member, local or diplomatic, will pass away, and this is like a bereavement in the family, where the ambassador needs to provide leadership and support.

Similarly, if citizens end up in jail the obligations become more serious. If visitors have broken local laws, even inadvertently, that is their responsibility: the embassy has no 'get out of jail free' card, and dual nationals are likely to be treated by the local government as their own citizens. But there is a responsibility to ensure that due process is followed and that the offender has access to legal advice, albeit at their own expense, so most embassies maintain a list of local lawyers willing and able to help foreign nationals. If due process or prison conditions are in doubt, consular officers should arrange to visit – if it is feasible. In Ghana, there was a British citizen of Ghanaian origin convicted of murder and waiting on death row. On this occasion, as High Commissioner, I arranged to visit myself. Britain ended the death penalty in 1965, and lobbies actively for its universal abolition. We had delivered a Note Verbale to the foreign ministry formally requesting that the sentence be commuted to life imprisonment, and ensured that the man was in touch with human rights lawyers in the UK who would take up the case *pro bono* and appeal it to the highest court in the country. This local process was still in course, but it was important for the Ghanaian authorities to see that this was a case the British government itself was following closely.

Another difficult question is that of children of British citizenship taken back to their family's country of origin, often against their will or by subterfuge, to arranged marriages – in accordance with local custom maybe, but contrary to British law. In Pakistan, the British embassy set up a special consular unit and emergency hotline to help such children return to the UK if they so wished. It was delicate and dangerous work, supporting a number of these returns, for which the team was rightly recognised with the FCDO's annual award for outstanding work.

Equally complicated are the cases of citizens taken hostage by terrorist groups. I was involved with the case of a British citizen kidnapped with a number of Frenchmen by a group linked to Ansar Dine, a Tuareg separatist movement with jihadist links that operated mainly in Mali but also across borders into Burkina Faso and Niger. The British government traditionally spares no efforts to get its citizens released, other than by force or by ransom, on the grounds that the latter only encourages further hostage-taking (though it cannot prevent families or employers making their own arrangements).

President Compaore of Burkina Faso, to which I was accredited as ambassador, was known to have back-channel contacts with the rebels, so I arranged to call on him with a UK government specialist. He offered to help by putting us in touch with his liaison man, a slight, quiet Mauritanian called Moustafa Chafi, whom we met in a scruffy café in the back streets of Ouagadougou. It felt very John Le Carré. Contacts continued, and the man was eventually released unharmed after nine months in captivity, though how much Chafi had to do with it was never clear.

The most difficult are cases of political imprisonment. The recent case of Nazanin Zagari-Ratcliffe illustrated the challenges. A dual British-Iranian citizen, she had been visiting relatives in Iran in March 2016 when she was arrested by the Iranian Revolutionary Guard Corps (IRGC) at the airport and subsequently put on trial for plotting against the government. She was later accused of spreading propaganda against the country through a BBC Persian training course. It was evident early on that she was being held as a political bargaining chip in the long-running dispute between Britain and Iran over sanctions that had blocked the re-payment of a nearly £400 million debt owed by Britain for refusing to deliver tanks bought and paid for by the previous Iranian government in 1979. Initially the British government sought to secure her release through quiet, behind-the-scenes lobbying in Tehran, judging that public protests would exacerbate the situation. It was clear, however, that the Iranian foreign ministry had little control over her case which was firmly in the hands of the IRGC. She was denied British consular access or legal help, despite efforts by the British Embassy to provide both, on the grounds that she was an Iranian citizen in her home country. In May 2016, her British husband, Richard Ratcliffe, therefore started a public petition for her release which received over three million signatures and began actively lobbying ministers and the media. Twice during her imprisonment he undertook public hunger strikes, once outside the Iranian embassy and later outside the Foreign Office. Questions were asked in Parliament, and in 2017 the then foreign secretary, Boris Johnson (who rarely read his briefing notes) told a Parliamentary committee that Zagari-Ratcliffe *had* been training journalists (she hadn't) – enabling the Iranian court to extend her sentence on the grounds that the British government had admitted her guilt. On another occasion there were press reports of a possible prisoner swap for an Iranian held in Australia, but that came to nothing. After six years of detention, Nazanin was finally released on 16 March 2022, the day after Britain finally paid the outstanding debt (Landale, 2022).

The case illustrates graphically that consular issues can very rapidly become political, so it is unwise to neglect them. It also points to the importance and sensitivity of official travel advice. The UK, like many western countries, now provides travel advice for tourists and travellers that indicates not only the safety of visiting any individual country, but also which parts of the country are safe. In particular it warns of areas where there is a risk of terrorist attack or criminal kidnapping, as well as wider threats to public order or from state action. This is done as a public service, but also as an insurance policy for the government, to discourage citizens from going to places where they may get into trouble and require extraordinary consular help. The travel advice itself can be politically sensitive: few governments are happy that another may publicly discourage visitors to their country, particularly if they depend heavily on tourist revenue. Changing travel advice, for example after the Westlands terrorist attack in Kenya in 2011, or for Sharm el-Sheikh in Egypt after an airliner was blown up departing from there in 2015, can be a very delicate matter that an ambassador needs to handle with great care. Anglo-Egyptian relations did not fully recover for some years, and governments have been known to retaliate by warning their own citizens against visiting London because of the prevalence of knife-crime. The art is therefore to make any change in advice as factual as possible – and ensure the ambassador gets to see it *before* it is published by the ministry.

Dealing with citizens permanently resident overseas is very different. As a rule, the responsibility increases in inverse proportion to the number. Where there are many thousands of British citizens, as in France, Spain, Australia or the US, they expect relatively little from the embassy. There is no expectation, for example, that every Brit in Paris would get a much sought-after invitation to the King's Birthday Party, the annual national celebration overseas. In Dar es Salaam, however, with barely a hundred British citizens in the capital during the 1990s, any citizen *not* invited would feel personally affronted and cause us grief for the rest of the year. In Brunei, one ambassador told me, the dozen or so Brits would feel entirely at liberty to turn up at the High Commissioner's residence every Friday night for a sundowner. One way to manage the community was to befriend the 'loyal societies', where they exist – the St George's, St David's and St Andrew's for the English, Welsh and Scottish contingents respectively. Usually they would come to life for just one event a year, Burns Night being a particular favourite for the Scots (and many others), with the local embassy enrolled to ensure a suitable supply of haggis, whisky and bagpipes. If there is an Irish community there will, without a shadow of doubt, be a St Patrick's Day event, though the Irish ambassador, if there is one, would normally take the lead.

For many long-term expats, ambassadors are mere transients, here today and gone tomorrow. The relationship is nevertheless important. Some foreigners achieve positions of real prominence in their adopted countries, culturally, academically, in business and even occasionally in politics. American universities are stuffed with eminent British academics; in Ghana one highly respected long-term British resident was the world expert on Ghanaian high-life music, while in Tanzania one British family had done business there for generations and knew many of the ruling party's leaders since they were at school together. Connecting with these people is important for a mission as they bring contacts and influence that an ambassador would struggle to achieve in three to four years at post. Getting on well with your community therefore matters. On one of my African postings, a newly arrived and ambitious young Italian ambassador was hastily withdrawn after he offended the local Italian community by holding, it seems, too many late-night pool parties attended by scantily clad models from a local 'agency'.

Your community of nationals also need to be borne in mind for disaster planning. Every mission needs an emergency evacuation plan: if you arrive in a mission without one, fix it fast. Disasters can strike at any moment and any place, particularly in our world where the climate is becoming more unstable, global terrorism knows no bounds, and pandemics can spread like wildfire. The unexpected and urgent need to evacuate citizens from Sudan when the civil war broke out in 2023 has been mentioned above; the same applied in Lebanon when Israel attacked in 2024. In the US in 2001, nobody expected an event like 9/11 and the embassy in Washington's emergency plan did not include the contingency. We made it up as we went along (see Chapter 8). The Pacific tsunami of 2004 killed over 230,000 people, including many tourists holidaying in Indonesian and Thai beach resorts. Getting consular help to the survivors was a nightmare when all normal infrastructure – phones, internet, transport – was utterly disrupted. But embassies in Bangkok and Jakarta did their utmost to help those stranded and destitute. Again, during the Covid pandemic in 2020, it was little reported and largely forgotten that the British diplomatic network, under firm ministerial direction, dropped almost all other work to evacuate around 38,000 British citizens back to the UK from 57 different countries on 186 charter flights (FCO, 2020, 7).

Countries' attitudes to their citizens abroad can vary. Some see their diaspora as a resource: Nigerian politicians invariably visit London in the run-up to an election to raise funds and secure votes; some see it as a threat, and have been known to assassinate opponents living in exile abroad (as Alexander Litvinenko and Jamal Kashoggi both found); others again see the diaspora as an extension of the nation to whom their real loyalty is due, with a duty to prioritise its interests over those of their country of residence. These attitudes can affect the role of the diplomatic mission, and indeed cause trouble for the host nation if illegal activities are supported by a foreign government. But these are exceptions rather than the rule.

Many countries appoint honorary consuls to help them where they are not represented. Normally unpaid volunteers, except for expenses, they are often long-time expats or nationals of the host country with some connection to your own. They do not normally have diplomatic status, though in some countries there are diplomatic benefits that make it an attractive role for businessmen. The British honorary consul in Burkina Faso was a Frenchman who had lived and worked there for decades. Whenever I visited Ouagadougou, he had no trouble getting me access to the President or other ministers I needed to see. He also managed impeccably the unexpected death of a British charity worker, the visit of her family and the repatriation of the remains. The Washington Embassy not only maintained seven consulates manned by British diplomats (in New York, Chicago, Los Angeles, San Francisco, Miami, Houston and Boston), but a network of a dozen honorary consuls in other cities, mostly American citizens, lawyers or businessmen, who provided invaluable contacts and intelligence about the state of local politics. So honorary consuls, contrary to Graham Greene's caricature, can be invaluable.

* * *

Visas are the other side of the coin: provided for foreign nationals wishing to visit your own country. Here governments have more discretion over how easy they choose to make it.

Many countries have agreements on visa-free travel for selected friendly foreign nationals, and for countries dependent on foreign tourists easy (if expensive) visas online or on arrival are often provided. But the political sensitivity created by growing numbers of foreign visitors and migrants mean that many, like the UK, have visa regimes for a growing number of other countries that have become progressively tighter, increasingly difficult and costly to navigate. This is a problem because the visa process is often a person's first encounter with your country. If it is difficult, it may not create the most positive impression; and if it is felt to be unfair, it can create bilateral diplomatic problems.

For many countries, visas are still issued by embassies, usually through a separate consular section with its own entrance and (usually packed) waiting room. Increasingly, however, the process is being outsourced to professional service providers and/or put online, though decision-making on individual cases remains under government control. Most British missions therefore no longer have a visa section but direct applicants to a separate Visa Application Centre (VAC), which sends the applications to remote processing centres (largely in the UK) where a decision is taken and the result sent back to the VAC for collection. This is costly, though the price of visas is often set to more than cover the costs, with different categories (for visitors, students, workers or settlement) attracting different criteria, documentation and prices. It remains a physical process for the UK because of the insistence on seeing original documents, and tends therefore to take weeks and occasionally months. Embassies have been almost entirely cut out of the process. Other countries have put the whole process online so you can secure a decision in days and arrive at the border with the proof of visa on your phone and get the stamp in your passport there. When it works reliably, this has greatly simplified life.

Where the process is still time-consuming, a fast track becomes essential for VIPs, especially heads of state and ministers who may need to travel at short notice, often with a large entourage. So ambassadors still need a way to influence decisions to avoid unnecessary political complications. It requires a point of contact in the visa processing mechanism where political factors can be inserted into the decision-making process and the whole thing speeded up. Having someone on the political team who knows how to do this is essential to avoid embarrassing situations.

The problem of illegal migration has also created an industry negotiating bilateral returns agreements: the ability to ship illegal migrants or unsuccessful asylum applicants back to their country of origin. These are difficult but essential to negotiate given their political priority at home. Some countries, like Eritrea, refuse to engage at all, claiming for example that the asylum seekers are all actually

Ethiopian. More often, the receiving country will seek some benefit themselves from accepting their citizens back, as well as ensuring that they are genuinely their own citizens, so again it will often fall to the ambassador to negotiate at a suitably high level where political influence can be brought to bear.

Multilateral diplomacy

Multilateral diplomacy is a wholly different ball-game.

As explained in the last chapter, it evolved only in the 20th century as a result not just of globalisation but of the international structures developed to manage it. The International Telegraph (later Telecommunications) Union – ITU – was the first such body, founded in 1865, with the League of Nations and its secretariat the first permanent political structure. A number of economic and political conferences were also initiated in the 1920s and '30s in an effort to solve the world's problems, but without lasting success. It was only after the Second World War that multilateral diplomacy came into its own under the auspices of the UN and new regional organisations around the world. Though the UN and EU are the frequent butt of nationalist criticism, with politicians chaffing at the constraints that international rules impose on national freedom of action, they also fulfil an essential diplomatic role without which the world would be a messier and poorer place. No multilateral bodies are perfect; they can be cumbersome, expensive and slow; all are constantly in need of reform; many diplomats as well as politicians complain about the endless hours spent negotiating intricate texts. Some even risk becoming redundant: what is the point of the WTO, for example, if the big trading powers simply ignore it and impose tariffs at will? But they all possess only as much power as their member states choose to give them and are needed more than ever as global problems multiply. So they still serve a purpose, and will always need diplomats to make them work. It is therefore important to understand how to operate successfully within them.

Contrary to the bilateral work described above, multilateral diplomacy is conducted primarily between diplomats and national or international civil servants acting as diplomats. Given the ever-wider spread of international rule-making, many areas of traditionally domestic policy have become subject to multilateral negotiation and officials from most ministries have at some stage become involved in UN, EU or other negotiations. So, as Lord Strang implied, we are all diplomats now. International NGOs have also come to play an important role in several areas of multilateral negotiation, from climate to human rights and humanitarian action, bolstering efforts to uphold global norms or rules when some governments try to weaken them. But the public rarely get a look in (see below, however) and politicians often appear only once a deal is done and there is something to celebrate. It is a world of committees, conferences and communiqués, drafting and drudgery, often over days and months. And yet I found it the most fascinating diplomacy of all – a kind of four-dimensional chess, where you are negotiating in all directions at the same time, and often to a tight deadline. Done well (like the Paris climate agreement), the results make a real difference; done badly (like the Brexit negotiations), everyone suffers.

Multilateral diplomacy has two underlying aims: firstly, to enable all to speak and all to be heard. That principally applies to the governments of nation states, those with the power and responsibility to negotiate binding agreements, though other interests agitate to participate too. Even so, the claim that multilateral institutions are 'undemocratic', that they exclude 'the people' because they are dominated by governments, is tautological. The purpose of government is to represent as well as govern people, and they do so in these institutions. Admittedly some governments represent their people more fully or effectively than others. But there has to be an international process that is manageable, and agreements that will be respected by all the governments concerned, of whatever political hue. Experience also suggests that governments reluctant to allow democracy or pluralism at home will be equally reluctant to allow the people a direct voice in international fora. As we saw in the last chapter, the multilateral system evolved partly to enforce some minimum global norms. But it only works if you accept the right to speak of other governments around the table. This is a vexed issue discussed in more detail in Chapter 6.

The second aim is to make unmanageable situations or problems manageable. This is the genius of the EU and why – despite all the complaints – it has been so successful: it turns problems of substance into problems of process, and thus enables them to be solved (Hannay, 2013, 121–72). The process is the key to it, and therefore understanding the process is vital.

That all speak and are heard, and that an inclusive process enables all nations to participate, does not mean that all are equal: some are, indeed, more equal than others. Successful multilateral institutions need to reflect power as well as principle; otherwise, they become toothless or useless. So at the UN, despite the historical anomaly associated with its founding in the aftermath of war, the existence of the five permanent members (the P5) of the Security Council has helped make it work. The antipathy between the US and the Soviet Union up to 1989 blocked progress on many dossiers, but not all. Where they aligned, things happened. China's inclusion in the P5 from the outset was a prescient decision, and in the last few years it has taken a visibly more active role in UN discussions. Britain and France have continued to justify their roles through activism, putting forward ideas, drafting resolutions and proactively seeking consensus while wisely refraining from wielding their (no longer credible) vetoes (Greenstock, 2016, 48–9). It is a symbol of the pragmatism that accompanied its founding that at the opening of the UN General Assembly in New York every September, it is not the US host that speaks first but Brazil – the result of a compromise to persuade Brazil to drop its bid to host the UN Secretariat in Sao Paulo. (For the UN, see Annan, 2012; Weiss and Dawes, 2020)

The Security Council stands at the apex of the UN system, the UN Secretary-General being unkindly defined (by one US diplomat) as 'more Secretary than General' (Chesterman, 2007). Besides the P5, it consists of ten temporary

Figure 3.2 Briefing the UN Security Council on EU policy on the Sahel, New York, December 2014.

Source: author's photograph

members, elected for two-year terms by regional groupings to ensure a geographi-cally balanced representation. The chairmanship rotates every month between the fifteen members, giving often small countries an unparalleled opportunity to influ-ence world events. It takes decisions by majority vote, as long as one of the P5 does not exercise its veto. Its remit is to act to prevent conflicts, though its track record is patchy. It is easier to act where one of the P5 is not directly involved – or if they are involved, that all are united, as during the original Iran nuclear negotiations. Nevertheless, passing a Security Council Resolution (SCR) can be a critical step in heading off conflict or, more often, paving the way for peace negotiations. When the Security Council is stuck, as it has been in recent years over Syria, Ukraine and Gaza, the UN General Assembly, on which all countries are represented and each has a single vote, will often step in to vote a resolution. These are adopted by simple majority and, while non-binding (unlike SCRs), give a clear impression of the collective view of governments world-wide. So knowing how to negotiate such resolutions (described in the next chapter) is an essential diplomatic skill.

Under the UN umbrella a whole ecosystem of international organisations exists. Some are direct agencies of the UN – UNDP (development), UNEP (environment), UNESCO (culture), UNHCR (refugees), UNHRC (human rights), UNICEF (chil-dren); others have specific functions – the FAO for agriculture, ILO for labour, IMO for migration, WHO for health, WTO for trade; and the Bretton Woods institutions, the IMF and World Bank, were created to provide affordable finance and prevent countries falling into the state of economic desperation that devastated so many lives and fed the growth of fascism in the 1930s. The International Court of Justice (ICJ) is an integral part of this structure, a court purely for states not individuals, established in 1945 to police the international rule of law. It is now complemented by the International Criminal Court (ICC), set up in 2002 to try individuals where national courts could not for the crimes of genocide, crimes against humanity, war crimes and the crime of aggression – though unlike the ICJ not all countries have adhered to it. The European Court of Human Rights (ECtHR) was also established in 1959 to interpret the European Convention on Human Rights (ECHR) to which all European countries have signed up.

There is a narrative that this whole multilateral structure was created to preserve the privileged position of 'the West' and that it needs to be struck down, replaced or at least drastically reformed. The case for reform is powerful, both to reflect the changing balance of economic, political and demographic power, and to enable the institutions to be more effective in supporting small countries (Malloch-Brown, 2011). But some advocates of this narrative are equally interested in undermining the principles and norms underpinning the UN Charter itself: of self-determination, individual human rights and the rule of law. These principles were established precisely to protect smaller countries and vulnerable populations from being dominated, intimidated or eliminated by bigger neighbours or authoritarian governments, and hence to prevent another world war. This battle of narratives therefore has real significance, and is being fought out day by day in the committee rooms and conference halls of the multilateral institutions themselves, as well as in social media and political meetings across the 'global south' (a recent term used as an imprecise shorthand for parts of the world not considered the 'east' or the 'west,' sometimes also referred to as the 'global majority'). Multilateral diplomacy is about more than just resolving specific problems: it is, often literally, about the future of the world – politically, economically and, above all, environmentally.

Separate from the UN, a wide range of regional organisations exists, varying significantly in their structure and ambition.

The EU is by far the most sophisticated and powerful of these, though it may look to an outsider like one of those mythical beasts with two heads, twenty-seven legs and a long tail. Founded by six nations in 1957 through the Treaty of Rome, it was explicitly designed to avoid the catastrophic wars that devastated Europe in the first half of the century. Through successive rounds of negotiation and enlargement culminating in the Lisbon Treaty on European Union in 2010, it evolved from a loose grouping of six focused on economic integration to a unique political structure of 27 member states in 2024 that is a mixture of intergovernmental, collaborative, federal and unitary elements, those in the Schengen border grouping and the euro zone having the most integrated cooperation. It achieved this by carefully managing the power balance between member states and the central institutions, and between the member states themselves through qualified majority voting (QMV) on the bulk of economic issues, but with unanimity reserved for foreign policy and institutional issues. The voting is 'qualified' because different countries have different numbers of votes to reflect their size and population – from Germany, France and Italy with ten each to Luxembourg and the Baltic states with two each. The European Council, composed of the heads of state or government of the member states, presides but does not formally decide: that is the prerogative of the Council of Ministers (meeting at ministerial level), supported by the Council Secretariat. The European Commission is the bureaucracy then responsible for implementing the decisions. Nevertheless the orientations agreed in the European Council conclusions are invariably reflected in the subsequent formal decisions, whether by the member states in Council through regulations, or by the European Commission through directives (Cooper, 2003; Patten, 2005; Van Middelaar, 2013).

This hybrid mixture of intergovernmental and unitary characteristics makes the EU a kind of voluntarist and democratic empire: states belong because they choose to join (or leave, in the UK's case), and agree to pool a degree of sovereignty which is exercised collectively by the institutions – the Commission, the Council, the External Action Service and the Court of Justice. A requirement of accession is that a country should be a functioning democracy, so every national government is elected by and represents its citizens. Council decisions can therefore be considered democratic. But to provide additional democratic accountability a directly elected European Parliament exists to which both the Commission and the Council report. Nevertheless, ultimate authority effectively remains with the heads of government in the European Council, which takes its decisions by consensus. This underpins the willingness of member states to remain within the EU. In theory, every member has a veto, enshrined in the 'Luxembourg compromise' which provides that if a member state claims a decision would damage its vital national interests, discussion must continue until a consensus can be found.

This structure drives a process where member states feel comfortable enough that there is a handbrake if their interests are too endangered, but there is a strong motivation to reach agreement, and a great incentive to build alliances so that the necessary majority can be found for the measures you want adopted. The fact that so much now comes within Community competence makes trade-offs easier to arrange: smaller countries in particular can trade their votes on things they are less concerned about for support on issues that are critical to them. It makes for complex, but rewarding negotiations. The single market was successfully built, the euro was launched, economies – and the EU itself – grew. Occasionally one member state will hold out against all the rest for national reasons (Hungary has made a speciality of it) – but there is a cost: they will find it harder to secure support for something else they do want in the future.

Since the early days, the EU has coordinated aspects of the external as well as internal policies of the member states. Trade fell within Community competence from the outset and was therefore handled by the Commission, but foreign policy remained a prerogative of the member states. They nevertheless found it useful to coordinate policies in relation to near neighbours, such as Turkey, or countries of particular interest to one or another member state, such as East Timor or Zimbabwe. Political Directors met monthly, meetings prepared by a network of 'European Correspondents' (of which I was one), and reported to the monthly Foreign Affairs Council (FAC) which would take decisions. The Maastricht Treaty of 1992 turned this informal arrangement into a formal 'Common Foreign and Security Policy', with a permanent team of seconded national diplomats in the Council Secretariat. The Lisbon Treaty of 2010 took this a step further, creating a permanent President of the European Council, and a High Representative for Foreign and Security Policy to chair the FAC and act as the representative and spokesperson on foreign affairs for the member states, where they agree, with a European External Action Service (in which I worked) to support them. Defence cooperation also took a tentative step forward, though NATO remained firmly in the lead on European defence. The coordination is far from total. In fact member states continue to pursue their own national foreign policies on many issues, and on some, like Middle East peace, they remain deeply divided. But for many of the smaller member states it gives them a far greater input to global diplomacy than they would ever achieve outside the EU.

A number of other regional organisations have aspired to emulate the EU, notably the African Union (AU), but none have yet achieved the EU's level of integration. Countries for which sovereignty is new and precious are often reluctant to share it to the extent of allowing a supranational body to set policy or police implementation. Most organisations have been set up to promote regional economic integration: ASEAN in south-east Asia, Mercosur in Latin America, Caricom in the Caribbean, and in Africa ECOWAS (West Africa), SADC (Southern Africa), ECCAS (Central Africa), IGAD (the Horn of Africa) and the East African Community. The AU also initiated the African Continental Free Trade Area (AfCFTA) to create an Africa-wide market that it is hoped will stimulate more rapid economic growth for all. Some of these have achieved more than others on the economic front. But for many the regular summits at head of state level have become an essential means of discussing (and sometimes dealing with) regional security and governance issues, so the diplomacy around each has become as much political as economic. A number of trade agreements also have a political purpose and have evolved over time: the North American Free Trade Area (NAFTA) has become the US-Mexico-Canada Agreement (USMCA); and the Asia-Pacific Economic Cooperation (APEC) has been partially superseded by the snappily titled Comprehensive and Progressive Agreement for Trans-Pacific Partnership (CPATPP).

Other regional organisations have always been primarily political. The Arab League, founded in 1945 and headquartered in Cairo, brings together all Arab-speaking nations, while the Gulf Cooperation Council (GCC) unites (some of the time) the Arab countries of the Gulf while the Organisation of Islamic States (OIC) includes all of these plus the Muslim states of Asia and Africa.

There is a plethora of non-regional groupings, ranging from the G7, G20 and BRICS (which again started as groups to discuss economic issues but have transmuted to a greater or lesser extent into political bodies) to the OECD, often described as a 'club for rich countries' that compiles and exchanges economic data, the IAEA, supervising the peaceful use of atomic energy, and the OSCE, designed after the fall of the Wall as a forum for inclusive discussions of security issues in Europe, but currently hamstrung by the war in Ukraine. The Shanghai Cooperation Forum, originally for China's partners in the Belt and Road Initiative (BRI), has been growing in importance. The ACP group exists solely as a counterpart to the (now expired) Lome and Cotonou Conventions with the EU. The Commonwealth and La Francophonie bring together countries that once formed part of the British and French empires respectively, but since independence have found some common purpose in continuing to meet. They have grown to include countries that were not former colonies, but are both searching for a stronger purpose. It is not just governments: the world's main central bankers meet annually at Jackson Hole, Wyoming, to share wisdom and discuss interest rates.

Finally, there are explicit military alliances, of which NATO is by far the most sophisticated and substantive. Others – the Warsaw Pact, the Central Treaty Organisation (Baghdad Pact) – have fallen by the wayside while others again, like the China-Russia 'no limits partnership', have sprung recently into uncertain existence.

This multiplication of multilateral bodies means that the diplomatic landscape is littered with the remnants of obsolete or redundant multilateral bodies. The axiom of Arthur Hugh Clough (in his poem 'The Latest Decalogue') that 'Thou shalt not kill; but need not strive/officiously to keep alive' could well apply to such organisations that have passed their sell-by date or lost their direction and purpose. Discretion (and space) restrain me from naming them, but most diplomats can finger a few. A clutter of zombie agencies lurk in the forgotten corners of capitals, consuming diplomatic time and resources in the hope that one day, like the Non-Aligned Movement (NAM), they will re-discover a purpose and can return to the land of the living.

Some areas of multilateral diplomacy, however, are growing. The most important recent evolution has been the growth of environmental diplomacy, conducted largely under the umbrella of the Conference of the Parties (COP) to the Paris Agreement on Climate Change. This has become the largest rolling multilateral negotiation in the world, the number of participants doubling at each of the major international conferences, from 3,000 in Rio in 1992 through Kyoto (1997), Copenhagen (2009) and Paris (2015) to over 80,000 in Dubai in 2023, of whom 40,000 had access to the negotiations and the rest to the related events (Muller and Gomez-Echeverri, 2024). Civil society, including numerous environmental groups and organisations, has played a growing role in climate negotiations, putting pressure on the government representatives, with more and more businesses following suit (albeit with different motives). A lot of the research and advocacy is being done outside government, and there is no question that 'the people' are an active and vocal part of the process. So too, of course, is business, which has found a global niche in the Davos meetings every January, where politicians are wined and dined and businessmen pick up the latest policy trends. But ultimately, it still requires governments to sign up to and implement commitments if they are to become effective. So that is where the negotiations and reality need to connect.

I spent 12 years, a third of my diplomatic career, working in or with the European Union, and a dozen more years liaising with UN bodies in the Middle East and Africa and the international financial institutions on global economic issues. This included organising the G8 Summit in Birmingham in 1998 (while Russia had, briefly, joined the G7). I found these roles the most engaging and rewarding of my career. Bilateral diplomacy is fun but multilateral diplomacy is fascinating – more challenging but more fulfilling.

Being involved in multilateral diplomacy at close quarters, I was struck by four things.

Firstly, it is time-consuming. It is the same principle as trying to get agreement in the family on what film to watch: the more people involved, the longer it takes. In a bilateral relationship, when the two sides agree, the deal is done. In multilateral diplomacy everyone needs to be consulted, listened to, and brought on board. So the convoy often moves at the speed of the slowest: no agreement can be reached until all, or a sufficient majority, have consented. Sometimes no agreement can be reached, so the issue is left on the shelf until something changes to unblock the process. Overcoming these challenges is part of the fascination.

Secondly, it is essential to keep the bigger picture in view and alert politicians to the wider ramifications of what is being discussed. It is easy to get engrossed in the minutiae of drafting agreements – the preamble, the clauses, the caveats, the accompanying statements. But without keeping the bigger picture and the end goal in clear view, negotiations will get bogged down. Politicians may insist on including issues that slow things down, or seek a quick fix that involves cutting corners that should not be cut. But they can sometimes see more clearly than officials what really matters. At the Birmingham G8 Summit, the official theme was tackling international crime – smuggling drugs or people and laundering money – on which a comprehensive communiqué was negotiated. But the real purpose was enfolding Russia as a partner in the group of global democracies. That Yeltsin joined Clinton, Blair, Kohl and Chirac and was given economic support for Russia's democratic transition was what mattered. The support was forthcoming, though Yeltsin's successor took Russia in a different direction, with the result that following its invasion of Crimea in 2014 it was suspended and the group returned to being G7.

Thirdly, it is important to distinguish between the individual representative and the country or cause they represent. As much as in bilateral diplomacy, building personal relations with your fellow negotiators is crucial to success. I used to sit on the EU's Budget Committee. Where the money goes is a sure guide to the balance of power, but each member state also had its own implacable political interests in specific sectors: farming for some, infrastructure funding or research grants for others. The discussions went on for hours and days, often late into the night. But the committee met so regularly we all knew each other personally and understood our different national positions so well we could joke about them and never allowed political differences to become personal animosity. It helped ensure that we always reached agreement, even if it needed the occasional bottle of Gammel Dansk (a Danish liqueur akin to drinking alcoholic mud) circulated at midnight to finalise the deal. It is more difficult when injured parties sit down together – the Assad regime and the opposition at the UN-brokered talks in Geneva for example. There is no trust and much bitterness. But still it is important to register that your interlocutor is a human being too, and from that realisation can come the beginning of a dialogue. Ultimately, diplomacy is all about relationships as much as interests.

Finally, those working for international institutions, though much maligned, are for the most part dedicated, hard-working and principled public servants, determined to carry out successfully the mission to which they are assigned. As the world becomes a more volatile place, too many have paid for their dedication with their lives – in UN peace-keeping missions, in terrorist attacks, or in the line of humanitarian work. My admiration for them never ceased, even if we had different perspectives on some issues. Representatives of the International Committee of the Red Cross (ICRC), for example, have responsibilities as independent guardians of the Geneva Conventions, seeking access to and safeguarding the rights of prisoners as well as delivering humanitarian aid to those in need. Their work is extraordinary.

One way or another, most diplomats will have to work in or with multilateral organisations, so it is as well to be prepared. The core skills needed for multilateral diplomacy are not significantly different from any other kind of diplomacy, but you need to use them differently. As a national representative it is all the more important to have the knowledge and the network to be effective: it is not a game for amateurs. More than in bilateral diplomacy, negotiations and discussions tend to take place between experts. If you don't know the details, you'll be out-argued; and if you don't understand the priorities and prejudices of the other participants, you'll be out-manoeuvred. If on the other hand you are working for a multilateral or international organisation, the skills are the same, but your objective is to deliver the mission of your organisation. This sometimes means finding out what its members, whether states or individuals, want to achieve so that you can implement it; sometimes it is persuading member states to do what they have committed to, but not actually done.

Working on humanitarian relief in the Middle East was especially challenging. The UN agencies trying to bring relief to displaced Syrians during the civil war (UNHCR) or to Palestinians during the Gaza war (UNRWA) faced not only a shortage of funds given the enormous needs of the people, but the necessity of negotiating with respectively Syrian and Israeli authorities to get access to those in need. The remit and the obligation of UN member states to allow it were clear; but for political and security reasons, those with local control were reluctant to respect it, and the UN Security Council was divided over enforcement. UN officials had to deal with realities on the ground and try through negotiation to get as much humanitarian aid to the victims as possible. Talking to reprehensible regimes or blood-soaked militias is not something you would normally choose to do. But sometimes it is what you must.

When you have to sup with the devil, they say, use a long spoon. After a career in diplomacy, I have a drawer full of long spoons.

Working for a multilateral or international organisation, there are three key relationships that have to be managed. Firstly, relations with others inside your organisation whom you depend on for support or cooperation. Secondly, relations with the members, whether states or individuals, and especially relations with the funders are crucial. People and governments give money for an organisation to fulfil its purpose, and you need to demonstrate to them on a regular basis that you are delivering that if the support is to continue. Thirdly, relations with those in the outside world you are trying to help or talk to. Working in the EEAS for the EU's High Representative for Foreign Policy (HRVP), we had to ensure that we had the other Commission services on board, liaising with them on a daily basis as they controlled the money and the trade and other policies; we had to have a clear understanding with the EU member states that what we were doing was in line with agreed policy; and we then had to interact with the third countries concerned to press the EU point of view or secure the agreements that were needed. Keeping all those relationships in good order felt like a juggler spinning ten plates simultaneously and ensuring none of them fell. The occasional crash showed it was not always as easy as it looked.

Soft power

Ever since Joseph Nye coined the term (Nye, 1990; 2005), soft power has been beloved of politicians and diplomats. At one stage after Brexit, the British government boasted of being a "soft power superpower" (MacDonald, 2018). Some have even tried to measure the scale of soft power that different countries wield (see for example the Pew Research Centre's regular Global Attitudes surveys). It is normally defined as the power of attraction, but taken to be primarily cultural as opposed to political or military, though Nye himself defines it more widely to include political attraction.

Britain does indeed have a good deal of soft power. The royal family are recognised around the world; London is a magnet for visitors, as is Shakespeare's birthplace; the BBC World Service remains a globally trusted source of impartial news coverage (though its independent coverage has irked a number of foreign governments); fans in every corner of the globe religiously follow the Premier League's football teams; British universities are world class and attract large numbers of overseas students who imbibe the culture as well as the education; and the English language enables the products of Britain's creative industries – music, literature, television, film and theatre – to find markets throughout the world. The British Council was for many years the standard-bearer for this soft power, though its role has shrunk with its revenues, and to make ends meet it has focused increasingly on its educational rather than cultural offering. British traditions of the rule of law and democratic practice were also widely admired, but took a severe beating in the years after Brexit, from which they have yet to fully recover.

The more attractive your culture, the more others want to share it and the more likely they are to have a positive view of your country. All countries have their attractions and all try to publicise them. Italy often comes top in international polls of popularity because of its cuisine, its culture, its climate, its antiquity, its fashion and design, and its people. France regularly tops the world tourism league table with around 80 million visitors a year. Switzerland, Sweden and Canada vie for the top slot in the 'Best country in the world' category. And the US asserts an overwhelming cultural dominance through its audiovisual and technological outputs. Apple products may be made in China, but they enhance the US's reputation. Many countries have cultural organisations that promote their brand – France's Alliance Française, Germany's Goethe Institutes, China's Confucius Institutes – and diplomats overseas will work with them to promote their culture. The national day is always a major opportunity to promote your country's unique attractions: the French 14th July celebrations in London are traditionally a cornucopia of the country's culinary specialities and invitations are eagerly sought after, while the King's Birthday Party at the British Embassy in Washington DC traditionally attracts the social cream, and the occasional royal.

For 70 years, it was always the 'Queen's Birthday Party' or QBP for short. In Accra we began planning it months in advance and the two to three days before saw the Residence wholly taken over with preparations: marquees erected, chairs hired, tables set out, lights and speakers wired up. Dozens of extra staff were taken on for the day. As budgets were squeezed, the FCO began to encourage embassies to seek sponsorship, so all major British companies in the country were approached for contributions in cash or kind – the latter especially from Diageo, the owners of Guinness who owned a brewery in the country. Some would set up stalls, others provide goodies for the goody bags. But the food was up to us, so for our 300 guests we would roast (over a pit, in a corner of the garden) one pig and two whole sheep, served with vast quantities of rice, steaming platters of *kelewele* (fried plantain) and a mountain of desserts. If we were lucky, BA would deliver a fresh cargo of best British cheeses. Music is a major asset, so we tried to time the visit of some British musician to coincide with the event. But if that didn't work out, there is little better than Ghanaian high-life to put people in a party mood. Equally important was to get senior Ghanaians along, and especially a senior minister to speak. Assiduous cultivation all year round helped deliver this: it could never be taken for granted, but it sent a powerful signal that the relationship mattered to both.

One of the most valuable and lasting forms of soft power is education. To get nationals from your host country to pursue education in your own country creates a bond that can last a lifetime. Setting up overseas campuses for British schools and universities has expanded this impact. Education is one area where the UK excels globally, and the annual competition for the very few Chevening scholarships – fully funded one-year postgraduate awards – was always one of the most popular and resonant connections with young people throughout the country wherever I was posted. The quality of students we were able to send to the UK was outstanding and the commitment that they return to their own country afterwards created an alumni network of immense value for the embassy.

Social media has provided new opportunities to amplify cultural promotion and impact. It is effortlessly global. 'Going viral' or working through influencers enables a global audience of millions within days, if not within hours or minutes. It has greatly enhanced the reach of celebrities and the attraction of the top sports clubs: my most popular tweet ever was a selfie with the Ghanaian midfielder Michael Essien, then playing for Chelsea. So governments also seek to use it to extend their influence. All foreign ministries and most diplomatic missions maintain social media accounts, but they find it hard to break into the big league in terms of numbers of followers because we tend not to supply what the market and algorithms encourages: outrage and controversy (though occasionally we get through on humour). Even Estonia, that most digitally capable country, has difficulty spreading its brand into the global market. What people choose to watch on their smartphones and computers is (in most countries) beyond a diplomat's control and social media can also compartmentalise and limit the diversity of views. So the cultural democracy that technology should enable is very partial and unequal – not all countries, industries or individuals benefit.

What social media *has* done is extend the soft power of *non*-state actors in international affairs. This can be benign and well-intentioned, for example through the work of Bono and Bob Geldof to promote action against debt, poverty and hunger, or the Syrian Observatory for Human Rights in spreading word about abuses during the Syrian wars; or it can be malign, as in the use made of it by jihadist movements in Iraq and Syria posting regular videos of their attacks and executions (Cooper, 2008). The diplomatic and political impact of social media posts can therefore be considerable, as Hamas demonstrated in Gaza and anti-French influencers (probably backed by Russia) showed in the Sahel. How this links to 'digital diplomacy' more widely is discussed below.

For all the value of popularity and attraction, however, soft power can only be turned into real power if there is a political gearing mechanism. Politicians and diplomats need to follow up the cultural attraction with a hard economic or political offer, taking political action to back it up. The equation that 'because everyone loves us, therefore we'll have influence' does not always add up. Soft power alone doesn't get you votes in the UN, success in negotiations or, ultimately, allies on the battlefield. All the soft power in the world will not protect you from a brutish neighbour. So while it is an essential implement in the armoury of diplomacy, do not be misled that it substitutes for real political or economic engagement. It may open the door, but not get you into the kitchen.

Digital diplomacy

Diplomacy has constantly adapted to new technologies – the telegraph, telephone, radio, television, air travel – but the revolution wrought by the internet, impacting the way we manage information and communicate with each other, is profound and, historically, only in its infancy. It is important to understand what has changed, what might change in the future, and what the implications will be.

Despite the hype, the revolution is one of *means* not *ends* (Westcott, 2008*)*. The purpose of diplomacy remains the same; and its practice still depends fundamentally on building trust between individuals and in organisations. One of the major challenges created by social media is the undermining of trust: who and what can you trust? What is fact and what is propaganda or disinformation? For this reason, just as in business, politics and culture, personal face-to-face meetings will remain an essential element of diplomacy. But the internet has enabled a whole new class of actors to become involved in diplomatic activity, as well as transforming the speed and spread of communication and the conduct of diplomacy itself (Seib, 2016; Fletcher, 2016; Bjola and Manor, 2024).

Even during my brief career, the transformation has been extraordinary.

When I joined the FCO in 1982, its working processes would have been familiar to a Foreign Office official from Harold Nicolson's day, 50 years earlier. We worked on paper. Information was kept on physical files which were held in the department's cupboards (the Registry, maintained by a Registry clerk) for five years and then sent to be weeded and consigned to the archives, from which they could be retrieved by the Office's historians or legal advisers if we needed to check a fact or a point of detail in a treaty negotiation. We exchanged information with our posts by telegram, sent from a central communications department and both incoming (white) and outgoing (pink) telegrams were distributed around Whitehall by an elaborate system of pneumatic tubes, along with European-wide messages, COREUs, which were green (Edwards, 1994, 54–62, describes it in loving detail). Computers arrived at the end of the 1980s and in UKREP Brussels it was regarded as eccentric that the Treasury official in the office next to me insisted on having his own computer on his own desk to type his own work rather than writing it longhand or dictating it to be typed up by a secretary. Unlike most of my contemporaries, I could type, so this suited me too. During the 1990s everyone began to work on desktop computers and communicate – like the rest of the world – by email. But two things slowed the transition: security, and working practices. Our information had to be kept secure from prying eyes, whether hostile, journalistic or just public, and the internet was not deemed a secure means of communication. Our work was also hierarchically bound: opinions, recommendations, submissions to ministers, advice to No.10 and instructions to posts all had to pass up through numerous layers, each giving their amendments or stamp of approval before it passed to the next layer and onwards or outwards. In principle IT speeded this up, but not if you simply tried to replicate paper-based processes, as senior officials wanted. We had to find different ways of working.

In 2002 I was appointed the FCO's head of IT Strategy, in effect the Chief Information Officer (CIO) as it became. My protests that I was not an IT expert elicited a reply from the Permanent Under-Secretary that that was exactly what they wanted. The FCO's first major IT project had failed abysmally, and the IT experts and senior officials were on such different wavelengths that they needed someone who understood diplomatic work to act as interpreter between them and devise a way of working and a new IT system (the fabled Firecrest) that took advantage of what the IT could do while preserving adequate security and sufficient control. IT costs money (our budget was £100 million a year) and takes time to roll out, so we needed to ask the FCO Board how the Office planned to work in 5–10 years' time – a thought that hadn't really occurred to them before. They eventually approved our new IT strategy and the British diplomatic service moved somewhat bumpily into the 21st century.

In practice, most people did most of their work by email as the quickest and most convenient way, whatever other systems you tried to impose. It just happens – just as, more recently during Covid, ministers started taking decisions by WhatsApp, whether officially permitted or not. Desktops have practically disappeared and everyone works on laptops, iPads or smartphones. The changes in our means of communication and ways of using information have continued to accelerate in this 'digital century', as Fletcher (2016) calls it. The complications this has created for record-keeping were illustrated by the UK inquiries into the Covid pandemic, when critical decisions were not part of the official record but had to be recovered from people's phones and other informal records.

Another revolution took place during the Covid pandemic when offices emptied, international conferences ceased and all work and meetings went online. The technology was available for work to be done remotely, but the habits had not until then been formed. Zoom, Teams and Webex suddenly became household names, and whereas video conferences with delegations had started to become more frequent, it now made no difference whether you were in Whitehall, Hackney, Berlin or New York – you all assembled for meetings on screen. The pandemic passed but many of the habits remained. Officials were encouraged, and sometimes required, to return to their offices, and the international circus that is the world of multilateral diplomacy resumed its relentless round. But the ubiquity of smartphones and mobile technology, meaning you are expected to be available at any time or any place, has only accelerated the speed with which crises emerge and responses are required, and has multiplied the number of actors involved (Seib, 2016).

There is a big advantage now in being able to set up virtual teams cutting across geographies, pooling the best available talent and information, who can work together in real time to deal with a specific issue or crisis. This is true across the board – in business, humanitarian and international organisations as much as national diplomatic services. For multilateral organisations it has actually been a boon in making it quicker and more efficient (and greener) to get people together to discuss a crisis. The only problem, as the world continues to turn, is finding time to sleep.

The openness and ubiquity of the internet has enabled far greater access to information for smaller nations and the wider public. Anyone with an internet connection (which still excludes a significant portion of the world's population) has access to the global store of knowledge and news that it contains, as long as their government allows it and they are not trapped, for example, behind the Great Firewall of China. Participation in international meetings has also become possible without the cost and disruption of travel. During the pandemic, European Council and UN Security Council meetings were held online. But it is significant that as soon as feasible, they resumed in person. Virtual meetings are better than none. But in diplomacy, they are still no real substitute for face-to-face meetings when difficult business needs to be done or other issues need to be settled in the margins.

One drawback has also become more evident. Information shared across the internet, even with end-to-end encryption or secured lines, becomes more vulnerable to attack from hackers seeking money, hostile forces seeking to disrupt a target, or those trying to steal secrets in order to make them public or use them for political and diplomatic ends. The publication of a vast store of secret US government information on Wikileaks in 2005 had a profound impact (Seib, 2016, 31). Cyber security has become a major preoccupation for diplomatic and government services, as it has for any organisation working in the international sphere. The UN and its agencies, the development banks, and international NGOs, especially those working on sensitive issues such as human rights or security, have all been subject to politically motivated attack at some point and have to try to find ways to protect their information and their ability to communicate.

At a global level, the internet has enabled a far more diverse range of actors to become involved in international relations. As Seib (2016, 29) puts it, the public is no longer merely a passive observer of diplomatic activity but expects to participate. The instant links between diaspora communities around the globe has made mobilising a world-wide campaign ever easier, as well as spreading local divisions globally, as we have seen in the Gaza crisis that followed the attacks in 2023. Chapter 5 explores how the instant dissemination of facts, non-facts and opinion has made it simultaneously more important and more difficult to dominate the public narrative, with a growing number of non-state actors, from terrorist groups to political dissidents to tech entrepreneurs, determined to influence the trajectory of international affairs.

Domestic diplomacy

To be an effective diplomat, you need to be just as adept at managing the internal mechanisms and politics of the foreign ministry and your national government as at dealing with foreigners. As 'global issues' such as climate, crime, health and migration have risen up the international agenda, diplomacy has become a whole of government enterprise. So managing these internal relationships is essential to successful diplomatic outcomes.

Any diplomat, whether working for a foreign ministry, an international organisation, a company or an NGO, will usually have to spend part of their career working at headquarters as well as abroad. Myself, I spent 50% of my career in London but for colleagues it would be anything from 30% to 70% depending on their circumstances, wishes, and luck (or skill) in securing overseas postings. For the ambitious, spending more time in the capital is rewarding if it secures jobs in the prime minister's or foreign secretary's private offices, or in key policy roles. Apart from a few ambassadorial posts, in New York, Geneva, Washington, Brussels and a few other centres, policy-making power resides in London, and if that is what you want to do, that is where you should be. But in my experience a more fulfilling career includes time both at home and abroad.

The work in a foreign ministry is very different from that abroad (Cooper et al., 2013, ch. 5; Hamilton and Langhorne, 2011, ch. 4). The hours can be more regular (though often longer), with working from home more possible, and the work itself more focused on policy and administration than representation and negotiation – except of course negotiation with one's fellow civil servants, which is an art in itself and different from negotiating with foreigners.

When it was created in 1782 to support the foreign secretary, the Foreign Office consisted of a Permanent Under-Secretary (PUS), a chief clerk, two senior and nine junior clerks, a Latin secretary and a 'Decipherer of Letters': fifteen in all (Nicolson, 1939, 203). In 2023, after multiple mergers with the India Office, Colonial Office, Commonwealth Relations Office and Department for International Development (DFID), it has around 7,500 UK-based staff plus 10,000 local staff at missions overseas. Of UK-based staff, roughly two-thirds are at home and one-third overseas at any one time (FCDO, 2023).

As a bureaucracy, the Office (as it was known) functioned well – at least when I worked there. The abrupt merger with DFID in 2020 caused severe disruption for a while, but things are now reported to be settling down (NAO, 2024). Responsibilities are constantly being reshuffled, but for most of my time, and in most other foreign ministries, they were divided geographically and thematically, with very hierarchical decision-making. One department would deal with South Asia, for example, managing bilateral relations with India, Bangladesh, Sri Lanka and Pakistan (sometimes hived off with Afghanistan). Another department would deal with climate negotiations, coordinating our dialogue with India alongside those with other countries and regions. Yet another (in DFID when it existed) would deal with humanitarian aid, keeping the regional department informed of its operations in Pakistan or Bangladesh in response to crises.

To get things done and decisions taken, three things are essential: firstly, a clear and concise analysis of the situation and recommendations for action; then to ensure that those who need to be consulted have been informed; and finally to get the proposal to the decision-making level as swiftly as possible. This means having good links with the minister's office. The foreign secretary's private office is the fulcrum around which the FCDO rotates (Henderson, 1984). The Private Secretary (effectively a chief of staff) is the person who manages the foreign secretary's workload, especially as they spend more and more time travelling, and who can make sure your request or advice is brought to their attention and a decision taken or discussion arranged. Getting access to the decision-maker is crucial, so having good personal relations with the private office repays the effort – especially if you are overseas and need an urgent reply. Of late, ministers have relied more heavily on their own special advisers, 'SPADs', who are brought in to give a political perspective alongside the official advice. Because they have the minister's ear and often understand their thinking, it is wise to get to know them. Most were happy to work with the civil servants, and it could help pre-empt potentially contradictory advice or anticipate strong ministerial views by talking to them in advance.

The same applies to the head of government. In the UK, Prime Ministers rarely have much time to devote to foreign affairs compared, say, to the French President, so getting to know people in No. 10 on both the official and political side was vital for getting issues raised with or action taken by the PM, and especially for getting time in their diary to see visiting heads of government from other countries or to attend essential summits overseas. As an ambassador it could be vital to have swift access to the Prime Minister's thinking in order to respond to a query from your host President's office about a visit, a crisis or a bilateral issue, and the swiftest way to get that was to ring the PM's private secretary responsible for foreign policy – usually a colleague on secondment from the Foreign Office. Such informal networks are vital to maintain one's credibility, access and effectiveness abroad.

A few foreign secretaries (such as Castlereagh, Bevin and Carrington) ran British foreign policy in fact as well as name. But more often than not, key foreign policy decisions have been taken by the prime minister because only the head of government can adjudicate the conflicting national priorities that often arise. So although British prime ministers traditionally enter office determined to focus on domestic issues, they are invariably dragged into the international arena sooner rather than later and either spend a lot of time on foreign policy, or fail to do so and suffer the consequences (as Boris Johnson and Rishi Sunak found). Occasionally prime ministerial involvement can prove disastrous, as Eden's role in the Suez crisis demonstrated (Kyle, 2011). But by and large, a diplomat needs to know the character, interests, policies and staff around the head of government better than most officials if they're to do a good job.

Of course, good relations with ministers are equally critical. They are the ultimate decision-makers and – at least normally in the British system – the ones who takes responsibility in public for the decisions taken. Professional politicians are different animals to professional diplomats. Some of them can be masters of diplomacy – Douglas Hurd, David Miliband, Cathy Ashton, Lynda Chalker, Alistair Burt among others in my time – but they can also be as focused on their political career, on reaching the top, as on the negotiations or issue in hand. I remember keeping an entire international conference of 40-odd foreign ministers waiting half an hour in Lancaster House because Robin Cook, the then Foreign Secretary who was due to chair it, was sitting in a back room on the phone to the editor of *The Observer* about a story for the weekend paper. Politicians' priorities can be different, and they tend to prefer officials who understand that. It requires a particular set of skills as a private secretary or chief of staff to get the minister to do the work needed *and* make them feel that officials respect their priorities, not just the ministry's.

The best way to get to know a minister is to travel with them or have them visit you in post abroad. This gives you more face time and far more social time with them than you would ever get at home in the office. Sharing a car, or a post-prandial whisky with them before bed, can lead to the most fruitful conversations and a good personal relationship that you can't achieve in the ministry. I got to know Keir Starmer when he visited Ghana as Director of Public Prosecutions investigating a corruption case involving a British company, and stayed a couple of days with us at the Residence. An intelligent and decent man. Looking after MPs and opposition politicians can be just as important: Tony Blair recruited Jonathan Powell as his chief of staff while still in opposition after Powell, as political officer in the Embassy, had escorted him round Washington DC to meet US politicians.

Foreign ministries, for all their particularities, are part of the national government and liaising with other ministries is now a crucial part of their work as more and more aspects of national life have an international dimension. There are formal coordination mechanisms, traditionally run in the UK by the Cabinet Office, which manages the various Cabinet committees on cross-cutting issues and prepares the most important issues for discussion and decision by the Cabinet itself. Since 2010, there has also been a National Security Adviser and National Security Council to coordinate the work of the Foreign Office, Ministry of Defence and intelligence agencies, supported by a Joint Intelligence Committee that assess the raw intelligence (Ricketts, 2021). Similar structures exist in most countries, some more coordinated, others less. The UK tradition is of relative internal transparency: most departments are willing to share information to ensure good decision-making. This is not always the case. In some bureaucracies, information is regarded as power: you share it sparingly, and only in exchange for other information (the situation in the European Commission when I worked there in the 1980s). The result can be decision-making silos where decisions in one sector (such as homeland security) can have unexpected or unanticipated consequences in another (bilateral relations with a targeted country for example). The US has a byzantine inter-agency process which often reflects the relative political power of the respective cabinet ministers as much as the relative weight of the national interests involved.

I often had to work closely with the UK Treasury. Relations between foreign and finance ministries are often difficult. Both tend to regard themselves as elite institutions and sovereign in their own field. So they tend not to get on. To get around this innate suspicion, I found it helped to (a) demonstrate an understanding of economics and finance, to earn some respect; (b) treat them as normal colleagues and build a good personal relationship;

(c) consult them on everything relevant *before* they got to hear of it by other means; and (d) show that the FCO could provide them with useful information they wouldn't otherwise get, so long as they involved us in the resulting decisions – trading information on the internal market as it were. This worked well, and meant that when the Asian financial crisis broke in 1998 we worked seamlessly as one team in handling it, with British embassies in Seoul, Jakarta, Manila and Bangkok giving the Treasury better information than they could get from open or other sources, and the Treasury keeping us informed about what the G7 Deputies (senior finance officials) were doing to solve the crisis.

One of the most complex negotiations I was ever involved in was that on the EU's Maastricht Treaty in 1990–1 (explained in the next chapter). This involved virtually every ministry in Whitehall: the Home Office on migration and borders, Justice on judicial cooperation, Agriculture, Trade and Industry, Work and Pensions on the social chapter, even Culture, Media and Sport on EU cultural policies. To manage this, we built a government-wide network of contacts in each ministry for the negotiations; we met often enough so that we knew each other well, and kept each other informed of both our own and other member states' positions on each issue. The negotiations within Whitehall on what the British government position should be were just as intense, complex and sometimes fraught as those with our European partners, and required just as much political and negotiating skill. Where ministers did not get on – and sadly this happens sometimes – officials needed to find a way to reach agreement so that ministers would not have to discuss it directly with each other, as this was likely to only widen disagreement. Where they did get on, putting a question to ministers to resolve could save months of otherwise frustrating bureaucratic wrangling.

This was also a case where Parliament itself had a significant input to the negotiations. The UK's relations with the EU had been contentious since it joined, and remain so to this day, even after it has left. Certain members of Parliament (MPs) took exceptionally close interest in the negotiations themselves and in the subsequent legislation to ratify the treaty. Though handling Parliament was primarily the task of ministers, officials, including me, were called to give evidence to explain why some of the treaty text had ended up the way it did, and what it meant. Regular interaction with MPs both bilaterally and in committee was therefore another part of the job. Sometimes, indeed, it felt like representing your government to a hostile power, so ferocious was the questioning. But in the UK, Parliament is sovereign and all MPs, whether from the governing party or opposition, deserve respect, so parliamentary delegations visiting overseas must also be handled with great diplomatic care.

Figure 3.3 Durbar Court in the Foreign Office, London, 2018.
Source: author's photograph

The extent of parliamentary involvement in foreign policy-making varies enormously from country to country. The British Parliament's foreign affairs and international development select committees follow major policy developments closely and have the power to summon ministers, senior civil servants and external experts to give evidence. Their meetings often provide opportunities to discuss complex issues in far more detail than can be done in debates on the floor of the House. In the US, Congress plays a major role in foreign policy and the Senate retains the constitutional power to appoint all US ambassadors and ratify all major treaties, powers that it guards jealously and which can act as a major constraint on the Administration. This makes it important for US diplomats to build good contacts and a good reputation on the Hill. The same applies in most European and other countries. Elsewhere, however, Parliamentary involvement with foreign policy can be perfunctory, episodic or absent, though governments will still reflect domestic political concerns in their foreign policy actions.

Whatever the precise arrangements at home, the good diplomat needs to be a master of domestic politics and bureaucracy as much as those of any foreign country. And whether at home or abroad, they need to be a master of negotiation, which we examine in the next chapter.

4 Negotiations

The most difficult day of my life as a diplomat was Monday, 20th September 1992.

It was the opening day of the UN General Assembly in New York. All foreign ministers and many heads of state were in town. The US President, George Bush Snr, would attend to give his opening speech (after the Brazilian, of course). The Middle East Peace Process was high on the global agenda, and as the UK held the rotating Presidency of the EU at the time it was our job to convene a meeting of the twelve foreign ministers to agree a statement on the issue. Douglas Hurd, the Foreign Secretary, had agreed to meet the Israeli foreign minister Shimon Peres afterwards to brief him on the EU's position. The EU ministers met at 7 am, the only time all were free, and we had booked the only available UN room which happened to be on the west side of First Avenue. The UN headquarters and Assembly buildings are on the east side, overlooking the Hudson River. We had to bring in our own electric typewriter and photocopy machine (this was 1992) the night before so we could produce revised texts to take account of any comments. The meeting, scheduled for one hour, went on for two as arguments and amendments went back and forth. The electric typewriter and its plug were British, the sockets in the walls were American. No one had an adaptor. We resorted to an old manual typewriter in a side room and used Tippex (remember that?) to correct it. As we were printing out the final version for each minister to take away, the photocopier jammed. Conscious that everyone had to be in their seats before the US President arrived in The Beast with security locking everything down, we took our one copy and dashed to the street. Too late. The New York Police Department had closed First Avenue and refused to allow anyone to cross it to the UN building – this a good 45 minutes before the President was expected. If you have ever tried arguing with a NYPD officer to explain that you have 12 angry foreign ministers trying to get to their seats in the UN General Assembly, most of them audibly cursing behind you, don't bother. They

DOI: 10.4324/9781003533436-4

were implacable, un-budgeable, and blunt. The stand-off lasted 20 minutes until phone calls (we did at least have brick-like mobile phones in those days) brought a UN Protocol officer to the rescue who escorted us over the road.

Once in the General Assembly building, I was dispatched to find Mr Peres and apologise in person that the Foreign Secretary could not make their bilateral as he had other important meetings that had been delayed. UNGA is a diplomatic circus. Like trapeze artists, ministers and their officials leap from one meeting to another, from one booth or level to the next, with split-second timing lest you miss a meeting and crash to the ground. I eventually tracked down the Israeli minister and his entourage between meetings and delivered the message to Peres. It was not welcome. They didn't shoot the messenger, but if looks could kill I would have died on the spot. The EU position was not popular with the Israelis, and scrapping the meeting felt like adding insult to injury. I couldn't even give them a copy of the text as my next task was to find a photocopier that worked and return with copies to hand round to each EU foreign minister in the Assembly hall for their approval before anyone else could see it. And this was all before 11 am. The day went downhill from there. By midnight, as we still worked on the report of the day (suitably bowdlerised to avoid embarrassment), I was shattered. Never again would I trust equipment without testing it myself. Practicalities can be as important to doing a deal as the substance. But you live and learn.

So negotiation is not all fun. And almost always it is hard work. As the Norwegian who mediated the Oslo Accords in 1993 said, a negotiation can be 700 hours of frustration followed by one hour of glory (Terje Roed-Larsen; see Powell, 2015).

But negotiation is at the heart of diplomacy: it is the means by which we seek to overcome disagreements without recourse to force. So the art of negotiation is central to our goal; and while diplomatic negotiation has some affinities with other forms of deal-making in the commercial world or in politics for example, it is different. The aim is not to win at all costs, not to make the most profit, nor (usually) to get one over your opponent. Game playing certainly has a role: for some negotiators it feels like a high stakes game of poker, or a chess game of indefinite length and breadth; and winning always feels good. As he walked out of the Maastricht Treaty negotiations the British Prime Minister, John Major, is reported to have cheerfully announced to his officials: 'Game, Set and Match!' The UK had achieved all its core objectives: the negotiations had been a success (*The Herald*, 11 Dec. 1991). But only because, in the end, everyone else had agreed too.

The purpose is to reach an agreement that all can accept and defend to their own authorities or public. They may not be happy with the outcome; it is very rare that a deal is ideal. But it has to be good enough for all parties to abide by it; otherwise, the problem will only return and a further negotiation will be needed. In the worst case, a failed negotiation will lead to war and disaster, as it did for the Melians. It is true that every war ends in a negotiation when one side wins or a 'hurting stalemate' is reached (Powell, 2015). But it is better if you can skip the war part and move direct from problem to negotiated settlement. Nevertheless, because negotiations are frequently not between equals, one side often believes it can achieve a more favourable outcome by force. The destruction of Gaza in 2024 was the result of a failure to implement the Oslo peace agreement and of both Israelis and Hamas believing that they could ultimately only achieve their objective by force – security on one side, an independent state on the other – although there were also those on both sides who simply wanted to eliminate the other.

Negotiations, of course, take many different forms. A bilateral negotiation between two countries over, say, an investment protection agreement, a migrant return scheme or a disputed maritime border is relatively straightforward. It becomes more complex where it involves a number of parties, like accession (or exit) negotiations between a candidate country and the EU, or the Iran nuclear deal, or climate negotiations at the UN. The most complex are the politically charged or indirect negotiations, often brokered by a third party, for example between a rebel movement and a government (as in Colombia, Syria or Sudan), or between two warring states, like Russia and Ukraine, or over some intractable international dispute, like the Western Sahara, Kosovo or Israel-Palestine. Negotiations can even be remote, as between two superpowers on the brink of war, such as the US and the Soviet Union during the Cuban missile crisis.

There are detailed studies on the art of diplomatic negotiation (Brownlie, 2009; Moore, 2014; Powell, 2015; Bonnafont, 2022). But in all circumstances, in my experience, there are certain essential ingredients for reaching agreement, discussed below. The most essential, and sometimes most difficult, of these is building mutual respect and trust.

The great skill of the Norwegian negotiators of the Oslo Accords, especially Terje Roed-Larsen, was to build a personal trust between the Israeli and Palestinian participants that the US had signally failed to do over endless previous rounds of negotiations. It was this more fruitful relationship that created the breakthrough (Aggestam, 2012). The same applied in the Northern Ireland peace process, where getting the IRA and DUP to talk to each other seemed at one stage a futile task, but eventually had Martin McGuinness and Ian Paisley dancing together (Powell, 2008, 308). On a less dramatic scale, working in the EU for 12 years, I learnt that it was the trust that officials and politicians from the different member states had in each other that always enabled an agreement to be reached in the end: a trust that they were ultimately committed to the same end, to making the EU work. That is why Greece is still in the euro, and why disputes over migration have not torn the EU apart (yet); and also why Britain's decision to leave the EU had such a devastating impact on its global reputation because it shattered the trust that had been built up over 40 years of working together. As Harold Nicolson said, 'the art of negotiation depends on reliability and confidence' (Nicolson, 1961).

Taking a predominantly transactional rather than relational approach to diplomacy makes it difficult to build this trust and respect. Not impossible: as an African diplomat told me, he liked the Chinese and Russians because you knew where you stood with them, the terms of engagement were clear – whereas the British tended to talk about values and then do something contrary to them. The charge of hypocrisy is just as damaging to a country's reputation as a breach of trust. But in my experience it is the building of *relationships* between people, and hence between governments and countries, that leads to successful diplomatic outcomes. It enables you to understand where the other party is coming from. As one of the Israeli negotiators in Oslo said: 'The more time I spent with our [Palestinian] partners, the more I discovered we may have known a lot about them but we understood very little' (Powell, 2015, 95). Since Edward Heath took Britain into the Common Market in 1973, many Conservative politicians have tended to regard the EU in purely transactional terms, devoid of either trust or respect, and, because they failed to understand it, made catastrophic mistakes as a result.

Besides building trust and showing respect, the other key elements for successful negotiation can be described under six headings: participation, location and process; preparation, persuasion and outcomes.

Participation

No negotiation will succeed unless you have the right people in the right place at the right time, 'in the room where it happens'. Without the right people, it just won't happen at all. So obviously, the first step is to identify who needs to be involved. It is rare that leaders themselves undertake a major negotiation except at the very end of a process; as Robert Cooper has pointed out, diplomats were partly invented to keep leaders apart as they invariably quarrelled when they met (Bunde and Franke, 2022, 27). There are exceptions: in the European Council, the top EU jobs are always decided by the leaders themselves in conclave, like cardinals choosing the Pope; Reagan and Gorbachev also came very close to cutting a nuclear deal at their summit in Iceland in 1986 (Boot, 2024). But generally, serious negotiations are left to trusted lieutenants. It matters that the people you are negotiating with, or the representatives you are bringing together to negotiate with each other, are those with the responsibility and authority to engage meaningfully. Ambassadors are traditionally designated 'Extraordinary and Plenipotentiary' to signal the authority they receive from their government or leader to negotiate on the country's behalf. The permanent representatives of member states who sit in COREPER, the EU's most senior committee of officials, are expected by their function to carry such authority. The sherpas who prepare G7 and G20 summits are also invariably close advisers to their heads of state or government; and most governments appoint as their ambassador to the UN in New York someone of senior standing who can carry the responsibility of representing their country in serious negotiations. The US Ambassador to the UN is traditionally a full member of the President's Cabinet, so at the centre of US decision-making.

Again, for regular international conferences, the relevant ministers of environment would descend on the conference venue and stay there until the deal was done. One challenge for such meetings is whether to include non-state parties in the negotiations, and if so, which, how many, at what level, and for how long.

In 1998, I was involved in organising the G8 Summit in Birmingham. The Jubilee 2000 Coalition, campaigning for debt forgiveness for poor nations, wanted to participate to make their case. Their chosen form of participation was to surround the leaders in the meeting venue with a human chain that would not be broken until the pledge was made to forgive all debt. Fortunately the leaders were meeting in retreat outside the city that particular Saturday, but the Prime Minister agreed that the Development Secretary, Clare Short, should receive the petition of three million signatures they had collected. This was appreciated, the message was passed to leaders, and the protesters left peacefully. Less peaceful was the WTO Ministerial in Seattle the following year, when anti-globalisation protestors reduced the city centre to chaos – shattered windows, looted stores, burning dumpsters, deserted streets – in what became known as 'the Battle in Seattle'. It is the only time I have been tear-gassed, as one of the delegates caught in the cross-fire. No agreement was reached. But at the following ministerial in Doha in 2000, the protesters were strangely absent, and a deal was done.

Governments have become more inclusive since then. At the COP meetings, as mentioned before, civil society, business representatives and lobbyists of every stripe are now an integral part of the process. It reflects pressure for the 'democratisation' of multilateral decision-making, but it is hard to find an acceptable formula. The argument that 'traditional' mechanisms are 'undemocratic', because diplomats hammer out agreements between themselves 'behind closed doors', is only true where the participating governments are themselves undemocratic – and the undemocratic ones are the least likely to want democracy to creep in through an international door when the domestic one is shut. It is nevertheless good for groups that feel unrepresented to be present and have a say before agreement is reached, to increase the inclusivity, credibility and public acceptance of international processes; and it is good for negotiations to be as transparent as they can be without undermining the potential for reaching agreement. This lies behind the recent 'UN-mute' initiative to bring civil society voices into UN debates. Wholly transparent negotiations, however, rarely succeed because official representatives then feel they must play to the gallery, showing their government or their supporters or their press that they are making no concessions to their principles or their national interests. '*On ne peux pas négocier devant le microphone*', as the negotiators found in Paris in 1919 (Otte, 2001, 171; MacMillan, 2001). Though President Trump has regularly done so, my experience is that that way lies stalemate, not agreement.

It gets trickier when you are negotiating to end a conflict. The key ingredient of successful negotiation, trust, is inherently lacking. But you have to get the people with the power to stop the fighting to communicate with each other and to explore ways of resolving the dispute, or at least pausing the war. As the veteran Finnish negotiator Martti Ahtisaari said: 'Reaching a solution that ends a conflict means talking to all those who are parties to the conflict' (Powell, 2015, 135). This is why a third-party mediator, some person or institution trusted by both sides, is so often essential for such talks. Very occasionally there is a protagonist who is completely beyond the pale, with whom no one is willing to speak. This was effectively the case with the Islamic State (ISIS or Da'esh) whose objective was to sweep away the world order and to do it in the most brutal way imaginable (Ghattas, 2020), who had no interest in negotiating and with whom nobody was willing to talk. So the war continued until ISIS was crushed, at least in Syria and Iraq. The same logic applied to the Allied decision in the Second World War ultimately to seek unconditional surrender from Germany: no one was willing to trust or negotiate with Hitler. But one of the great lessons of both the Northern Irish and Colombian peace processes is that talking to those whom many states categorise as terrorists is often essential to achieve a peaceful outcome that benefits everyone (Powell, 2015). The IRA were committed to a united Ireland, anathema for many years to a majority in the north who wanted to retain British sovereignty there. The PLO for many years, and Hamas still, were committed to the destruction of Israel whose government were consequently unwilling to talk to them. Liberation or secessionist movements often have only one objective and an uncompromising approach to achieving it. If they choose to do that through violence rather than discussion or democratic decisions, it is hard to find common ground. But where a military stalemate has been reached, or crushing their ideas as well as their fighters proves impossible, talking has to start.

For such negotiations two groups are needed: the warring parties themselves, whether terrorists, rebels or governments; and people who are willing and able to talk to them, mediate, or negotiate on their behalf. For Hamas, for example, the state of Qatar acted as an intermediary in discussions with the US, and the US acted as an intermediary for Israel. In the case of the Iran nuclear agreement, the three European countries (E3) plus the EU acted as interlocutors with Iran on behalf of the US, which had broken off diplomatic relations since its Embassy staff were taken hostage during the 1979 revolution, at least until a secret back channel was established between the US and Iran through the good offices of Oman, where the talks were held, and negotiations could proceed face-to-face behind the scenes. The two parties returned subsequently to the full forum to finalise the deal as buy-in from the P5 and E3 was essential to ensure the deal stuck (Ashton, 2023). This was an example of a successful diplomatic negotiation which reduced the risks of war, and would probably have continued to do so had not President Trump subsequently repudiated it, with consequences that are still playing out.

In the past, it has often been the UN that stepped in as intermediary, usually at the explicit request of the UN Security Council through a resolution mandating the Secretary-General to use his good offices to find a solution to some intractable conflict. On occasion, the Secretary-General would undertake this task himself, as Dag Hammerskjold fatally did in the Congo in 1960–1, or Kofi Annan on Cyprus in 2003–4. But more often he would appoint a Special Representative of the Secretary General (UN SRSG) to contact the parties to the conflict and try to get a negotiation process going. There may be a dozen or more of these in existence at any one time, covering conflicts from Libya and Lebanon to Haiti, Myanmar, the Western Sahara and the Horn of Africa. In trying to resolve the Syrian civil war, successive SRSGs worked thousands of hours bringing together as many of the parties as possible (except for Al Qaida and ISIS) in Geneva to seek a solution, but without success. In some conflicts, like Israel-Palestine, the UN is *persona non grata* to one or other party, and others take on the mediation role. This need not necessarily be a state. Churches, NGOs and simply trusted individuals have played leading roles, often behind the scenes and out of sight, like the Catholic St Egidio community, based in Rome, the Anglican Church involved in South Sudan, or Humanitarian Dialogue based in Geneva, who have all specialised in the international mediation of conflicts. The Quakers also have a long tradition of seeking the peaceful resolution of disputes and they work quietly behind the scenes in a number of places to find common ground (Bennett, 2020).

Finally, a critical role in negotiation can be played by the sponsors of either party to the conflict. In Syria, for example, little progress could be made without involving Russia and Iran as the primary backers of Assad, or Saudi Arabia, Qatar and Turkey as supporters of different factions of the opposition, though none were formally part of the Geneva process. I remember meeting the Russian Deputy Minister responsible for the Middle East, Sergey Vershinin, during the talks to persuade him to put pressure on the Assad regime to show more flexibility: 'Ah Nick,' he said. 'You know we don't really have much influence on them. They are difficult people. But I will try my best.' They never budged, and I never believed him. I had no doubt that if Russia had wanted Assad to move, he would have moved. So we needed Vershinin there.

With the Geneva process stalled, a wider forum was established – the International Support Group for Syria (ISSG), co-chaired by the US Secretary of State John Kerry and Russian Foreign Minister Sergey Lavrov – to bring together all international parties involved, but excluding both the Syrian government and opposition. It too got nowhere. Instead, Russia demonstrated its influence by initiating a rival set of talks in Astana, capital of Kazakhstan, involving only Iran, Turkey and themselves, being the three external powers with troops on the ground in Syria, in other words, with skin in the game, plus the US as observers. A deal was eventually struck in Astana that left Assad in power and the opposition confined to Idlib province under Turkish protection. Without Russian backing, the UN was powerless (Phillips, 2020).

The Northern Ireland peace process would also never have succeeded without the active involvement of both the Irish and US governments in applying pressure on the parties involved, and pushing them towards a settlement. For the diplomat, what matters is to identify who are the critical players that need to be involved, as well as who can play the role of mediator, and ensure that they are all brought into the process at the appropriate time.

Location

The location of negotiations can also play a critical role. Finding the right place is not always simple.

Multilateral organisations have their designated seats where most meetings and negotiations take place. The EU, which is in effect a perpetual negotiation machine, meets mainly in Brussels, Strasbourg or Luxembourg, with occasional meetings (welcomed by participants) hosted by the country holding the rotating Presidency. The European Parliament's travelling circus, with its home in Strasbourg, a secretariat in Luxembourg and meetings in Brussels, illustrates the kind of costly and time-consuming compromise necessary to keep all member states happy. NATO meets in Brussels, the UN in New York or Geneva, the IMF and World Bank ministerial meetings alternately in Washington DC and an external location. Major international conferences like the COPs and Commonwealth are hosted by those willing and able to bear the cost, while the G7, G20 and BRICS rotate between their members.

But for more difficult negotiations you need a place acceptable to all parties, one where decent facilities are available, and if necessary out of the public eye. There are regular venues like Geneva or Vienna, accepted as neutral, where the UN can provide meeting rooms and secretariat support. Although the margins of the UN General Assembly are a regular spot for informal and sensitive meetings and the Security Council is in constant session, it is rare for New York to be used for other negotiations; this is because it is in the US, it is expensive, and it makes the talks very visible. Sometimes the sponsor of peace talks will want to host the negotiations, as the US has for many Middle East peace process meetings. Camp David, the Presidential retreat in rural Maryland, has repeatedly been used as a venue for such negotiations because it provides a secure and informal setting for the talks, where the press and public can be easily excluded. More extreme was the choice of Dayton Air Force Base, Ohio, as the location for talks between Serbian, Bosnian and Croatian leaders in 1995 to resolve the Bosnian civil war. The accommodation was sparse, the facilities minimal and the chance of going out for the evening excluded. It was part of the plan by Richard Holbrooke, who chaired the meetings, to deprive the leaders of any alternative to reaching an agreement. He reputedly even postponed meals at the final hurdle until the deal was done (Chollet, 2013). I can see why. Having sat behind John Major when he chaired the London Conference on the Balkans in 1992 which tried, unsuccessfully, to stop the war breaking out in the first place, the leaders of the former Yugoslav republics – Milosevic, Izetbegovic, Tudjman – were a fractious lot, focused as much on their own political careers as on the welfare of their people. Depriving them temporarily of food and liberty may indeed have been the only way to get them finally to focus on the bigger picture. But it was risky, and took the full authority of the US in its unipolar moment to pull off.

More recently, China hosted the talks between Saudi Arabia and Iran in 2023 that led to the restoration of diplomatic relations between them, the whole deal doing as much to emphasise China's growing power in the Middle East and its role as broker as to signal the de-escalation of tension between the two protagonists. In 2025, Saudi Arabia itself played host to the start of Ukraine-Russia talks mediated by the US.

When complete discretion is required, somewhere far from the regular diplomatic track is needed. Israeli and Palestinian representatives made progress when they met secretly in Oslo, not publicly in Washington; the US and Iran began their secret talks in Muscat, supported by the Omani foreign ministry, where it was easy not to be seen or recognised. Qatar provided the location for the US to meet secretly with the Taliban, designated a terrorist organisation by the US, as both had representation there and meetings could take place without Congress or the press noticing. One of the most famous conversations in diplomatic history took place in 1982 during a 'walk in the woods' outside Geneva when US negotiator Paul Nitze had a frank one-on-one discussion with Soviet Ambassador Yuliy Kitinsky which paved the way for arms reduction talks between the two superpowers (Graham, 2016). The phrase has become a diplomatic term of art, 'to go for a walk in the woods' meaning to have a personal and private meeting, usually unrecorded, at which both negotiators can go beyond their brief and look at where a realistic landing point for the negotiations might be. So location matters.

Process

Just as important as the location is establishing a process and managing the choreography of a negotiation.

Every successful negotiation needs a process. In international organisations, such as the EU, WTO, IMF or NATO, this is already defined and accepted by all parties through years of practice. But for ad hoc negotiations it is essential to establish an agreed process early on so that the parties have a framework to work within and realistic expectations of what will come next. As Shimon Peres explained years ago, everyone knows the outline of an eventual peace settlement in the Middle East in terms of territory, refugees and even Jerusalem, but the problem is the absence of a process to get there: 'The good news is there is light at the end of the tunnel; the bad news is there is no tunnel' (Powell, 2015, 205). When the post-Oslo peace process ran into the sand in 2014 and the Israelis and Palestinians ceased to meet or talk directly, it became in hindsight inevitable that violence would return, as it did, appallingly, on 7 October 2023. It is often essential to keep a process going despite recurrent outbreaks of violence so that there is still a place where exchanges can take place. If negotiations are public, it may be politically necessary to break them off in response to some blatant aggression, but all the more important in those circumstances to have a back channel where work can continue and private messages still be sent.

Within each process the choreography will vary, depending on the purpose of the meeting or negotiation. But in all circumstances ensuring the smooth running of the administrative arrangements is crucial to a successful outcome. Nothing will put a negotiator into a less accommodating mood than a squalid bedroom, a sleepless night, a car that fails to turn up, a protocol badge that has not been prepared, a security process that requires endless queuing or a meeting that misfires because one party went to the wrong place. In the conferences I organised, the last-minute crises tended to be organisational rather than substantive: the minister who brought a 'companion' on his plane without telling anyone; or the delegation of militia leaders from Somalia held up at the airport by immigration officials who wanted to deport them because the protocol officer sent to meet them had gone to the VIP suite instead of the arrival gate.

Summit meetings, attended by heads of state or government, are usually the most fraught, particularly if the US or Chinese President is attending. Security and protocol requirements then become overwhelming. One country house we had selected as the retreat venue for the Birmingham G8 Summit was suddenly withdrawn by its owner after an unannounced visitation by the US President's security detail, who trampled all over the house and garden and ordered the owner to make this and that rearrangement before the summit could be held there. It is a paradox that leaders themselves often want the simplest, most informal arrangement for their meetings, the traditional 'fireside chat' among themselves with no advisers – the intention behind the G7 summits when they were initiated (originally as G5), and a key ingredient for all Commonwealth summits. But such meetings inevitably grow as the leaders want good press coverage, and officials want to use the occasion to get some serious agreements reached and recorded. So the delegations to such events now consist not of seven leaders plus seven sherpas, but seven leaders plus 5,000-odd officials, security, press and police. Creating within that a space of some hours during which the leaders can talk frankly and privately among themselves and build the personal relations essential for cutting difficult deals remains crucial to success. We fortunately found another country house for the leaders' retreat (the very beautiful Weston Park), kept the presidential security recce under control this time and limited attendance to the bare minimum. It helped us reach agreement on a number of difficult issues, including discussion of debt relief for highly indebted poor countries (the HIPC initiative), and a major increase in support for the campaign against malaria. Of course, it did mean the leaders missed the Jubilee 2000 protest, but nobody minded too much as everyone got what they wanted in the end.

True, this desire for informality does not go for all leaders, some of whom glory in the pomp and circumstance of glittering dinners, military parades and massive meeting tables to advertise their power and importance to the world. If flattery and bling are needed to put the leader in the right mood, then that is what needs to be delivered. President Xi Jinping's state visit to Britain in 2015 is a case in point. Though President Xi was delighted with the state banquet hosted by the Queen at Buckingham Palace, there are few pictures more excruciating than the look of puzzlement on his face at being forced to clutch a pint of warm English beer in Prime Minister Cameron's local pub near Chequers. Wrong move: President Xi has not visited Britain since.

For major conferences and summits you also need to match the choreography with the venue, wherever it is decided to hold it. If the leaders' meeting place is small and intimate, you may need to erect a temporary media centre or offices nearby to accommodate the hangers-on. The UK's G7 Summit in 2021 was held in the Cornish village of Carbis Bay – very charming, but a logistical nightmare given the winding single-lane roads that led to it and the lack of nearby accommodation. Delegations, accommodated a mile or two away, were annoyed not to be close to their leaders, locals were fed up at being locked down for the duration, and the police had a monstrous job managing the traffic. Summits in Africa always amazed me that from seeming chaos, last-minute order was miraculously plucked. Nevertheless, at a particularly chaotic AU-EU Summit in Abidjan, a single small doorway led from the conference hall to the rooms where the leaders' group photo and subsequent dinner were to be held. This led to impossible congestion as soon as the formal session ended, with leaders being pushed and shoved out of the way by other presidential security details determined to get their man through first. The dinner was not a success. Bad choreography often leads to bad outcomes.

The choreography of peace negotiations can require even more careful handling. As mentioned, these will often be between two sides that have no trust in each other and no wish to meet face to face. 'Proximity talks' are a common way forward, in which the protagonists come to the same location but stay separate while an intermediary shuttles back and forth between them, carrying proposals and counter-proposals from one side to the other, as happened in the Syrian talks in Geneva. Sometimes the two sides are not even physically close: Henry Kissinger pioneered the concept of 'shuttle diplomacy' when working on Middle East peace in the early 1970s, travelling between Tel Aviv and Cairo, testing out his ideas and pushing both towards common ground. Occasionally the two sides are willing to talk, but cannot politically be seen to do so. Negotiating with terrorists may seem like rewarding violence, so complete secrecy is required to avoid provoking opposition at home that would stop the contact from taking place. This requires complex choreography: Kissinger's first visit to Beijing to discuss opening US relations with China took place while he pretended to be convalescing from a stomach bug in Pakistan (Cooper, 2021, 373–401); and Jonathan Powell describes the elaborate ruses needed to keep contacts secret during the Northern Irish and other peace negotiations (Powell, 2015). These behind-the-scenes contacts are often referred to as 'track two' talks as opposed to the public 'track one' ones. But eventually, for the talks to deliver an agreement, they have to become public, and managing that transition from informal to formal talks is a critical part of the process.

Apart from those rare occasions mentioned above, leaders are normally only brought in once the bulk of an agreement has been finalised at official level. Preparing G7 summits, sherpas will meet several times in advance, often virtually but at least twice in person, to decide the issues for discussion, who else to invite (African, Asian and Latin American leaders have all been included in the past) and to negotiate a communiqué. The final session takes place on the spot the night before the summit, with the aim of having a clean, agreed text for heads to bless the next day. The EU has COREPER to prepare the European Councils, which now follow a standard choreography in Brussels, but the most intractable issues invariably remain for the heads to settle, as only they can make the political concessions necessary for agreement. The pressure for them is time: how long does it take to reach a consensus? Occasionally the EU has had to 'stop the clock' while talks continued because agreement was needed by a certain date to meet legal obligations.

The European Council also suffered the longest dinner in history. It had been agreed to settle the candidates for the top EU jobs over dinner in June 2019, but negotiations and bilateral consultations continued long into the night, past dawn and through the next day, heads abandoning the dinner table and resting in their delegation offices waiting for the summons to return and approve a final deal. One by one, proposed candidates were dropped and others put forward, Council President Tusk undertaking one bilateral after another. The 'dinner' which started on 30 June finally ended on the morning of 2 July when an agreed slate of appointments was wearily approved. The dessert was quite spoiled, but all the coffee had been drunk.

Getting the right pace to negotiations is also important. Agreements only emerge when the stars are sufficiently aligned. But this does not mean the talks should stop; as Roed-Larsen observed, it can require infinite patience while ideas, proposals and the political context evolve. The Geneva talks on Syria and the UN-brokered negotiations among Libya's warring factions achieved no breakthroughs, but they were kept going so that when political forces begin to shift, there would be a forum in which negotiations could resume – unless overtaken by events on the ground, as in Syria. Seemingly intractable problems can eventually be solved, as in Northern Ireland and Colombia, through persistence, patience, persuasion and waiting for the propitious moment. The trick is to know when to pick up the pace and turn up the heat. The Iran nuclear negotiations, having dribbled along for some years, suddenly accelerated in 2015 when President Rouhani came to power and President Obama proved willing to take risks (Ashton, 2023). Such moments pass, so seizing them is something that takes diplomatic judgement and political courage. These are not always present: a number of Middle East peace agreements never happened because the opportunity was missed by one side or the other – most notably at the Camp David negotiations in 2000 (Bregman, 2014).

All processes need a timetable, even if it is a flexible one. Where there is a fixed date – a summit, a visit, a conference – the deadline is hard and negotiations normally accelerate towards it, with a final text only agreed just before or at the meeting. Peace negotiations are more tricky. Deadlines here can be counter-productive as the politics is more fluid, and missing a deadline can set things back rather than move them forward. Better, then, to define progress in terms of milestones: moving on to the next phase once one has been achieved, whenever that is. Nevertheless, it is sometimes necessary to create a deadline to accelerate things, as Holbrooke did at Dayton. To bring the warring Somali factions into agreement on a federal political structure, the UK held a London summit in 2012, the EU a Brussels one in 2013 and the Danes a Copenhagen ministerial in 2014, at each of which the Somali parties would only reap the benefits of international support if they could reach agreement among themselves in time for the meetings. This worked.

Finally, to keep up momentum and avoid a logjam at an early stage over some intractable point of principle (recognition, ceasefire, disarmament, whatever), it is often wise to allow parallel negotiation on each of the main areas of a deal rather than sequential discussion of each in turn. This allows issues on which agreement can be reached relatively swiftly to be settled and parked. As the areas of agreement grow, so does the sense that there is something to be gained from concluding the negotiations, and that the tough issues are resolvable too.

Preparation

For negotiations, as for exams, good preparation is always a key to success. Whoever is best prepared and best briefed has a far better chance of achieving their objectives.

For individual encounters, between one minister and another for example, where you are not negotiating a text, it is important to remember that most ministers will not use notes. They may or may not have read the brief in advance, but it is critical for all the key points to be on the front page of the brief, so that they can be seen at a glance. That is all that will be used during the discussion itself. Some officials seem to find this hard to grasp: working for the EU's External Action Service, I would regularly receive a brief of 5–10 densely written pages, packed with facts about the issue and its background, with a few negotiating points to make right at the end. For the High Representative, I would have to re-arrange and edit it drastically to be any use. The Foreign Office disciplines, honed over decades, were rather better in this respect, more attuned to the political needs of the minister. The art is to put up front as concisely as possible all the information that is essential and add the context, background and detail behind, just as a good journalist will write a story so that you get the key information in the first paragraph and it will still make sense wherever the editor cuts it off further down. Even then, many ministers will simply look to the Ambassador, senior official or their private secretary to give them a two-minute summary of the key points to make immediately before the meeting. So always be ready with the shortest possible summary and the most vital issues to raise. Also work on the assumption that in formal meetings, only the main representative speaks unless others are specifically invited to do so. As in *The Godfather*, for junior members of the team to butt in may wreck the negotiating tactics, and maintaining discipline and the authority of the spokesperson on your own side is essential to getting a good outcome.

For more formal negotiating sessions, where a text *is* being discussed, more elaborate briefing is needed. It is essential to define two things at the outset: your starting position, usually your preferred outcome; and your bottom line – the minimum acceptable outcome. In the EU, French negotiators were masters of the art of setting an ambitious target, resisting all efforts to water it down and ending up, after a few final concessions, with an outcome well above their bottom line (as we discovered afterwards). But to resist all concessions throughout risks either a breakdown in negotiations or growing pressure to make major concessions at the end that push you below your bottom line.

The brief prepared for the negotiations needs to reflect this, explaining the specific amendments to the text needed. The most elaborate brief I ever prepared was for the final Maastricht Treaty negotiations at the European Council in 1991. The whole 200 pages of the final draft treaty were set out with the treaty text on one side and our commentary and brief on the facing page, including how other states were lined up on the key outstanding points. The demands from other Whitehall departments for all their amendments to be included were ruthlessly pared down to the bare minimum by a committee of officials so that the Prime Minister had a realistic number of points to pursue. Though the negotiating session was strictly limited to heads and foreign ministers only, Sir John Kerr, Britain's Permanent Representative to the EU (who knew the text backwards), smuggled himself into the meeting and squatted down beside the Prime Minister's chair to advise him on the spot, his presence betrayed only by the occasional curl of smoke from his cigarette and his hand emerging to tap the ash off into an ashtray. The outcome was deemed a great success, as John Major said.

Most useful for a negotiator to know in advance is where the other party or parties are coming from and what their objectives and red lines are. Some of this will be apparent from earlier discussions, or reports from your own embassies. Occasionally other means of finding out are used. During the Lancaster House conference in 1979 to negotiate Rhodesia's transfer to majority rule, Lord Carrington, the British Foreign Secretary who chaired it, received daily briefings from British intelligence on the ZANU negotiating position, gleaned from devices previously positioned in the delegation and hotel rooms of Robert Mugabe and Joshua Nkomo. It helped him bring the conference to a successful conclusion leading to a peaceful transfer of power. But normally you have to rely on more conventional means of getting the information.

Persuasion

Negotiating is fundamentally about persuading the other side to accept your position or to reach a mutually acceptable compromise that meets enough of your objectives to be acceptable. Bilaterally, this is done face-to-face or with the help of a mediator. Multilaterally it is a question of creating, or joining, a consensus or, in some cases, a majority for what you want. The arts of persuasion are therefore vital.

To make your own case as convincing as possible, you need to know your audience through the preparation you have done, and listen to the other side. In fact listening is critical to the art of persuasion. The more you can couch your argument in terms that appear to meet the other parties' objectives, the easier your task becomes. Lecturing the other side about the sins of the past may be a necessary step to assert the moral justification of your case, but it doesn't always help set up a fruitful conversation about the present or future. Understanding how you got into the mess may be useful, but the negotiation is about how to get out of it. It is also very different from a debate, where you listen to your opponent in order to refute their argument, not to reach agreement.

This is, if you like, the 'soft' approach. It is a good place to start. But where agreement proves elusive by this means, a 'hard' negotiating stance may be needed, *in extremis* like that of the Athenians before Melos. Blunt truths about where power lies and what the alternatives to agreement might be will sometimes bring concessions or more flexibility on the red lines. But not always. As we saw in the 2024 negotiations over a ceasefire in Gaza, where neither side accepts the validity of the other, no amount of force, arm-twisting or persuasion will bring agreement – and that way lies perpetual war.

There has, particularly since 1945, also been a desire to put one's case in terms of respecting universal norms: the right to self-determination, the application of human rights principles, the unacceptability of genocide, the responsibility to protect (R2P as it is known), or the principle of non-interference in the internal affairs of other nations (once a favourite of Chinese negotiators, though less so these days in relation to their neighbourhood). It enables a moral or normative pressure to be put on the other side, and in particular gives smaller, weaker states added leverage in trying to hold larger countries to principles they may have signed up to but may not reliably practise. In reality, many states are selective about which principles they choose to apply and when, which can lead to charges of inconsistency, hypocrisy or imperialism. Sometimes you can win the argument on principles, but fail in the negotiation because the other side chooses not to recognise them. Increasingly in the 2020s, as we argued in Chapter 2, these global norms have been eroded or ignored, particularly by some powers for whom they are inconvenient constraints on repression at home or aggression abroad. These powers have sought to redefine a multipolar world based on alliances of convenience or narrow national interests in contrast to what they perceive as a 'western-dominated post-war multilateral system' skewed against the 'global south'. The US too has become increasingly selective, refusing for example to accept WTO rules on trade in order to protect domestic industry, and asserting its right to seize others' territory. The EU, being based on such principles from the outset, has been firmest in their defence, but even its member states are finding that the competition with the US on trade and with authoritarian states on territory makes consistency both more important and more difficult.

These arguments, however, illustrate that ideas continue to matter in foreign policy. Espousing different models for how the world works, putting out competing narratives, matters because they are reflected in states' positions on specific issues, on their alliances in case of conflict, and on who votes with you at the UN. The conflicts in Ukraine and Gaza have highlighted this question. Basing your negotiating arguments on principled or ideological positions only works if the framework is accepted by all parties. This the Melians found, to their cost.

A particular challenge is negotiating with a partner who does not tell the truth. Britain's Prime Minister Neville Chamberlain faced this challenge in his talks with Hitler in 1938, but most diplomats have encountered it at some point. I remember sitting with Federica Mogherini (when she was the EU's High Representative for Foreign Policy) listening to Russian Foreign Minister Lavrov say things about Russian involvement in Syria that were demonstrably untrue, which he knew were untrue, and which he knew we knew to be untrue. But he said them unashamedly, to make the point that he didn't care and would continue to impose his version of reality on the world. French President Macron later found the same in talking to Putin about Ukraine. The Russians are by no means alone: I have heard a number of governments assert baldly that they had no intention of killing civilians, or blowing up humanitarian convoys, or using poison gas, or suppressing freedom of speech, or locking up opponents, or sending ethnic minorities to labour camps, or forcing them out of the country, before proceeding to do so. There was always an excuse: it was an accident, or was necessary to combat terrorism, or to preserve the state, or to prevent foreign subversion. As Aesop's fable of the wolf and lamb illustrates, the wolf can always find an excuse to eat the lamb however innocent it is. Yet even lies have meaning – you just have to understand why they are telling you this. It is unwise to dismiss others' bluster: when Putin said Ukraine does not or should not exist, we would be wrong to think he doesn't believe it. After years of dealing with Nazi and then Soviet propaganda, Harold Nicolson concluded sadly in 1961 that 'Truth itself has lost its significance' (Nicolson, 1961), an assertion which is also being tested in certain (currently) democratic countries.

The one person who can never afford to lie is the mediator or chair of the talks. That is because they have to be trusted by all sides, so honesty is their main weapon. A mediator has to maintain neutrality and trust while trying to nudge the two sides closer together by not only relaying messages from one side to the other, but indicating areas of flexibility and sometimes introducing ideas of their own, on their own authority, that might help find a way through. They must painstakingly build up areas of common ground, and suggest how outstanding obstacles could be overcome, or worked around. The role of a chair in a multilateral negotiation is similar: finding the ground for compromise, pushing, sometimes quite hard, to bring recalcitrant parties on board. It is tough work and mediators, including many SRSGs, often do the role only for a year or two before moving on.

In the preparations for an EU-Africa Summit in 2014, we had a very difficult argument on migration in the senior officials meeting I was chairing – a big meeting with 53 African and 28 European countries all represented. Gradually we adjusted the text, using some creative ambiguity, until all parties were on board except the South African, who stuck to a hard line. Fortunately I knew their representative well, the Permanent Secretary at the Foreign Ministry, so I addressed him directly: 'Jerry, we can put in a footnote saying South Africa doesn't agree with this paragraph, but then everyone else who has accepted the compromise will want footnotes too. It'll become a Christmas tree, footnotes hanging off every paragraph. And in any case you wouldn't want South Africa to become just a footnote?' 'Nick,' he replied, 'South Africa will *never* be merely a footnote . . . But I take your point. I will recommend this text to my authorities.'

The next year we had a similar problem at the EU-Africa summit on migration in Valletta, Malta. The European side had got tougher and at the senior officials meeting there was gridlocked on the asylum text. Around 2 am (with the summit due to begin at 11 am that morning) Pierre Vimont, who was chairing and a man infamous for working 24 hours a day refreshed only by five-minute catnaps, announced that he himself was perfectly happy to work through the night, as he usually did, but he felt sorry for others who were used to getting some sleep, and would still have to brief their presidents. He appealed for flexibility. We got some, but not enough. While we continued work on the rest of the text in plenary, we therefore created a small working group with the two hardest-line protagonists – Hungary on one side and Egypt on the other – plus the Irish and an EEAS official and sent them off to work on the text in a side room. An hour later they returned cheerfully to the plenary having not only agreed a text, but struck up a friendship. With the two hardliners on board, everyone else accepted it – and we went back to our bedrooms for a few hours' sleep before the summit.

Vimont was the essence of that quality identified by Nicolson as key for successful negotiation: keeping calm and carrying on.

Not only must the negotiator avoid displaying irritation when confronted with the stupidity, dishonesty, brutality or conceit of those with whom it is his unpleasant duty to negotiate; but he must eschew all personal animosities, all personal predilections, all enthusiasms, prejudices, vanities, exaggerations, dramatizations and moral indignations.

(Nicolson, 1939, 116)

Or as Talleyrand put it: '*Et surtout, pas trop de zèle.*'

Outcomes

Getting from discussion to agreement invariably requires compromise. For many 'compromise' is a dirty word: it implies weakness, abandonment of principle, giving in to the other side. It smacks of 'appeasement', which the press at least regard as one of the greatest sins in diplomacy. Diplomats know compromise is necessary to reach agreement, but politicians hate it. They prefer to be seen winning, 'battling for Britain' (or wherever) and coming out on top against the foreigner who was forced to make all the compromises. More than once, post-negotiation triumphalism or, even worse, pre-conclusion triumphalism, leaking the deal to the press or announcing it on social media before anyone else in order to claim the credit, has undone months of negotiation and sunk a hard-won agreement.

In such negotiations, therefore, it is important to recognise that while everyone will have to make concessions to reach a consensus text, all sides want to avoid being publicly embarrassed. So the final deal needs to have something for everyone. All should win and everyone must get prizes, as Lewis Carroll put it in *Alice in Wonderland*. Each negotiator can then highlight their successes and slide as silently over their concessions as the press will let them.

As a chair, therefore, the art is to build consensus point by point, getting delegates to drop their minor issues and raise only the major ones. As a negotiator, you aim to build as wide a coalition among the other parties as possible for your point of view, through separate bilaterals before or in the margins of the meeting itself. But who controls the drafting of the text is vital. In the EU it is the Presidency or Council Secretariat who try to balance the views of the member states. In the UN Security Council, one of the five permanent members traditionally 'holds the pen' in drafting resolutions on specific subjects – the UK for Sudan and Somalia, France for the DRC and Lebanon, the US for Haiti and Iraq, for example – and works with the rotating chair to build consensus, or at least a sufficient majority, and to avoid a veto. In peace negotiations, drafting the agreement can be the most valuable role a mediator can play as each side is often hostile to anything proposed by the other. But the parties still need to take ownership. The negotiations to re-unify Cyprus failed in 2004 largely because the final text was seen as 'the UN's', not a product of the parties. As we noted at the beginning, one of the diplomatic skills is 'letting the other side have your own way': seeding an idea that they decide to propose as their own, which you can then accept.

The last chapter identified that the hardest negotiations are sometimes with your own side. Negotiators, if they are listening intelligently, will understand why some elements of an agreement need to be there, even if they don't like them. For those not in the room, whether back home in the capital or in the bush, it is not so evident, and it can be hard for the negotiator to go to his colleagues and argue the other side's case without being accused of going soft. There's a fine balance between keeping your colleagues fully informed so that they keep up with the shifting ground of the negotiations (at the risk of them insisting you stick to a harder line), and keeping them in the dark until a full package can be presented with the argument that the gains outweigh the concessions. Each negotiation and each protagonist will have its own specific context and dynamic, and a judgement on the right balance can only be taken at the time. In the Maastricht Treaty negotiations, the British Treasury set out an extremely tough line on budget discipline to rein in what it saw as EU profligacy. The senior Treasury official was included in the PM's delegation for the final European Council to ensure they would sign up to the deal. In the end, keeping the UK abatement (worth several billion pounds a year) was by far the most important objective, and to secure it the PM had to concede more generous funding for the structural funds – an essential objective for other EU members. Through gritted teeth, the Treasury had to agree.

This illustrates how final agreement can sometimes only be reached by enlarging the package under negotiation so that there are more prizes to go round and all can gain something. The EU is masterly at this, which is why the European Council is often the only place where such trade-offs can finally be made. (Leaving the EU means that the UK no longer has so many cards to play, has less to trade off with others, and therefore has more difficulty securing what it wants from its European neighbours.) This need for trade-offs also underlies the principle that 'nothing is agreed until everything is agreed'. This enables participants to make provisional concessions on a text or a deal which, it is understood, can be withdrawn if other parts of the deal don't come out satisfactorily for them. This helps negotiators focus on what really matters and fend off pressure from others in their own camp who want to hang tough on less crucial issues.

Sometimes creative drafting is necessary to get opposing negotiators to accept a single text. The British have a particular reputation for this, one American general in the Second World War expressing his wonder at their facility in 'the use of phrases or words which were capable of more than one meaning or interpretation' (James, 2024, 71). The English language has a uniquely wide range of words that mean almost exactly the same thing, but with the very slightest nuance, which can be invaluable in drafting agreements. The problems often come when it is translated.

In peace negotiations, particularly after civil wars, a deal that will stick has to be agreed between the parties themselves. But the point may come where, though they are close to a deal, one side or the other refuses to budge on a critical issue. This is where external pressure can help force a conclusion. Both parties may have external sponsors, or depend for support on neighbours, who need to be mobilised to apply pressure at these times. To give two contrasting examples: in 2012–14, the interminably divided Somali factions had been given some breathing space by the success of AMISON in clearing Al-Shabab out of Mogadishu and the coastal areas, and Somali pirates had been effectively driven off the seas by an EU-led multinational naval force. The international community, including neighbours, donors and the UN Security Council, were united in wanting to stabilise the country, and therefore cooperated at the series of conferences in London, Brussels and Copenhagen mentioned earlier to put pressure on the clans and factions to agree a political way forward, effectively adopting a loose federal structure. The combined pressure worked, and the resulting political structure, while not exactly stable, has survived so far.

By contrast, Libya's civil war between rival factions in the east and west of the country proved impossible to resolve despite all the UN's efforts because the international community was divided, with some (Turkey, Italy) supporting the government and militias in Tripoli, and others (Egypt, UAE) supporting General Haftar's forces in Benghazi. Without a sufficiently united international community, the peace process has stuck and the country remains divided. The same appears to be the case in Sudan's civil war between generals Hemedti and Burhan in 2023–4, which drags on as long as international sponsors continue to support rival factions.

While failing to reach a deal is usually bad for everyone, in any conflict situation there are some who benefit from the status quo, who profit from the conflict itself, or whose political power depends upon it. This has been true in Libya where the absence of any effective authority has enabled a criminal economy to flourish, creating vested interests that do not want a settlement. As a result, many peace negotiations fail. In fact, most successful negotiations have been preceded by a number of ones that failed, from which the protagonists and mediators each learn lessons. Occasionally a major failure, like that of the UN to achieve a reunification of Cyprus, rules out a deal for years to come. But often a failure can be a precursor to success. So patience, perseverance and tenacity are essential for any negotiator.

Surprisingly frequently, there will be a last hold-out who threatens to veto the whole deal without some concession that would upset the delicate balance that everyone else has agreed, and the use of the veto in the UN Security Council has become depressingly common in defence of one or another client of a P5 member. Sometimes the block is placed by a party who is not even central to the dispute, but seeks some narrow sectional benefit and has little to lose if the deal fails. Mediators have therefore developed the concept of a 'sufficient consensus' where, if the main parties have agreed a deal, the minor ones just have to live with it. In the EU in 2024, one particular member state (Hungary) opposed increased EU assistance for Ukraine, but was persuaded to leave the room while the European Council voted through the support package so that Hungary could avoid having to explicitly endorse it but did not block the agreement. Abstentions or deliberate absences have also been a regular feature of UNGA votes on sensitive subjects like Ukraine and Gaza.

One last word on reaching agreement: beware of partitions, or of power-sharing deals between fundamentally opposed parties. They rarely work. They may bring temporary relief, a cessation of hostilities or a 'government of national unity'. But frequently they simply store up trouble for the future, freeze a conflict rather than resolve it. They may seem the only way forward at the time, but they can come back to bite you.

Equally critical to reaching agreement is to record it and explain it. It is good diplomatic practice to record all encounters with your host country or with the other negotiators, even if only for internal consumption, to inform your superiors and to protect your back later if ever accused of doing something you should not, or not saying something that you should. In negotiations it is not only important to have an approved text of the agreement, but to record how you got there and why it took the final shape that it did – essential for later interpretation. Often enough, diplomatic reports will highlight the role of the author: the telegrams from the British Ambassador to South Africa in the early 1990s might lead you to believe that the agreement between Mandela and de Klerk on the transition to majority rule was primarily due to the Ambassador's personal intervention (he went on to a distinguished career). It is natural to highlight one's own role, but to have credibility, keep it real.

Spinning the deal – how it is presented in public – can also be critical to its success. There will invariably be unhappy parties and if their voice dominates the media, even a good deal can begin to unravel. Hence it is helpful to agree with all parties the main lines for the press before they emerge into the public eye, ideally through a joint communiqué. But be sure to communicate it swiftly and persuasively. And then ensure that you celebrate success with the team that made it possible, especially those behind the scenes. At the end of weeks or months of relentless work, they deserve it.

Implementation

Negotiations rarely end when the agreement has finally been reached. The implementation of any agreement invariably involves issues that still need to be negotiated: those carefully drafted ambiguities that enabled the deal to be done need to be clarified on the ground; the separation and demobilisation of forces has to be achieved; the mobilisation and deployment of monitors organised; implementing legislation enacted. For a deal to stick, it needs to have a clear sequencing of follow-up actions, a means of monitoring implementation and a way of holding the parties to account. It helps the credibility of the deal and the negotiators themselves if there are some early and visible benefits, to fend off critics back home keen to unpick the agreement or blame those who signed it for not achieving more ambitious aims.

Peace-keeping operations are particularly challenging and require diplomatic skills of the highest order. These used to happen under a UN umbrella, but in recent years others have taken a lead: the African Union was responsible for AMISOM (later ATMIS) in Somalia, even if it was funded by the EU and supplied by the UN. It proved very effective in 2011–12, as did the UN operations in Liberia and Côte d'Ivoire, which were withdrawn once democratic rule had been embedded. But peace-keeping is more difficult where there is no peace to keep. The UN operation in Mali (MINUSMA) had the highest casualty rate of any UN operation, until that of UNRWA in Gaza, because their role was primarily to protect the civilian population from terrorist groups with whom no peace agreement had been reached. So they became a primary target, and received little support from government forces who resented their role in monitoring *all* human rights abuses committed against civilians, including by the army. There, as in the DRC (MONUSCO), the operations became so unpopular or ineffective that the host government eventually demanded their withdrawal. In 2024, UNIFIL in southern Lebanon even came under direct attack from the Israeli Defense Forces. The head of a peace-keeping operation has to face all ways at once: deal with rebels, liaise with the host government, coordinate with regional actors and troop contributors, and report back to the UNSC. In addition they need to care for their staff, ensure everyone has 'hostile environment training' (HEAT in the jargon) and can cope with their tasks. The skills to fill such a role are scarce and precious, and those who do them successfully deserve recognition and reward that they only rarely receive.

Continuing to communicate on the implementation of a deal is important to help keep all the parties up to the mark, especially when the searchlight of media publicity sweeps on from this crisis to the next. Given the centrality of communication to all diplomatic activity, it deserves a chapter to itself.

5   The media and the message

Communication is at the heart of diplomacy, both public and private. A diplomat's purpose is persuasion and words are the weapons they use. Knowing how to use them well, with discretion and appropriateness, is critical to success. Getting the right message to the right audience at the right time can make all the difference, and with public information becoming a more contested space world-wide, ensuring your message is persuasive and lands well with the public is equally critical. It is now an integral part of a diplomat's job to be visible in public as a representative of their country or organisation. Some specialise in public relations or media management, but sooner or later everyone will need to know how to present to a public audience or handle the media. As one American diplomat put it: 'There has never been a good diplomat who was a bad communicator' (Stearns, 1996).

This chapter looks at how to craft your message, how and where to deliver it and ensure that it sticks, and how to deal with audiences that disagree with your message, or may not even want to hear it.

A good deal has been written about 'public diplomacy' and 'propaganda' (e.g. Cull, 2019). This area is one where, though the substance remains the same, the forms by which we engage with the public are evolving fast and will continue to do so. With instantaneous globalised public information flows, all diplomats everywhere are engaged not just in promoting their country or organisation and its policies, but in the battle of narratives to influence governments and public opinion. This was true in the Cold War: the 1950s, '60s and '70s, as much as the 1930s, saw competing ideas for how the world should be run, promoted by all available means. Would the future be communist or capitalist, authoritarian or democratic? More recently Islamist and jihadist ideologies have been spread with the purpose of changing the political and international order. What has changed is that the means of propagating ideas has expanded and accelerated through the use of the internet, as well as through radio and television, meaning that the public is more directly involved. Joseph Nye argues that:

> In an information age, communications strategies become more important and outcomes are shaped not merely by whose army wins, but also by whose story wins.

> (Nye in Cooper et al., 2013, 563)

DOI: 10.4324/9781003533436-5

Two recent examples have been the regime changes in the Sahel in 2020–3 and the Israeli-Palestinian war in Gaza from October 2023.

In Mali, Burkina Faso and Niger, public disillusion with democratically elected governments that had failed to create more jobs for young people or to ensure security against jihadist and separatist violence – despite help in Mali and Niger from the UN, US, EU and France – encouraged military juntas to take over and legitimise their rule in all three countries by promoting a narrative that they were liberating the country from foreign, and specifically French, influence. In spreading this narrative they were actively helped by a unit of Yevgeny Prigozhin's Wagner Group that specialised in online information campaigns and helped spread anti-French disinformation widely through social media. Public opinion was turned against 'the west' and 'western-backed' neighbouring countries; UN, US and French forces were expelled, and Russian mercenaries were brought in to help protect the juntas from internal and external threats. The diplomatic, information and military actions were well coordinated to bring the three governments firmly into a pro-Russian camp, at least for a while (Brown, 2024b).

Gaza is a clear example of Nye's dictum on the global stage. Despite having started the most recent war on 7 October 2023, Hamas was predictably outgunned and out-fought by the Israeli military which took effective control of the whole of Gaza (at least above ground). But the battle for world opinion, and particularly US opinion, was crucial to the ultimate outcome for both sides, and Hamas and the Israeli government both devoted great efforts to getting their competing narratives out. At the time of going to press, the situation remained unresolved.

A more encouraging example of using a compelling narrative to change things was the campaign to write off the debts of highly indebted poor countries, mentioned in the last chapter. During the 1970s and '80s, many countries had accumulated massive debts to the international financial institutions (IFIs), especially the IMF and World Bank, and to private lenders. Servicing the debts weighed heavily on their budgets, curtailing spending on health, education and other services. A number of NGOs launched a campaign to write off the debts, citing the biblical custom of a 'jubilee' once every 25 years when all debts were forgiven and people could start from a clean slate. The 'Jubilee 2000' coalition recruited celebrities such as musicians Bob Geldof and Bono to their cause and lobbied leaders relentlessly, including at the G8 Birmingham Summit in 1998, to support the initiative. British ministers Gordon Brown and Clare Short took up the case and, with the IMF, persuaded both official and private sector lenders to forgive a large part of the debt under the highly indebted poor countries (HIPC) initiative, finally adopted in 2001. Without the mobilisation of global public opinion, it is doubtful that the poor countries would have secured such a satisfactory deal, which was of significant economic benefit in the following decade (Amoako, 2020, ch. 7; Hamilton and Langhorne, 2011, 252).

Whatever the issue or the context, four things are needed for an effective exercise in persuasion: a clear message; the right medium; a persuasive method of delivery; and a constructive engagement with potentially hostile or sceptical audiences.

The message

For the diplomat, when communicating with governments or the public, though the words may be your own the message is normally not. You are the messenger, representing your government or organisation and following a script usually written by others in the capital or at headquarters. Jerome Bonnafont (2022) describes the diplomat as like an actor, choosing how to deliver the script but not choosing the content. The analogy is good because as a diplomat you are never just representing yourself, you *are* your government. Like an actor, you are constantly observed and constantly judged. You can decide the means of delivery – where, how and with what nuance – but not the substance. The diplomat's role is therefore to ensure it is presented in as clear, concise, comprehensible, respectful and resonant way as possible. We will look at each of these in more detail.

Firstly, this means knowing your audience. Who are you addressing? What will resonate with them? What should you avoid, to ensure people aren't distracted, put off or alienated?

During the Cold War, for example, the battle of narratives between the Soviet Union and its communist allies on one side and the United States and its western allies on the other revolved around whose cause really represented 'freedom': to simplify, for one side it was democracy, human rights and a capitalist free market; for the other it was freedom from imperialism and capitalist exploitation, with a state that served the collective interests of 'the people' not the individual. For many countries emerging from colonial rule, the latter narrative was attractive as the advocates of the 'liberal' global order included their former colonial rulers from whom freedom had been reluctantly wrung. The debate still resonates today, particularly in Africa where poverty and external exploitation remain live issues. Though the two decades after the fall of the Wall in 1989 saw a strengthening of the multilateral, norm-based system, disappointment that progress has not been faster has reopened the argument. As the debates over Ukraine and Gaza have shown, arguments based on universal values or norms will not get much traction if those values do not appear to have been consistently applied, or have not delivered anything useful for those still suffering.

So to have impact, you need to have strong arguments, a compelling narrative, and to address other people's realities. That is what knowing your audience means and, as in negotiations, it requires listening carefully to those you want to persuade and taking account of their point of view.

Secondly, the message must be respectful. While criticism of others' positions is sometimes both necessary and useful, insults have no place in diplomacy, though they are still used occasionally as shock tactics or to provoke a response. Normally, however, it is more effective to criticise policies rather than people. Personal attacks tend to be counter-productive, as you never know when today's pariah will become tomorrow's partner – so better not to risk alienating the individual. It is often easier to change policies or change minds than to change people.

Thirdly, make sure the message is consistent and credible. To reverse a policy, as the UK did over the EU in 2016 or over its aid spending in 2020, or the US did in pulling abruptly out of Afghanistan in 2021 or the Paris climate agreement (twice), is always damaging to credibility. Sometimes, the message you are instructed to give is not the one you would like to give or it may in your view be counter-productive, in which case you may need to push back against instructions to make it more credible (see Greenstock, 2016, on British Iraq policy). But this is not always possible. Remember also that an effective message is one that has a compelling narrative, a story that will fix it in people's mind. If official instructions don't provide that, you may have to find one yourself.

Fourthly, keep the message short. Not necessarily the 180 characters of a tweet, or the three-word slogans beloved of politicians – but concise and simple enough for people to grasp what it is and remember it. A good turn of phrase, something memorable with resonance, helps. But there are times when the message is more complicated and over-simplification obscures rather than illuminates, puts off rather than persuades. 'Structural adjustment' for example started as a phrase that summarised a policy approach by the IMF and World Bank designed to rein in profligate and protectionist policies and restore financial stability to poorer countries. But it came to be seen as a neo-colonialist imposition that hobbled governments, destroyed industries and impoverished the vulnerable. There were problems of substance with the adjustment policies, as there were with the policies they replaced, but rather than an intelligent debate about how to adapt economic policies to improve the outcome, it became a slanging match between proponents of rival slogans.

Fifthly, be conscious of the difference between internal and external messaging. What is useful at home may not go down well abroad. As a diplomat, you are expected to send frank and honest reports to ministers and colleagues back home: it is what they need to make well-informed policy decisions. But it can be a problem if they become public, leaked by accident or design to the media or to the host government. During the 2008 US election campaign, a confidential report from the British Ambassador in Washington, Sir Nigel Sheinwald, describing Barack Obama as talented but aloof and uninspiring, found its way into the public domain. Once elected, Obama indicated privately that he held no grudges, understood that diplomats had to give their personal opinions, and received Sheinwald as if nothing had happened. Embarrassing for the British, but no harm done. Not so with President Trump. An internal report on the Trump White House from Sheinwald's successor, Sir Kim Darroch, describing Trump as 'insecure' and his administration as 'clumsy and inept', was leaked to the press in 2019. At a subsequent press conference Trump castigated Darroch as a 'pompous fool' and refused to meet him. Boris Johnson, then Foreign Secretary, failed to back his ambassador in public, effectively forcing him to resign (Doyle, 2008; Sparrow, 2019; Wintour, 2020). No system is ever 100% secure, and some diplomats now report as if anything they say could unexpectedly appear in public. But it has the result of making internal reporting less valuable to the recipient. Sometimes you need to run the risk, while never forgetting what the risks are.

For politicians, there are similar but different challenges. It is all too easy to forget that a message designed for a domestic audience will also be heard, and interpreted, more widely. Bashing foreigners may win you votes at home, but will not win you friends abroad. Diplomats have become all too accustomed to picking up the pieces after incautious political statements: 'What the Prime Minister *meant* was . . .' not what he or she actually said. This makes it particularly important for diplomats to be involved with the drafting of political speeches on foreign policy issues, or those with impact on foreign relations, such as immigration rules or trade and investment decisions. A classic case was Mrs Thatcher's Bruges speech in 1988. The Foreign Office sent No. 10 an anodyne draft for a relatively routine event, but the Prime Minister was keen to vent her frustration with Commission President Delors's ambitions for a more federal Europe and penchant for greater economic intervention. When the more robust revised draft, crafted by her Private Secretary Charles Powell, was received in the Foreign Office it caused consternation. Alarmed that it would precipitate a rupture with European partners, senior officials tried to water it back down by taking out some of the more incendiary language and trying to moderate the message. The final version was not anti-European: it praised the Single Market, which Thatcher had always supported, and did not question Britain's membership. But it still made clear her opposition to a federal, interventionist Europe which became the story, and did indeed aggravate her relations with other EU leaders (Clark, 1993, 224–7). The speech met its domestic objectives, becoming an object of veneration for Tory Eurosceptics who formed themselves into a 'Bruges Group' to resist further European integration. But it did not enhance British interests or influence abroad, and after Thatcher's fall in 1990 her successor John Major signed the Maastricht Treaty, announcing that he would put Britain at the 'centre of Europe' (at least for a while).

Finally, for a message to work it needs to resonate with the audience and reflect the world as they see it. Boris Johnson's rhetoric about 'Global Britain' may have had a nostalgic appeal at home, but persuaded few abroad because it was so baldly contradicted by the facts: a weakened, introverted Britain that abandoned its friends in Europe and cut its aid to the developing world. Similarly, US rhetorical support for democracy has always fallen flat in the Middle East given their close alliance with the monarchies of the Gulf and the fiasco of their intervention in Iraq. Where you are trying to change minds, the message needs to be sufficiently related to people's perception of reality to be effective. Unless, of course, you are trying to change their perception of reality itself.

Disinformation has become increasingly common as a way to muddy the waters of truth, to make people question their existing beliefs and influence public opinion in favour of one side of an argument rather than another. Information warfare has accompanied the physical kind for hundreds of years, but technological change has made disinformation and propaganda easier to spread and harder to stop. Conspiracy theories are a favourite way to make people doubt the information they receive from the media or their own government, or question the independence and motives of the UN or other international bodies. Such theories have existed for centuries, and infamous forgeries like the Protocol of the Elders of Zion, first published in Russia in 1903, and the Zinoviev letter published in the UK in 1924 have had major political and diplomatic impacts (Clarke, 2004, 127). Social media, however, has enabled both disinformation and conspiracy theories to spread faster and further than ever before. As always, they are most effective when they tap into existing suspicions or prejudices, making the fabrications sound plausible to inno- cent or interested ears, with AI making fakes harder and harder to identify. If you throw enough 'chaff' into the ether, people will not be sure what is true and what is not, and will then follow their gut instincts.

For the diplomat, counteracting such disinformation about your own country or organisation is both critically important and extremely difficult, as France found in the Sahel. Getting your truth out and getting it heard can be chal- lenging. Swift rebuttal of accidental or deliberate misinformation is essential to avoid your own messages being distorted or undermined, and constant moni- toring is invaluable – if you have the resources to do it and access to the right media. In countries governed by autocratic regimes, freedom of the press and therefore access to it can be strictly limited, and such governments often have their own sophisticated propaganda machine to generate 'useful' content. So your own access may be limited and your message not be heard. More liberal regimes, with greater press freedom and transparency, also pose a problem as you may get your message out but it is not always heard amidst the cacophony of divergent views, gossip, selective reporting and outright deception. As bad money tends to drive out good, persuasive disinformation can drive out the truth, as the British found during the Brexit debates.

The medium

This is where using the right medium to get your message across is vital. You should be ready and able to use all the media available, but in any individual case pick the most appropriate for the audience you want to reach.

The majority of people now get most of their news digitally. The lines between print, TV, radio, websites, podcasts and social media posts have become almost impossibly blurred, with most big media institutions operating multiple chan- nels simultaneously. It is therefore a question of identifying which brand reaches the audience you want. As of 2025 (and it changes constantly), to influence, for example, global decision or opinion-makers, getting your news, story or spin into conventional British outlets like the BBC, the *Economist* or the *Financial Times* is worth dozens of individual conversations. They remain popular and respected among the global elite for their journalistic standards and broadly objective reporting – as long as you accept their premise that order is better than chaos and an open capitalist world economy remains desirable. For one part of the US elite, the *New York Times, Washington Post, Newsweek, Time* and *New Yorker* remain influential, though less so than in the past. To reach more right-wing opinion, how- ever, Fox News has been the dominant voice since 2010, with a plethora of other dedicated channels that speak to a divergent range of true believers. In francophone countries, France 24 and Canal+ get the most access, and in the Arabic-speaking world Al-Jazeera has carved out a particularly influential position, though it has been accused of an Islamist bias or of being a Qatari mouthpiece (Cooper et al., 2013, 213–21). China and Russia each have an international broadcaster and media channels and have been making efforts to build news outlets with global impact, but are constrained by their unwillingness to host alternative or independent views.

To influence public opinion more widely depends where you are. Wherever I travelled in Ghana I would try to arrange an interview with the local radio station as this was the most effective way of being heard by local audiences who rarely saw newspapers and (back then) had little internet access. It meant adjusting the message to whatever would be relevant or interesting locally – football (always), music, visas, the royal family, British investments in mobile phone networks or in Ghanaian fruit and cocoa production, or conservation and education projects. Nationwide, Ghanaian television still had reach and impact, so an interview on one of the main channels would be quoted back to me for weeks afterwards.

Increasingly, though, social media reaches the widest public audience. This creates a dilemma for diplomats and others representing more than themselves. If that is where people, especially young people, go to get their news and exchange opinions, you cannot afford not to be there, on Facebook, YouTube, X(Twitter), TikTok, WeChat, Instagram, Linked-In, or whatever is trending by the time you read this. On the other hand, they are all crowded fields; to be noticed it helps to be constantly active and preferably provocative. That does not sit well with diplomatic decorum and discretion. This is why, though every British Ambassador has social media accounts, they tend to the anodyne – relaying events, photographs of meetings and visitors, comments on places they have been, the weather, their garden, pets, sporting activities and similar safe subjects. They will relay official statements on matters of global and local interest, royal events and the like. But it is rare that you will see anything controversial or critical. The exceptions tend to prove this rule. A former colleague built a huge following in one African country by commenting extensively on Premier League football, a local obsession, but was drawn into tit-for-tat disputes with members of the public supporting other teams, so that one local told me in exasperation, 'That man, he tweets *too much* . . .' While he achieved high rates of public recognition, he became better known for his Twitter controversies than for his promotion of British interests. Another former colleague in the Middle East built an impressive following by tweeting in Arabic about football, local culture and pithy commentary on local events, none of it particularly controversial but still managing to irritate the government, to the extent that he was no longer able to get meetings with the president or foreign minister. For an ambassador, a million social media followers is no substitute for talking to the government. Even China reined in some of its 'wolf warrior' diplomats who proved counter-productively controversial (Xiaolin and Yitong, 2023). Controversy and jokes may be meat and drink to internet influencers, but are problematic for diplomats. As a result, you have to be there, but be square (as they used to say).

This inhibition does not apply to those actors who *aim* to disrupt traditional diplomatic activity, whether terrorist organisations pursuing global jihad, civil society activists pursuing climate action, politicians trying to stir up public outrage, or governments seeking to undermine their opponents' legitimacy by spreading rumours, rewriting history and propagating their own narrative. The Ukraine war illustrates this, Russia actively propagating its narrative that their invasion was merely a justified response to NATO's aggressive expansion into Russia's sphere of influence, that it threatened Russia, and that Ukraine was never really an independent country anyway. Those opposed to this narrative have struggled to counter it in the global digital space, with the result that the Russian view gained traction among public opinion outside Europe. This trend towards exercising digital influence is also evident in national politics, but the absence of control in the international sphere can make it even more damaging there. It has led to serious questions about the editorial control of content by the companies dominating digital platforms – Google, Facebook, ByteDance, X and the like. The argument between freedom of expression on one side and stopping hate speech and deliberate falsehood on the other has no firm resolution, but the pressure to shift the dial towards more control (for better or worse) is growing. Some governments already exercise national control over the internet to exclude 'disruptive' foreign content, of which the 'Great Firewall of China' is the most elaborate and effective – even if, like the original Great Wall, it will inevitably fail to keep barbarian ideas at bay forever. Ideas, like people, will find the weakest spot and pour through when the time is ripe – as Marxism-Leninism did in China itself.

The debate over the impact of social media on foreign affairs echoes the panic over the impact of wireless in the 1930s. Hitler's extensive use of the media, and his realisation that if you tell a big enough lie and tell it often enough, people will start to believe you, have obvious parallels today – in democracies as well as autocracies. This is not to underplay the impact of the internet and social media, but to underline that human nature has not changed, and politicians will use whatever media is available to make whatever case they want. As Nicolson put it in his ineffably aristocratic way 80 years ago, the result is that 'the old courtesies of diplomatic intercourse will wear a trifle thin'. Even so, he still believed that 'the best antidote to the hysterical school of broadcasters is a policy of truth, under-statement and calm' (Nicolson, 1939, 169–72).

The modern diplomat needs to adjust to the unreliability of digital space: objective truth about a situation is giving way to subjective truth, 'my truth', which is whatever I choose to believe or assert whether supported by facts or not. This makes it all the more important that, to be trusted, the diplomat does stick to objective truth and continues using *all* available means of communication, and not over-rely on digital means given their fallibility. Traditional public diplomacy involving personal meetings with officials and the public throughout the country, spreading the same message from the top to the grass roots, gives you the chance to listen and discuss as well as project your own message, enabling you to craft a message that will resonate with each audience, in a way that social media alone does not. Even then, *how* you say it matters too.

The method

How do you make your message stick?

First and foremost, say it in a language people will understand. As I explained earlier, if you're in a foreign country, use their language wherever you can. It is true that English has become in practice the language of diplomacy and a global standard on the internet and in international media. But many of the people that you want to hear your message are neither diplomats nor journalists. Politicians and the public will not only understand better, but appreciate the effort to speak their own language. This is not always easy. Some languages take years to learn fluently, and not all foreign ministries or organisations have the resources that the FCDO puts into hard language training in Arabic, Chinese, Japanese, Russian, German, Farsi or Turkish. If you can speak English, French and Spanish, you have a fair part of the world covered, and with Arabic you can reach another key segment. But your credibility as a communicator will be high if you can speak at least some Urdu, Hindi, Thai, Malay, Korean, Hungarian, Polish, Finnish or – in my case – Swahili.

Speaking to politicians is similar to speaking in public: keep the language simple and the message clear. Not that they are stupid; quite the contrary. Many will have a far cannier appreciation of you than you do of them. But they are always busy and appreciate something that is easily accessible and doesn't take too long.

Secondly, be memorable. As Walter Bagehot said, 'An Ambassador is not simply an agent: he is also a spectacle' (Bagehot, 1867, ch. 4). There are good and bad ways of doing this, and once again you need to adapt to the circumstances and cultural norms of the country. The job of British Ambassador to Washington is a plum one, so all the incumbents have been intellectually whip-smart. But not all were memorable. Sir Nicholas Henderson happened to be the Ambassador during the Falklands war, a tense moment in Anglo-American relations because the US, even under President Reagan, would not automatically support the UK on questions that involved a legacy of empire. With his languid aristocratic manner, antique dress sense and floppy bow ties, Henderson was almost a caricature of what Americans thought of the British, but this actually helped him get onto every American TV chat show in town to make the British case with an intellectual acuity, eloquence and humour that helped Britain win the battle for US public opinion (Henderson, 1994).

During my time at the Washington Embassy, the Ambassador was Sir Christopher Meyer whose natural flamboyance manifested itself in wearing, every day of the year, bright red socks with whatever suit or outfit fitted the occasion. Others found equally distinctive ways of being remembered: the High Commissioner I worked with in Dar es Salaam had a surprising repertoire of bawdy sea shanties from his time in the Navy that were sung with gusto on suitable (and unsuitable) occasions. In Brussels, the senior British official in the Council Secretariat was instantly recognisable by his taste for colourful ties and ability to recite paragraphs of poetry from memory; and Scottish colleagues always seemed able to turn out in full kilt and regalia when an impression needed to be made. US Secretary of State Tony Blinken is known for his skill with the electric guitar; President of the African Development Bank, Akinwumi Adesina, is never seen without a smart bow tie; and Ngozi Okonjo-Iweala, head of the WTO, is always immaculately turned-out in traditional Nigerian dress with matching headgear. Hats and scarves can make otherwise conventional dress more memorable. If people are interested in the way you look as well as how you speak, they are more likely to remember what you say.

But still, it is important to be appropriate and respect local sensitivities. This can be particularly taxing for women, for whom rules are more complicated than for men. It used to be the case that diplomatic services hesitated to appoint women to countries where the culture remained male-dominated in public life. This is less so now, but in some countries women diplomats or representatives are still expected to dress 'appropriately' in public or official meetings by covering the arms, wearing skirts rather than trousers, and sometimes covering the head. There is a dilemma whether to refuse such constraints and dress as you would in your home country, which you are of course representing, or to adapt to local custom even if on a personal basis you may not agree with it. In one country, a lone female ambassador found on arrival that she was expected to retire with the women at the end of a diplomatic dinner. She made clear she was there in her professional capacity, and would stay to take cognac with the men – as she did for the next three years.

Besides the language you speak and the way you look, your style of speaking should be appropriate to the occasion. A formal speech to a seated audience is very different from a policy presentation to a committee, an intervention at an international conference, an after-dinner speech to a well-fed room, or indeed from an extended interview on live radio or TV, or a one-minute sound-bite on the morning news. A good diplomat needs to be able to pick the appropriate tone and style for each occasion. There is no point trying to prescribe a format for each: better to watch carefully those who do it well and learn the style. But shorter is almost always better than longer. Humour in the right context and with the right tone makes people surprised, interested and happy (Christopher Meyer was the only diplomat I knew who could make the most respectable American audience enjoy a risqué joke, told with such charm and panache they found it irresistible), but you need to be sure of your ground, know the audience and pick the right context. Even for impromptu speeches, it is always useful to think in advance what is the one point you want people to remember from what you say. PowerPoint is almost always a killer: sometimes it is unavoidable, but use maps, charts and pictures to illuminate what you are saying rather than screeds of text that repeat it.

Except for major set-piece speeches, or formal statements in Council where the words and phrases have to be precisely right (especially if in a foreign language) it is best to work from the shortest notes possible or, even better, without notes at all. If actors can learn their lines, so can you, though it does need time. Otherwise, condense the notes down to a single page, or even to one-word headings. In preparing, be clear what you want to say and don't worry too much about the words you will use to say it. It will sound more convincing if you make your case as you would in a normal conversation. In giving speeches, it is sometimes useful to imagine giving it to a single person: it helps make it direct and personal, and people relate to the personal. The largest audience I ever addressed was a gathering of five thousand young business men and women in a vast open-air conference centre in Accra. What some told me afterwards they remembered was not my message about British help to Ghanaian entrepreneurs, but the story of my father setting up his own business while teaching electrical engineering at university, and how he made it work because other business people recognised he knew what he was talking about. If you don't know what you are talking about, people will spot it pretty quickly, and it's best to shut up.

But always be prepared and know what you want to say: winging it is risky and can be a disaster.

Talking to journalists is an integral part of a diplomat's job, far more so than for a home civil servant, a businessman or a development or humanitarian worker, unless explicitly employed to liaise with the media. Journalists can be your best friend, and your greatest threat. For one thing, you are both in the information-gathering business and may have information the other wants, so a mutually beneficial exchange can be effected, as long as the rules are clear. To understand American, German, French, Ghanaian or Tanzanian politics I found talking to local journalists invaluable. Most politicians have a point to make, as indeed do some journalists; but by and large journalists want to understand what is really going on behind the scenes and, having lived in the country all or most of their lives, know better how to find out. On diplomatic or international issues journalists from the major agencies are almost always happy to exchange notes with diplomats and share facts that help build a better picture of what is going on. In negotiations, some of those involved will brief journalists more fully than foreign diplomats. True, it helps if you can offer some information in return, but be very clear from the outset whether you are talking on the record or off, and whether you know the journalist in question well enough to trust their confidentiality. With less scrupulous journalists, or those you don't know, never say anything that you are not willing to see in print – it is never good to be the source of a shocking headline. But trusted contacts among the press can be very helpful in providing insights and helping you get your side of the story out. It can be more impactful to get a respected journalist to make your arguments in an op-ed than for you or a senior government official to do so.

Hostile audiences

There will be times when people do not want to hear the message you want to give them, and vice versa. This is one of the reasons for the formality of diplomatic exchanges, so that uncomfortable messages can be given and received with respect and restraint. However blunt the message, Notes Verbale always begin and end with time-honoured traditional formulas of respect, though there is something surreal about being expelled from a country through a Note Verbale that ends with the words: 'The Ministry of Foreign Affairs avails itself of this opportunity to extend to the Embassy the assurance of its highest consideration.'

This respect is not always adhered to. On an official visit to Zimbabwe in 2013, where the EU had difficult and delicate relations, I had asked to call on President Mugabe. We were told first to call on the foreign minister who proceeded with a vigorous 45-minute interrogation. Shouting would be an unkind word to use but it was, shall we say, more aggressive than usual. Preserving dignity and sticking to the script while not provoking an escalation of rhetoric or volume was tough. But having weathered that storm, we were immediately summoned to the Presidential residence, cancelling planned meetings with the opposition on the way, to wait upon Mugabe's pleasure. That turned out to be three hours after we arrived, when we were finally admitted to the presence. Mugabe himself was perfectly polite, though we received the ritual lecture about the iniquities of the British, Tony Blair, Claire Short, land issues and the rest (even though I was there representing the EU) before we could get down to business. This was to discuss the prospects for free and fair elections in Zimbabwe. It seemed best not to tackle the subject directly, so I started with history. We discussed the independence struggle, which engaged his interest, so I asked which African leaders he most admired. He proposed Nkrumah and Nyerere. And which did he think was most successful, the former ousted in a coup and dying in exile, or the latter who handed over to his successor and died on his farm? He got my drift, and we had a useful and relatively open discussion about what constituted real stability and progress. Not that it changed his mind; but at least the message was delivered and I wasn't evicted.

Even so, my success rate at persuading leaders to stick to term limits or allow their people a free choice in elections has been limited. Similar conversations with Presidents Blaise Compaore in Burkina Faso and Yoweri Museveni in Uganda didn't yield any better result than in Zimbabwe, with similarly predictable consequences. But you have to try. The question is how to put it persuasively while avoiding paternalist pontificating. When you don't have a big stick, and someone doesn't care about the rules, your power of persuasion needs to be adjusted to the person you are speaking to. Other leaders (Obasanjo in Nigeria in 2007, Macky Sall in Senegal in 2024, eventually) were persuaded to stand down by international pressure when many at home were urging them to hang on to power as well as to leave. So persuasion can work.

All these conversations took place behind closed doors, where you can be frank. All too often there is pressure to make a public statement: to condemn rigged elections, human rights violations, the arrest or murder of journalists, or constraints on free speech. The UN faces this pressure constantly, especially in circumstances like Syria or Gaza where one side of the organisation is trying to call out human rights abuses while another side is trying to talk to the governments concerned about humanitarian aid delivery. There is no right answer, no magic solution in these circumstances: it is a matter of judgement for those concerned who have to take a decision what to say in public, balancing the pros and cons in that particular situation, though it can often help the diplomat on the spot if the statement comes from headquarters rather than having to make it themselves – as long as they are informed in advance and are prepared. The ICRC has managed to keep its privileged role in accessing prisoners held by the most heinous regimes by staying studiously silent in public on the grounds that speaking out would prevent them doing their primary job. Diplomats too need to keep lines open even to the most reprehensible regimes, though sometimes the pressure – and the moral obligation – to speak out becomes too much. Then you have to be prepared for the blow-back.

Facing a hostile media is often more intimidating than sceptical presidents or aggressive foreign ministers, unless you are ambushed in public, as President Zelenskyy found in the White House in 2025. The journalist's job is to try to expose facts or comments that will make a story. To handle the situation, first, know your facts – ideally better than they do, though journalists love nothing better than to spring a surprise on their interviewee, so get the most up-to-date news you can before you go on. Second, keep cool, never get angry, and don't get into a shouting match if the interviewer or another speaker keeps interrupting. You will keep the moral authority by staying calm. Third, never walk out: that is effectively admitting defeat and makes great television or social media clip so will be endlessly replayed. Fourthly, never let them put words into your mouth; 'So are you saying that . . .?' is a common ruse. But fifthly, do try to answer the question posed: circumlocuting diplomats evading the issue or trying to change the subject will not persuade anyone of their case. Finally, if you find yourself without an answer, offer to come back once you've got to the bottom of it and have another discussion so that you don't miss the chance to make your case.

The media are always interested in peace negotiations, but often saying anything in public risks precipitating a breakdown. Best to avoid saying anything potentially prejudicial to journalists, though – occasionally – carefully scripted public messaging can be used to nudge the negotiations along.

Delivering unwelcome news to a host government is always difficult: a change of travel advice that will put off tourists, the imposition of sanctions on some person or enterprise, or the arrest of one of their nationals. There is no way round this, and you have to be prepared for a hostile reaction. Remember that you are the messenger for your government and acting on instructions, so present the issue in as straight and factual a way as possible. Then report the reaction to your authorities, and ensure you have a press line to cover any queries or to put out on social media. Sometimes, as we saw in an earlier chapter, you may be summoned to receive unwelcome news, in which case make sure that you have a line from HQ before saying anything to the press in response.

Most difficult is finding yourself in disagreement with your own country's policy or actions. This happens. Brexit proved a particular challenge for quite a few British diplomats: the policy itself was obviously the result of a democratic process and pursued by a government duly elected by democratic means. It was therefore the civil servant's duty to deliver it, as almost all accepted (despite the accusations of a deep-state plot to block it). But some of the arguments that diplomats were asked to present to foreign governments explaining the British approach to the exit negotiations, for example, were simply not true. In these circumstances, if the instructions cannot be changed and you cannot in good conscience carry them out, the honourable course is to resign. In a well-known case, one of the FCO's senior Legal Advisers, Elizabeth Wilmshurst, resigned over the Government's decision to ignore her legal opinion and join the US in invading Iraq in 2003 without a second UN Security Council Resolution authorising it. One British diplomat, responsible for explaining Brexit to US audiences, resigned when the cognitive dissonance between the government line, legality and reality grew too wide (Hall Hall, 2021). Others quietly decided it was time for a career change and stepped away from diplomacy to jobs in the private or non-governmental sectors. To ask a diplomat to lie or ask them to deliver a blatantly non-credible message, even though it happens, is to rob them of their greatest asset – trust – and thereby undermine the very instrument a government is using. I spoke to American colleagues who faced similar dilemmas during the first Trump Administration, made all the more difficult because policy changes could be communicated late at night by Twitter, or off the cuff in public remarks before the official structures had any time to prepare a rationale or line to take. Even some European colleagues in Brussels could be reduced to shrugging their shoulders with a despairing look when delivering some of their instructions in committee meetings, and would come over afterwards to apologise and suggest ways to help them get their instructions changed so that they could join a consensus.

Public diplomacy is not always easy, and managing the media, as it multiplies and diversifies, is becoming ever more challenging. But diplomacy still operates by rules, and these rules are, surprisingly perhaps, still normally respected. The next chapter explores what they are, and why they exist.

6   Diplomatic rules

Diplomacy is a strange game. As we saw in Chapter 2, though diplomacy is funda-mentally about power, with diplomats the ultimate pragmatists, it has a set of rules that most participants still respect and which, whether written or not, a diplomat is expected to know.

The Vienna Convention on Diplomatic Relations provides the basic rules of the road for diplomats, and though signed only in 1961, it codified practice that had evolved over centuries (details in Feltham, 1982, and Roberts, 2017). Two years later it was followed by the Vienna Convention on Consular Relations, the two making up what are known as 'the Vienna Conventions'. They were preceded by the founding Charter of the United Nations and the Statute of the International Court of Justice (ICJ) adopted at or following the San Francisco conference in 1946, and subsequently by the Geneva Conventions in 1949 setting out the rules for humanitarian treatment of people in times of war and peace. These four are the basic texts from which the current rules of diplomacy stem.

There is no space to explore here the intricacies of international law or the role of the ICJ: there are books aplenty for the curious (see for example Brownlie, 1998). My aim is to outline how they impact on a diplomat's everyday life and work. Those with an insatiable appetite for the legal details should read Sir Ernest Satow's *Guide to Diplomatic Practice* (first published in 1917, its most recent edi-tion edited by Sir Ivor Roberts in 2017), the comprehensive, indispensable and regularly updated guide to all manner of diplomatic activities from how to write a treaty to the orders of diplomatic precedence at ceremonies. Like 90% of diplo-mats, I never looked at it once during my diplomatic career: if in doubt, we could ask the Foreign Office Legal Advisers. But it was nice to know it was there. This chapter is no more than a plain man's lightning guide to the basics.

Origins and recognition

Chapter 2 explained the historical origins of the current states system in which diplomats operate, but we need to expand a little on some of the elements of that system to understand how it works now.

The first diplomats were in effect heralds or envoys from one leader to another, given a privileged and protected status to enable them to come and go in order to

DOI: 10.4324/9781003533436-6

discuss potential alliances, deals or conflicts before they happened. This was not always respected: in 614 CE, the Byzantine emperor Heraclitus sent envoys to the Persian king Khusraw to sue for peace after his army was defeated. Khusraw listened carefully to the offer they brought, and then had the envoys executed. The message being clear, Heraclitus raised another army and this time defeated the Persians (Frankopan, 2015, 69). But by and large the injunction not to kill the messenger held good, and most envoys returned whence they came in one piece, rather than in bits.

The first key shift happened when such envoys stayed put: rather than just visiting to deliver a message or negotiate a treaty before returning home, they took up permanent residence at the court or in the capital of the other country for years at a time. Between European countries this started in the 15th century, though Byzantines and Venetians had made use of resident envoys a couple of centuries before that. These were broadly welcomed as providing a permanent means of communication between monarchs, as between the Tudor monarchs of England and the Holy Roman Emperor Charles V of Spain across the water. The correspondence of Eustace Chapuys, the Emperor's ambassador to the court of Henry VIII from 1529 to 1545, is a crucial source for the history of England at that time (Mackay, 2015).

An envoy's protected status as representative of a foreign monarch was in due course extended to their residence; these were, in effect, the first embassies. Some rulers gave land to foreign ambassadors, as an indication of favour and protection. The British were granted such privileged plots, for example, in Istanbul, Tokyo and Addis Ababa, on which they built imposing residences. Elsewhere, the embassy in Paris was acquired in 1815 when allied forces occupied Paris after the fall of Napoleon. The Chinese emperor, when finally forced to accept foreign missions in 1860, required that they were all confined to the 'Legation Quarter' in Beijing. In 1985 you could still wander the streets, peering through rusting gates at dilapidated western buildings, overgrown courtyards and the occasional church. Some of the period buildings survive, spruced up, but the embassies themselves have moved elsewhere.

The second key shift was in the mutual recognition of states. This acceptance that another authority has sovereign control over a geographical space beyond your own is the basis for international law (Brownlie, 1998). What establishing diplomatic relations implies is the recognition of the other state's sovereignty, and a mutual understanding that those relations will be conducted in accordance with international norms. According to Article 38 of the Statute of the ICJ, those norms, the rules of international law, are set by three things: international conventions (duly deposited), international custom (meaning 'general practice accepted as law') and 'the general principles of law recognised by civilized nations'.

This is why recognition remains such a critical question. It is the sovereign decision of every state whether to recognise another, but membership of the UN is a seal on the general acceptability of a state and is decided by a two-thirds majority vote in the General Assembly on the basis of a recommendation from the Security Council. It was not until 1971, following the US's opening towards China under Nixon, that the Communist government of the People's Republic of China was recognised as the country's legitimate representative at the UN, replacing the Nationalist Kuomintang government based in Taiwan (Calvocoressi, 1982, 70–3). China holds religiously to the One China policy, insisting that Taiwan is an integral part of a single country, only temporarily out of its control, and that no state can recognise both. Taiwan is now recognised only by an ever-shrinking number of small island states. Even messier were the manoeuvrings around the (non-) recognition of the Khmer Rouge as the government of Cambodia/Kampuchea from 1974 when they seized *de facto* control until the UN-brokered agreement in 1991. During that time Prince Sihanouk's government continued to represent the country in the UN though without any presence in the country itself, while rival Khmer factions physically fought over control of its embassies in third countries (Widyono, 2007; Hamilton and Langhorne, 2011, 213).

These illustrate that recognition is dictated by global politics as much as by international law, a reality that is clear to other self-proclaimed states which remain unrecognised by the international community. Somaliland proclaimed its independence from Somalia in 1991 but has yet (in 2024) to receive a single formal recognition, so its envoys have no diplomatic status, though they receive representational assistance from an NGO called 'Independent Diplomat' (Ross, 2017). The Turkish republic of northern Cyprus has likewise been unrecognised by everyone except its guarantor, Turkey, since 1983, so its envoys travel on Turkish passports. The 'states' of South Ossetia and Abkhazia that broke away from Georgia are recognised only by Russia and a few of its closest allies. Disputes continue over Western Sahara and, of course, over the state of Palestine – widely recognised, widely represented, including at the UN, but without agreed borders or other basic elements of sovereignty (Geldenhuys, 2009).

It is nevertheless quite common to maintain diplomatic representation in unrecognised states. Many countries, like the UK, are represented in Taiwan by a 'Trade and Cultural Office' (now known simply as the 'British Office Taipei'), headed by a senior diplomat, but implying no recognition of the Taipei government as sovereign. The UK maintains a representation to the Palestinian Authority (PA) through its Consul-General in Jerusalem, who is not accredited to Israel but is (normally) allowed to pass freely into the West Bank to visit Ramallah where the PA is based. The British representative to Somaliland currently resides in Addis Ababa, and visits from there. In other countries where a sending state has difficulty or objection to recognising the government of the receiving state, they can still be represented by a chargé d'affaires who can operate without presenting credentials to the head of state, thereby avoiding implied recognition – provided, of course, that the receiving state will give them a diplomatic visa. Chargés d'affaires enjoy full diplomatic privileges and immunities, but without the status of ambassadorial rank. Where that is problematic, or relations have been ruptured, a country can still maintain some representation for consular or other purposes through an 'interests section' in the embassy of another state.

In short, the politics of recognition is complex and contingent on the circumstances. What matters for the diplomat is to understand the sensitivity, and frequently the ambiguity, of these situations. Where sovereignty of a territory or region is disputed, the diplomat must proceed with caution, lest one side or another take a visit as implicit recognition, or use it for propaganda purposes. The government of Cyprus in Nicosia allows diplomats to travel across the green line into northern Cyprus precisely because they still claim sovereignty over it. But visiting disputed territories like Abkhazia or Western Sahara is a very delicate matter on which guidance from headquarters would be well-advised.

What to do when a revolutionary or terrorist organisation seizes a state, or a military coup overthrows a government, is a more frequent problem. The UK has a policy of recognising states not governments, so even if a legitimate government with which we have relations is removed, the embassy would not normally be withdrawn unless it was at physical risk; however, normal diplomatic relations with the new junta or revolutionary government may be suspended. When the Taliban took control of Afghanistan in 2021, most western embassies were withdrawn on security as well as political grounds and formal diplomatic relations were broken off. In Niger in 2023, coup leaders arrested and imprisoned the democratically elected President Bazoum, whom many in the international community continued to recognise as the legitimate head of state. Most embassies nevertheless remained in Niamey, though relations with France deteriorated rapidly and a few months later the French Ambassador was declared *persona non grata* and all French diplomats and military were withdrawn. US troops were also subsequently asked to leave. President Ali Bongo of Gabon, ousted in a similar coup the same year, received less international support partly no doubt because he had just rigged the elections to stay in power, which then precipitated the coup. Diplomats in Gabon quickly established contact with General Nguema, while in Niger relations with General Tchiani remained patchy and scratchy, except with the Russians, who swiftly came to help. For accredited diplomats in these countries, the situation can be difficult. Is it safe to stay? Is it safe to leave? If you do, will you be allowed back in? Will the new government respect your diplomatic privileges and immunities? Who can and should you talk to?

My experience in these circumstances is that the diplomatic corps as a whole tends to stick together and, through the Dean, liaises with the *de facto* authorities, whoever they may be, to ensure all are protected and treated respectfully and equally. In 2010, Côte d'Ivoire held long-delayed elections, designed to resolve the ten-year conflict that had broken out following a coup d'état in 1999 and been frozen by a temporary peace deal in 2007 that left Laurent Gbagbo in place as President – to whom I duly presented my credentials the following year. The UN were supervising the election, backed by a military peacekeeping mission, UNOCI. As the British Ambassador I worked closely with the UN, the EU and other monitoring missions to encourage a transparent and peaceful process. After two weeks of painstaking compilation and cross-checking, the chairman of the Electoral Commission, under heavy UN guard, announced the result, and then fled the country. Gbagbo had lost and one of the opposition leaders, Alassane Ouattara, was declared President. Gbago refused to accept it, persuaded his placemen on the Constitutional Court to declare the results invalid on a technicality, and called his supporters onto the street. The opposition *Forces Nouvelles* mobilised their own forces in the north and marched south on the capital, Abidjan, to enforce the result. Ouattara, already in Abidjan, was holed up in the Golfe Hotel, protected by UNOCI troops. In late December the diplomatic corps en masse (except the Chinese) sped through the night to call on Gbagbo at the Presidential Palace in a last-ditch effort to persuade him to stand down and hand over. After we had waited for two to three hours, he finally agreed to see us around 1 am. We delivered our message, but he preferred to talk about football and the pleasures of the night. It was clear he had no intention of going. The next day I called on Ouattara at the Golfe Hotel to assure him of British support, and returned to Accra. Two days later, Gbagbo declared me *persona non grata* and, with the Canadian ambassador, expelled us from the country. This was gesture politics as we were both already out of the country; the French Ambassador, far more active in trying to push Gbagbo out, remained. When the *Forces Nouvelles* (with a little help from the French military mission, Licorne), took Abidjan the following March and captured Gbagbo in the ruins of the Presidential palace, I was able to return to the country where Ouattara declared that I was now *persona* very *grata*.

This was a clear case where international diplomatic intervention made a difference. Without UNOCI supervision of the election, without a united international response, there is no doubt that Gbagbo would have remained president whether the Ivorians wanted him or not, and Côte d'Ivoire's stagnation and probably conflict would have continued.

Where a country succumbs to full blown civil war, like Sudan in 2023–5, most embassies are simply withdrawn once citizens have been evacuated, as little official diplomatic work can be done. Resolving the conflict is a task for special envoys and track-two contacts, rather than formal diplomacy, and in the heat of battle rival forces tend not to pay much attention to diplomatic immunities.

The case of Afghanistan illustrates well the difficulties of dealing with revolutionary take-overs. During the Taliban's first stint in power, from 1996 to 2001, following the lengthy civil war that followed the fall of the Soviet-backed Najibullah regime in 1992, it was recognised only by Pakistan, Saudi Arabia and the UAE and was never permitted to take Afghanistan's seat at the UN. Following its return to power in 2021, after the US withdrawal, it was clearly the *de facto* authority throughout the country, but as of 2024 it has not yet been formally recognised by any other state, or allowed to take Afghanistan's seat in the UN. China, however, has exchanged ambassadors, and both Pakistan and Qatar have regular official, even ministerial level, contact. Even so, most countries that evacuated their embassies will not go back any time soon, and non-recognition could last for some time, inhibiting Afghanistan's re-integration into the global community (Bristow, 2024).

One recent case stands out as an exception. In June 2014, Abu Bakr al-Baghdadi, the leader of the Islamic State in Iraq and Syria (ISIS, also known locally as Da'esh), proclaimed its caliphate from the pulpit of the Grand Mosque in Mosul. At the time ISIS had physical control over around 40% of Iraq and 30% of Syria, and yet no one recognised this self-proclaimed state. This was not merely a revolt that sought to overturn and replace local governments, but one which challenged the founding principles of the international community of states by refusing to abide by any of its established rules. Any diplomat or envoy trying to reach al-Baghdadi would have been not just turned back but probably taken hostage and gruesomely executed. The states of the world, increasingly divided over Middle Eastern issues at the time, united to eliminate this threat to the established order (Phillips, 2020).

One footnote: in countries with heavily devolved constitutions, regional governments often want to set up their own offices in foreign capitals. The German Länder and Canadian states have done this for many years, and while Britain was a member of the EU the devolved administrations of Scotland, Wales and Northern Ireland all maintained offices in Brussels to liaise with the institutions on issues of interest to their region. Just opposite my EU office near rond-point Schuman there was also, prominently advertised, the office for Catalunya, the Catalan region of Spain. US states have done this less frequently, though I used to enjoy going to a burger bar just off Trafalgar Square that called itself 'The Texas Embassy'. Though such offices will liaise closely with the embassy, they are nevertheless not normally part of the official representation of the sending state and therefore not entitled to diplomatic privileges or immunities.

Protection of persons

The principle of inviolability for diplomatic envoys was established at an early stage, and the 1816 Congress of Vienna recognised the principle of diplomatic privileges and immunities for ambassadors. For the public this may appear slightly quaint and, well, privileged. Diplomats traditionally pay no taxes in their country of accreditation, can access duty free alcohol, are immune from prosecution, and are therefore able to avoid parking fines. It all sounds very cushy. But it is important to understand what these privileges and immunities are really for.

A diplomat should be free from any undue pressure in the receiving country which might be used to influence their views or their advice in favour of the host government. The purpose of diplomatic immunity is therefore primarily to protect the diplomat from legal or physical pressure or harassment, or indeed from inducements of any kind that might prejudice their opinion of the host country (Athens used to execute on their return envoys who had succumbed to bribery while abroad). They need to remain wholly loyal to their own government and be free of fear or favour from the country where they are living. They are exempt from tax to ensure they are not penalised, and immune from prosecution so they cannot be threatened or the subject of malicious suits brought not just by governments but by individuals who want to put pressure on an embassy for whatever personal reason they may have.

When serving in friendly, allied or like-minded countries, such protections are rarely needed. But not all countries are like-minded or friendly, and it is vital to maintain the global rule so that diplomats are indeed protected in countries where, given the chance, a government or faction or individual would not hesitate to put pressure on foreign diplomats to secure their own ends. In particular, it is essential to ensure they are not effectively taken hostage and used as a bargaining counter for some objective the receiving country may have. Such hostage-taking has occurred, as we saw in Chapter 3, but not among diplomats – apart from the US Embassy staff held hostage in Iran in 1979 (see below). Some ambassadors have also been kidnapped, but by terrorists not by states (Jönsson and Hall, 2005, 115).

This privileged status is reflected in the use of diplomatic passports. In many countries, all members of the diplomatic service are issued with such passports whether they are working at home or abroad. The British government, for reasons of equality and vanity, refused for many years to issue its diplomats with such passports, arguing that a British passport alone should be sufficient to ensure that the bearer was allowed 'to pass freely without let or hindrance' and be afforded 'such assistance and protection as may be necessary' – as the preamble printed at the front of every passport requests and requires. Reality, however, proved otherwise, and British diplomats and their families were regularly inconvenienced by the absence of such passports, particularly in difficult posts, even if they carried a diplomatic visa from the receiving country in their regular passport. In 1994, Parliament was finally persuaded to allow diplomats to carry diplomatic passports, but only while they were accredited to an overseas government or organisation, and to their families only if resident and accredited. For British diplomats based in the UK who travelled frequently on diplomatic business overseas, the most that was conceded was a short phrase typed on the 'Observations' page of the passport saying, 'The holder is a member of Her [now His] Britannic Majesty's Diplomatic Service.' This always raised eyebrows at immigration desks: 'Never seen that before. Why don't you just have a diplomatic passport?' was the usual response when I tried to avoid the queues and go out the diplomatic channel in order to get to my first meeting on time. The EU at least allowed me a diplomatic *laissez-passer* for international travel while I worked for them.

Diplomatic immunity nevertheless does come with obligations. There is a presumption that diplomats will respect the laws of the land where they are living. So although legally they cannot be prosecuted for minor speeding or parking offences, they are expected to stick to the speed limit and park only where it is permitted. In London (not a great place to have to drive or to park), they will receive tickets for these offences and are required to submit them with a Note Verbale confirming the transgressor's diplomatic status to avoid subsequent prosecution. The Marshall of the Diplomatic Corps would occasionally read the riot act to ambassadors if too many tickets were being issued, and for some years maintained league tables of parking fines issued in an effort to shame them into making their staff stick to the law. Most ambassadors do care about the reputational impact of staff constantly in trouble with the local police, and may even suggest the culprit be sent home.

But there are three areas where diplomatic immunity applied to persons can become problematic.

Firstly, it is occasionally the case that someone with diplomatic status commits a severe transgression. In these circumstances the host government will usually ask for the individual's diplomatic status to be waived by their government so that they can be brought to court. On 17 April 1984, a demonstration outside the Libyan People's Bureau (effectively their embassy) in St James's Square, London was attacked by two figures who appeared at upper windows of the building and sprayed the crowd with machine gun fire. A policewoman who was monitoring the demonstration, WPC Yvonne Fletcher, was killed on the spot and eleven Iranians were wounded. The building was sealed off and the British government demanded that the perpetrators be handed over to be tried for the murder by British courts. The Libyan government refused, and after a tense 11-day stand-off the whole staff of the Bureau were expelled from the country and diplomatic relations were broken off. A memorial still stands on the spot where Yvonne Fletcher fell.

But such problems can arise even with friendly countries. In August 2019 a recently arrived US diplomat, Anne Sacoolas, set off by car from an RAF base in Northamptonshire driving on the wrong side of the road. She immediately hit a young motorcyclist, Harry Dunn, coming the other way, killing him instantly. Sacoolas fled the scene and, claiming diplomatic immunity, left the country before she could be arrested. This led to a three-year quest by Dunn's family to bring the case to court. The British government asked the US to waive Sacoolas's immunity and return her to the UK, but they steadfastly refused to do so, mainly, it seems, because she was working for a US intelligence agency at the time. The issue became such a *cause célèbre*, and Harry's family so justifiably determined that their son's death should be properly prosecuted, that it was raised by the British prime minister with the US president at the G7 Summit in Cornwall. It was finally resolved by agreement that Ms Sacoolas would take part in British court proceedings by video-conference where she pleaded guilty to a lesser charge (causing death by dangerous driving) and was given a suspended sentence (Cooper, 2024). Though the case never imperilled wider UK-US relations, it preoccupied people at the highest level and illustrates how the rules of diplomatic immunity can entangle allies as well as enemies in delicate legal negotiations.

Secondly, there is the whole question of spying. Diplomats and spies are closely related but fundamentally different. In the 16th century, the two roles may have been hard to disentangle: diplomats of the day gathered information and sought to exert influence by whatever means they could, including through bribery and blackmail. But as ambassadors became permanent and their privileged status was confirmed, it was assumed that although gathering information remained a core part of their role, they would do so only by legal means; and that while their job was to liaise with the government on matters of mutual interest or concern, they should not interfere directly in the internal politics or affairs of the receiving state. Interference and spying were considered activities incompatible with their diplomatic status. Some countries post intelligence staff to their country of operation under diplomatic cover. Where this is in a friendly or allied country and their primary purpose is liaison with the local intelligence services, these staff are 'declared' to the receiving state who will enable the necessary access and contacts. Where the government may be less friendly, or itself the target of operations, they remain under cover and do intelligence work alongside their official diplomatic role. If the receiving state discovers that such work is being done, or more commonly decides that they wish to make a point to the sending state, they will expel the individuals 'for activities incompatible with their status' (Cormac, 2021).

Thirdly, it can be particularly difficult if the laws governing certain aspects of life in the receiving state are different from those in the sending one. It has become an issue with same-sex partnerships, which remain illegal in a number of countries. These governments may be reluctant to provide diplomatic status for a same-sex spouse in the way that they would for a husband or wife of the opposite sex, even though gay marriage may be fully legal and recognised in the sending state. When I joined the British diplomatic service in 1982, it was still illegal for homosexuals to belong to it – though a blind eye was often turned as long as it was not overt. One colleague in Brussels, however, was unceremoniously ejected from the service in the 1980s when his boyfriend went to the press about their affair over some disagreement. By and large, same-sex partners do now receive equal status (and since 2024 are also entitled to carry diplomatic passports when overseas), though foreign ministries might still limit the range of postings available to avoid the risk of rejection. Nevertheless, if a diplomat on a posting engages in same-sex relations with a national of a receiving state where that is illegal, it may not end well for either of them.

There is also a fourth area which we will discuss in more detail later as a part of diplomatic life: some countries forbid family members of those on diplomatic visas from working while resident, or using diplomatic premises, including their homes, for commercial activities. I encountered a case of this on one posting overseas where the spouse of one of our diplomats, unable to take paid employment, wanted to set up a tailoring business in the garage of their diplomatic house, employing a few local citizens to help. This was understandable, but not permissible: the local authorities would have been very unhappy at what they would see as a deliberate evasion of diplomatic rules and labour regulations on diplomatic premises, so we had to close it down as a commercial enterprise. As a diplomat in a foreign country, you may not like some of the local laws but the understanding is that, in return for your immunity, you try to respect them.

Protection of premises

The embassy buildings and ambassador's residence are both covered by the principle of inviolability in two ways: firstly, it is the responsibility of the host country to provide external protection for the property so that it is not attacked; and secondly, the embassy itself is effectively treated (*de facto* even if not *de jure*) as part of the sovereign territory of the sending state, so that it cannot be entered by agents of the host state except with the ambassador's permission (Roberts, 2017).

The receiving state's responsibility to protect diplomatic premises is clearly stated in the Vienna Convention, but is applied rather variably. Some countries maintain a specific diplomatic protection unit; others rely on the local police force in the capital. In both cases their physical presence outside embassy buildings tends to be the exception rather than the rule, only provided when there is a specific threat from public disorder or a potential terrorist attack. It can also, occasionally, be used to intimidate, both the diplomats of the sending country themselves and, more often, their visitors. Foreign diplomats cannot be prevented from entering their embassy, but running the gauntlet of armed 'protection forces' can be intimidating. There is also a tendency for such protection to evaporate when it is most needed – after a coup d'état, during a civil war or when a raging mob are clamouring at the gates. This happens. In 1967, at the height of the Cultural Revolution in China and following the arrest and imprisonment of pro-China activists in Hong Kong, first the British Consulate in Shanghai and then the embassy itself in Beijing were attacked, sacked and in the latter case burnt to the ground by thousands of Red Guards. The offices were ransacked, including all the confidential correspondence the staff had been unable to destroy in time, and a number of staff were physically assaulted. The Chinese diplomatic police made no efforts to stop the mob, though they did eventually ensure that all staff were evacuated from the building without serious injury (Carter, 2021). The attack on the US embassy in Tehran by students in 1979 is perhaps the most infamous case, resulting as it did in the US diplomatic staff being held hostage, illegally, for 444 days and a complete rupture in US-Iranian relations that persisted for years (Axworthy, 2013, 167–73). As recently as 2011 an Iranian mob invaded and sacked the British Embassy in Tehran in response to the imposition of severe financial sanctions targeting Iran's nuclear programme. Though the Iranian police stood aside to allow the rioters into the Embassy, they did protect British diplomatic staff from the mob, and the incursion was swiftly condemned by the Iranian government, who did not want a full rupture in relations at that time.

Given this history, it is unsurprising that many embassies ensure their own protection. All US Embassies have a contingent of US Marines to protect the premises; British embassies used to recruit their own security guards locally, overseen by a UK-based security officer, but now rely mainly on commercial security companies to guard both the embassy and the ambassador's residence. None of this would repel the kind of assault described above, but it does deter casual violence and provide a first line of defence against potential terror attacks.

Whatever happens outside an embassy, the inviolability of diplomatic premises requires that agents of the host state, whether officials, police or military, may not enter an embassy except at the express invitation of the ambassador or chargé d'affaires. This is to prevent them entering by force or subterfuge and seizing persons or confidential documents or intimidating the staff. Diplomats need to know they are safe inside their mission, able to speak and write in confidence to their own government. There are exceptions: in emergency situations, should a fire break out in the ambassador's absence, firefighters would have a right to enter to tackle the blaze; and if a receiving state has reason to believe that criminal activity is going on inside the embassy they can ask the ambassador for permission to enter to investigate.

But this provision also has complications. Most notoriously, as mentioned earlier, in October 2018 the dissident Saudi journalist Jamal Kashoggi was murdered, dismembered and disposed of inside the Saudi consulate building in Istanbul. The Turkish authorities were justifiably furious that such a crime could be committed in their country and that Saudi Arabia invoked the diplomatic immunity of their premises to prevent Turkish authorities entering the premises to investigate the disappearance. It led to a diplomatic rupture between the two countries that lasted nearly two years. The Saudis eventually admitted that Kashoggi had been killed and in a trial behind closed doors in 2019 convicted eight people of involvement. A UN investigation concluded it had been an extra-judicial killing (BBC World, 2021). Some other states have also engaged in the extrajudicial killing of dissidents abroad, but none have so blatantly abused the diplomatic immunity of premises to do so. Given the international furore to which this gave rise, they may hesitate to do so again in the future.

More common is for dissidents or others who feel their life is at risk in their own country to seek asylum at a foreign mission. It is something ambassadors dread. The most high-profile case of this recently has been that of Julian Assange, founder of Wikileaks, who in 2012, having just lost a court case against his extradition from the UK to Sweden to answer charges of rape, walked into the Ecuadorian Embassy in London and claimed political asylum. The then President of Ecuador, Rafael Correa, was sympathetic to Assange, agreed to grant asylum, and instructed the Embassy to allow him to stay as he would be arrested as soon as he tried to leave. So he stayed, for seven years, provided with a small office turned into a bedroom. In 2019 the Ecuadorians could bear it no longer and asked him to leave. Throughout the Metropolitan Police maintained a presence outside the Embassy ready to arrest Assange should he ever set a foot off the premises. The Ecuadorian diplomats were allowed to enter and leave, as was Assange's cat, but not Assange himself. When he finally left he was indeed arrested and taken to Belmarsh Prison to await extradition proceedings, by this stage to the US on spying charges. His total stay at the Embassy is reported to have cost the Ecuadorians over £5 million ($6.5 million) (Melzer, 2023). In 2024, the leader of the opposition in Venezuela took refuge in the Spanish embassy after elections that he claimed to have won, but which the government refused to accept and sought to have him arrested. He eventually was allowed to leave the country into exile.

The lesson is – be careful who you let into your mission. It is one reason some embassies keep their consular and visa offices, the ones most frequented by members of the public, separate from the main Embassy premises so that people cannot just walk up to the counter and claim asylum.

In 2012, while I was working for the EU, an opposition leader and his wife arrived one Sunday morning at the EU delegation offices in Guinea Bissau saying that he feared he was being targeted for assassination by his political rivals. The Head of Delegation, without consulting headquarters, admitted them. In that country at that time it was a credible threat, but it put the EU in a difficult position: if we asked them to leave the mission he would quite likely be detained by the authorities and, if killed, we would be considered culpable. The EU, however, has no sovereign territory, so cannot offer asylum – only member states can do that, and in this case none were willing to take him in. Various avenues were explored, and we were eventually able to negotiate their safe passage from the delegation to the airport for them to leave the country. But it was an uncomfortable time having an asylum seeker on the diplomatic premises and an unhappy government outside: not a situation I would recommend, even if occasionally it may be unavoidable.

Protection of information

The Assange case of course arose from Wikileaks publishing a vast trove of confidential US government papers leaked to it by Chelsea Manning. The question of the confidentiality of government information, official secrets acts, transparency and whistleblowing is far wider than we can discuss here. But it is relevant because the Vienna Conventions explicitly provide that communications between a state and its missions overseas should be inviolable, in other words not intercepted or interrupted by the host state where missions are based (Roberts, 2017, 81–5).

When engaged in delicate negotiations or reporting sensitive situations, secure communication is essential. Early diplomatic envoys would use elaborate codes, invisible ink or subterfuge to get their messages safely back to their own authorities and keep them from the eyes of others. This transitioned into the tradition of the diplomatic bag, carried in person by a special courier, known in Britain as a King's (formerly Queen's) Messenger. These have existed since the 16th century, though they were officially instituted as a cadre in England by King Charles II in the 1660s, when he broke off a silver greyhound from a royal dish for the messenger to carry as a sign to his ambassadors that the messenger was genuine (Moorhouse, 1977, 183). Originally the diplomatic bag was meant to contain only written material, dispatches and code books sent between capitals and embassies, securely sealed at one end and carried in person by the messenger until delivered to be unsealed at the other. The Vienna Conventions specify that customs officers may not open or examine the bags in transit. Over the years, however, some diplomats succumbed to the temptation to use the bag to smuggle prohibited items through customs, whether guns, drugs, money, watches, cheeses, bacon or fresh fruit. In 1964, Italian customs officials violated the immunity of an Egyptian diplomatic bag because it was emitting groans: inside they found a drugged and kidnapped Israeli (Edwards, 1994, 59).

The romantic days of messengers and bags, however, are almost over. They still exist, but primarily to transport IT and communications equipment in bulk, even by the container-load, to ensure no one slips a few extra chips into it en route. Protecting the information itself remains as vital as ever, but is now done primarily by electronic means. That by no means ensures its security: the vulnerability of our online information is familiar to all. VPNs are penetrable and encryption remains a constant struggle between governments and hackers, though the greatest vulnerability of IT systems remains human, as Manning demonstrated. States have always spied on each other, but in our virtual world there are many other actors seeking to break into email systems, access financial data, deny access or listen to the conversations remotely. Though the risk is far less in friendly countries, there will still be third parties present who will seek to take advantage of the lower security there: Nazi Germany's most valuable intelligence on British intentions came from the Ambassador's valet at the British consulate in Istanbul (Parris and Bryson, 2012, 90). The wise diplomat assumes that nothing is wholly secure, and might choose to hold the most sensitive conversations in a secluded corner of the garden. The kind of unexpurgated views on host governments expressed by past British ambassadors in their valedictory despatches (now made conveniently public in Matthew Parris and Andrew Bryson's book) are less frequently heard; and as British ambassadors in Washington found, even far milder criticism can find its way into the public domain and cause offence these days.

The fact remains that to make good foreign policy a foreign minister needs good, well-informed and honest advice from posts overseas; and this may often be unflattering to those commented upon. So to preserve good diplomatic relations the advice needs to be confidential, and well-protected.

The unprotected

Diplomats are in many ways now an exception. A growing number of people work in international relations without the benefit of diplomatic privileges and immunities.

Apart from the Secretary-General and the most senior UN staff, United Nations officials have only limited diplomatic immunity (immunity from prosecution, tax exemption and travel privileges), not the full privileges of the bilateral diplomat. They carry a 'UN Laissez-Passer' which provides a degree of diplomatic access and protection. This extends broadly to the whole family of UN agencies, including humanitarian organisations, who badly need such protection in many of the places they work. But like national diplomats, if the UN is dealing with unrecognised authorities in a country or region, it is hard for UN staff to get from them visas or agreement to protected status. In 2024 in Syria, whether operating in areas under government control or not, UN staff needed to get agreement from the Assad regime in Damascus as the *de jure* authority over the whole country; in Afghanistan no operations are currently possible without the permission of the Taliban authorities; and in Gaza and Lebanon, the UN's neutral and protected status has not been respected by the Israeli forces in the recent conflicts. So even for the UN, it is tough.

Other international organisations have negotiated varying degrees of diplomatic recognition and protection in the 'headquarters agreements' they sign with their host government when first established – with the US for the IMF and World Bank, France for the OECD, Austria for the OSCE, Ethiopia for the AU, Egypt for the Arab League, and so on. These tend to have similar provisions, though there is no standard template; and all states are wary of granting diplomatic privileges too freely lest they be abused by organisations over which they have little control.

The EU fought a long campaign to secure full diplomatic status for its staff in third countries (outside the EU) equivalent to that of its member states' diplomats, on the grounds that it is more than a mere international organisation, though distinct from a sovereign state. With the united support of all EU member states it has succeeded – even in the UK after Brexit – so all EU diplomats, whether from the institutions or the member states on secondment, have the same status.

International NGOs and businesses, however, have no such privileges. Visas have to be obtained from the due authorities and residence, taxation, family status and the rest need to be sorted by the organisation's local administration as for any expatriate worker. In many countries this is not a problem, and it can come with fewer constraints on what they do in a country than those bound by the Vienna Conventions under the watchful eye of the local foreign ministry. But in fragile or authoritarian states, diplomatic status can provide significant protection from arbitrary actions. Though most organisations recognise a duty of care to their staff in dangerous locations, people still go at their own risk. Liaison with your national embassy becomes more important the more insecure the situation; and, as we have seen, though few states will guarantee to protect or evacuate all its citizens in times of crisis, they have an obligation to help where they can.

* * *

The principle of inviolability and the application of diplomatic privileges and immunities therefore remain crucial for the conduct of diplomatic relations and are enshrined in treaties accepted by all sovereign states. They matter. Though they are less legally binding, so too do the rules of that other preoccupation of diplomats – protocol.

7   Protocol

It is said that three things can kill a diplomat: alcohol, cholesterol and protocol.

Stifling, enervating, insufferable flummery it can be, but I have never yet found protocol actually fatal. In fact, its true purpose is to keep diplomats alive. Before its rules were laid down, disputes over diplomatic precedence were known to have led to injury or even death in the days when honour took precedence over self-preservation (Nicolson, 1939).

As we have seen, until the 18th century envoys and ambassadors were regarded very much as the personal representatives of their monarchs, and it was therefore the monarch's status and honour that had to be preserved in the order of precedence at the great courts of Europe. The same rule applied in the ancient Near East, where the Egyptian Pharoah would only agree to exchange envoys with other 'Great Kings' whom he could regard as his equal: all others had to come to him as supplicants (Cohen and Westbrook, 2002). This led in the 16th and 17th centuries to endless disputes between the ambassadors of the kings of France, Spain and England over who should take first and second place at ceremonial events, leading to the violent clash of carriages in royal processions (Hamilton and Langhorne, 2011, 69–73). Samuel Pepys's diary for 30 September 1661 records one such affray in which the Spanish Ambassador's party 'killed three of the French coach-horses and several of their men, and is gone through the City next to our King's coach', leaving the French Ambassador immobilised, crestfallen and fuming; Pepys adds, 'it is strange to see how all the City did rejoice. And indeed we do all naturally love the Spanish, and hate the French' (Pepys, 1995).

To avoid such unseemly fracas, the monarchs of Europe agreed new rules of precedence for ambassadors at the Congress of Vienna in 1815. They would henceforth be ranked by the order in which they arrived at post, the longer-serving having precedence over the newer arrival however great their country of origin or grand their monarch, with the longest-serving taking the role of Dean of the diplomatic corps (unless that role was reserved to the Papal Nuncio as representing a higher authority). The Dean is the point of contact for the host government for all general issues affecting the corps as a whole, such as participation in state events or the security for diplomatic missions in a crisis. The Dean also acts as convenor and chair of meetings of all resident ambassadors when these are required, for example to discuss government proposals affecting them or the security situation in the capital.

DOI: 10.4324/9781003533436-7

The purpose of protocol is to enshrine in behaviours the qualities we identified earlier: to ensure that respect is shown to all, and that diplomatic relations remain orderly even when there may be political tension between the participants. They are in effect the rituals of international life, and rituals matter (Jönsson and Hall, 2005).

Presentation

To be a successful diplomat you need to look, act and speak like one. This is not laid down in the rules of protocol, but it is common sense. It does *not* mean that you need to look stuffy or old-fashioned, even if diplomats tend to the conventional. As mentioned in Chapter 5, it is often useful to be noticeable and look memorable. But you do need to remember that it is not just you but your country that is being judged by how you look – so know what is appropriate to wear, and when.

As in all things, it is important to show respect to your colleagues and those you are dealing with by wearing clothes that are suited to the occasion and respectful of local custom. For men that will often mean wearing a suit and tie, even where the climate may not make this especially comfortable. In both Tanzania and Ghana, for official functions, by day or night, inside or out, suits were expected. In the hot or rainy seasons this felt rather like wearing a suit in a sauna, and required a long cold shower afterwards. In other respects Tanzania was more relaxed – part of Nyerere's legacy of antipathy to colonial pomposity – but even there colleagues and I would always wear a tie when calling on ministers. Times and habits change of course: in Britain, ties are almost unknown in business circles these days, and are only rarely seen in government offices. But abroad it is wise to assume more conventional dress until you know the individuals you are dealing with and the culture of the place you are working. In Ghana, ministers would often wear a traditional smock, agbada or dashiki at work and receptions, but the British High Commissioner was always expected to appear in our (apparently) national dress of suit and tie. The same I gather in the Gulf.

If you are given local clothing to wear as a gift in the course of your diplomatic duties, it is polite (and fun) to put it on: just be aware who is taking photos of you that may appear instantly on social media. By the time I left Ghana I had accumulated half a dozen traditional smocks and two or three sets of *kente*, most of which I donated on departure. I still have a couple in the wardrobe for suitable occasions: Ghanaians always greet me as a brother when I do wear them, though these days one needs to be careful to avoid accusations of 'cultural appropriation'.

For women diplomats, as mentioned, what is considered respectable attire is often a more complicated question. Customs and conventions differ more widely and in some parts of the world the covering of arms, shoulders, legs and/or hair remains important. Trousers are now considered normal, though always check locally. An elegant scarf worn around the neck can be drawn over the hair when necessary for meetings. But the wider range of styles available to women can be an advantage when travelling outside the capital and can certainly be better adapted to the climate than the suit. In countries where the roads are good and the climate kind, there is little or no difference in dress in the capital or hinterland. But when travelling in rougher or more remote places, practical clothes make more sense, as long as you take something respectable in case of diplomatic need.

Working in an embassy itself tends to be more relaxed. In Accra ties were out and short sleeved shirts in, though we had a lively debate over whether shorts were acceptable office wear. The 'shorts-are-fine' faction was strong amongst expatriate men with hairy legs, but they were outnumbered by local and female staff whose opposition carried the day (with firm support from the head of mission who pointed out that even in the High Commission we had visitors coming in from the outside for whom we – all – had to present a respectable face, and legs). In foreign ministries, again customs vary, but at least in London the extension of home-working during Covid and the FCO's amalgamation with DFID has almost made 'office wear' a thing of the past, except among senior staff who have representational duties during the day.

Once essential for ambassadors at major posts and for the governors of overseas territories, full dress regalia, plumed hat and all, is no longer required except on the rarest occasions: the traditional London tailors who made them have lost a lucrative line of business. For the Marshall of the Diplomatic Service in London and for ambassadors to countries with a crowned head of state, some state occasions still require morning suits or white tie and tails. But for the most part these can be hired, and in your own wardrobe you can get away with having only a dinner jacket and selection of sober or flamboyant bow ties to see you through the many formal dinners that it is still the diplomat's lot to attend. If you have a defence attaché, however, they can usually be relied upon to turn out in something spectacular for special events such as the King's Birthday Party and local military ceremonies; it greatly enhances the colour-mix and the prestige of the occasion.

NGOs have a dress code all their own. Foreign correspondents' attire and aid workers' chic can sometimes have an Indiana Jones quality to it, but is normally dictated by practicality: pockets to put things in, back packs for carrying laptops and water, hats for protection from the sun, boots for tackling dusty tracks. This is fine for the field, but when calling on governments or meetings in capitals, something less rough is recommended to avoid inadvertent disrespect or suspected arrogance.

Modes of verbal address should also be kept respectful. Ambassadors are traditionally addressed as 'Your Excellency', and while this may sound cringingly pompous or sarcastic to some of us, it is often wise to begin by using it with ambassadors you don't know as they may take their dignity seriously and it would foolish to risk showing disrespect. You can dial it down once you know the individual and how attached they are to ceremony.

Credentials

Presenting credentials is the essential first step for any ambassador arriving in a new posting, and one driven entirely by protocol.

The conventions agreed in 1815 did not for some time extend beyond Europe. Lord McCartney's mission to open British relations and trade with China in 1793 was stalled in Beijing for some weeks while negotiations were conducted over whether McCartney should perform the traditional prostration (*kowtow*) required of all visitors to the Emperor or not. McCartney insisted that the two rulers, King George III and the Emperor Qianlong, were of equal status and he would remain standing. The compromise was reached that he would show the Emperor the same level of obeisance he would do his own sovereign – a single genuflection on one knee, though without the traditional kissing of the King's hand as touching the Emperor was beyond the pale. The ceremony then proceeded cordially though unproductively, the Emperor refusing to open China to British trade (Peyrefitte, 2013). The British envoy sent in 1838 to Emir Nasrullah of Bukhara, Colonel Stoddart, was less lucky, or skilled: on arrival in Bukhara he rode rather than walked up to the Emir's palace, which was taken as a great insult and he was duly flung into the palace's infamous 'Bug Pit', full of scorpions, snakes and decaying corpses, from which he was hauled five years later to be executed (Hopkirk, 1992). The moral of the story is to do your homework *before* you meet the head of state.

Broadly, though, there is now a regular process for presenting credentials even if the local forms of the ceremony can vary.

Every ambassador receives an official letter of credentials from their own head of state to the receiving head of state, nominating them for the post. These can be wonderfully flowery, full of 'our Trusty and Well-beloved servant . . . in whom we have full confidence and whose high character and abilities recommend them to us to send as our Ambassador Extraordinary and Plenipotentiary . . .' Before their departure to post, the late Queen Elizabeth II was assiduous in meeting personally all her outgoing ambassadors and their spouses. In her many decades on the throne, there were very few countries or world leaders about whom she knew nothing, and her insights, particularly on the personalities, could be extremely astute. So this ritual was far from purely ceremonial: it was important for you to arrive at post with the host government knowing you had spoken to the monarch before you came. The King maintains the same tradition. A call on the Foreign Secretary is also normal, though often brief, but a call on the Prime Minister is reserved only for those going to particularly high-profile or sensitive posts – such as Washington, Moscow, Beijing, Paris or (at one time) Port Stanley. When I presented credentials in Ghana and gave President Kufuor personal greetings from the Queen and Foreign Secretary, he immediately asked: 'And the Prime Minister? Does Gordon Brown send greetings too?' I had asked for but not received a call on the PM, but sometimes it is politic and polite to pretend that you have. You need to keep your credibility intact. So chat to the PM's Private Secretary beforehand and take his (surrogate) greetings with you.

Once your appointment is approved at home, you cannot travel to post until you have received *agrément* (approval) from the receiving government. This is not a mere formality. It is customary for the receiving government to accept whomever the sending government chooses as its ambassador, but there are ways of indicating dissatisfaction either with the government or the individual, usually through delay rather than outright rejection. It is the job of your departing predecessor to ensure you receive *agrément* as swiftly as possible before they leave so that, if necessary, any problems can be ironed out at a higher level.

On arrival in post, the first call is on the Foreign Minister to hand over the *copies figurées* (working copies) of the credentials, have an introductory chat and (normally) be allowed to start appearing around town, though not at official state functions until after the full credentials have been duly presented. Many heads of state hold credential ceremonies only occasionally, dealing with incoming ambassadors in batches rather than individually, so it can be weeks or even months before this happens. Nevertheless it can be a sign of the importance attached to your own country how quickly you are summoned to see the head of state; a good relationship with the local Head of Protocol can be invaluable in ensuring an early date. If you are a non-resident ambassador to neighbouring countries, it can take longer to arrange visits to their respective capitals for the credentials ceremonies. When I arrived in Accra I had four additional sets of credentials to present in neighbouring countries, which required some logistical skill and diplomatic perseverance to complete in the first year. When you finally get the call to see the President, drop everything and go. To turn down an invitation could lead to a very long wait indeed.

Credential ceremonies themselves vary enormously. In Britain, the arriving ambassador is collected from their residence and ridden through the streets of London to Buckingham Palace in an open horse-drawn carriage, accompanied by a detachment of mounted Horse Guards. On arrival, they are greeted by a military band playing their national anthem before ascending to the Credentials Hall, being announced to His Majesty and invited forward to present (respectfully, with both hands) the letters of recall for the previous ambassador and credentials for the new arrival. A brief statement of amity and conversation follows before the newly accredited ambassador returns the same way they came. It is customary to offer a *vin d'honneur* afterwards at the residence or embassy to one's fellow ambassadors, staff, friends and relations to mark the occasion.

The structure is much the same everywhere, but with local variations. In Accra, I was summoned to Christiansborg Castle (known Kafka-like just as 'The Castle'), originally a slave fort before becoming the seat of British colonial government and then the presidential palace under Nkrumah. (The Presidency has now moved to Jubilee House, built in the shape of a traditional Akan royal stool, and The Castle is being turned into a museum.) I was allowed to bring a small entourage consisting of my wife Miriam, the Deputy High Commissioner and the Political Secretary. As well as the military band playing both national anthems, we were greeted on arrival by thunderous

Ghanaian drummers and a traditional priest who poured a libation to the gods (in best schnapps, as is the tradition) before going up to greet President Kufuor, accompanied by Foreign Minister Akufo-Addo and senior officials. After handing over the credentials, the President and I sat on a sofa, were handed glasses of champagne (don't drink it all at once) and had a friendly conversation about bilateral relations for a quarter of an hour.

This is crucial. In many countries there will not be many chances for a one-on-one conversation with the head of state, and first impressions always count. So it is your opportunity to build a personal relationship and ensure that the president or monarch remembers who you are. This is especially so where relations may not be so cordial and access to the head of state in person is very limited.

In Lomé, we arrived at the Togolese Presidential Palace ten minutes early and caught the band relaxing on the front lawn. We did a discreet U-turn in the drive, drove back out the gates, round the block and back in again, by which time they were properly assembled, only to break into the wrong national anthem (the German Ambassador was also being credentialled that day). Another pause, and then a slightly ragged version of 'God Save the Queen' rang out while I stood to attention in the noonday sun. Niger proved most difficult to pin down, and, with no direct flights, took two days travelling from Accra. We were given only three days' notice, so arrived at the palace only just in time. We were greeted (after the correct national anthem) by President Tandja standing alone at the top of a steep, wide set of steps up to the palace, magnificent in a traditional embroidered white *djellaba*, red *kofia* hat and heavy dark glasses, looking down at me as I walked up the steps with as much dignity as I could muster. After the formal handing over of the credentials, we proceeded to sit in the vast audience hall where, Chinese-style, we sat side-by-side in two massive armchairs with our entourages arranged face-to-face down each side. The acoustics were so bad that I could barely hear what the President said, let alone my note-taker sitting fifty yards down the hall and almost invisible in the immensity of her armchair. No champagne here: strictly non-alcoholic fruit juice.

A few months later, Tandja was toppled in a coup. What happens in such a situation is ambiguous. Your accreditation is to the state rather than the individual, so an ambassador's functions should continue unaffected. But, as we identified earlier, relations with a military or revolutionary regime can make official contact difficult. Ambassadors who have arrived and not yet presented credentials can be left in a frustrating diplomatic limbo, with nobody acceptable to present credentials to – another good reason to present credentials as soon as possible in a state that may prove fragile.

Following the ceremony, you are free to arrange courtesy calls on relevant ministers and fellow diplomats you have not yet met. This is strongly recommended. It may appear time-consuming, but pays dividends as most feel flattered to be called upon and it helps build the personal relations that will be the basis for your future work. Of course, in major capitals like Washington and Beijing few ministers have much time for calls by diplomats unless there is specific bilateral business to conduct, but it is always worth asking. If offered an alternative, be careful not to debase your currency by seeing someone too junior – your staff can do that. The antiquated habit of circulating business cards to all fellow ambassadors on arrival, already fading when I joined, has now disappeared completely. Nevertheless, have plenty of cards to hand round when you meet people as most will reciprocate and give you valuable contact information. If you are in a country where visas are much in demand, it can be wise not to print your mobile number on the card to avoid the risk of unsolicited calls on this issue at all times of day and night. Write it on personally for those you want to have it.

Ceremonials

As a diplomat, and specifically as an ambassador, you get privileged access to state events. Use it: it may be tedious, but it is invaluable in building a network and establishing credibility.

Politics is all about access. Travelling with Tony Blair on Concorde in 1997 to his first G7 Summit in Denver, Colorado, I was sitting down at the back, being the bag man with the briefs. I asked his Principle Private Secretary, Alex Allan, if I could have five minutes beside the Prime Minister at the front to talk him through some agenda points. 'Nick,' he said, '*everybody* wants "just five minutes" with the PM. I'll see.' In the event, Blair spent the flight talking with Alistair Campbell. It was a lesson. Next time I briefed Alastair Campbell. But the point is that time with heads of state and government is rare and precious. You need to know exactly what points you want to raise and what outcome you want to achieve, while avoiding boring them by leaping straight to the business. Getting that balance between good personal relations and doing business can only be judged in the specific circumstances. President Tandja was not a man for jokes, whereas President Barroso at the European Commission rather enjoyed them – as long as they were good – and it made getting your business points across easier.

Attending state and other ceremonial occasions not only shows respect to your hosts, but can be an invaluable opportunity to meet political figures who are not otherwise easily accessible. State openings of parliament, state banquets and receptions for visiting dignitaries, investitures and inaugurations, royal weddings and political funerals all provide long hours of tedium – the Protocol office invariably demands you be there far in advance – but also rare moments of access. The only time I had a chat with a US President was at the state banquet for George W. Bush's visit to Ghana in 2008. Sometimes you need to be a bit entrepreneurial about putting yourself in the way to be met, spotting the right place to stand, or taking a message (real or not) to the foreign minister, or your own minister, at banquets to get yourself inside – without in any way being pushy or underhand, of course. Being in the right place at the right time, to pass a message or make an introduction, is one of the most vital diplomatic skills they don't teach you in school (though many FCO colleagues were masters of the art: see Westmacott, 2021).

In Ghana, as in many other cultures, funerals have an outsized importance and attending them gives you credibility with local politicians and the public. In the UK, memorial services fulfil the same political function. Again, get there early, as the milling around beforehand is often the best time to catch important people when they having nothing much else to do. Once it is over, many will be swiftly on their way.

In April 2012, and as official representative of the EU, I attended the funeral of President Mutharika of Malawi after his sudden and unexpected passing (a result of witchcraft, some believed). Flying from Brussels to Lilongwe, we drove to Blantyre, stayed the night in an old colonial bungalow-turned-hostel, and rose early the next day to drive for an hour or more down dirt roads to the field outside the President's ancestral village where a monumental mausoleum in white marble, pillared and domed, had been constructed to house his remains (well in advance, one imagined). Thousands were gathered from 8 am in the morning, the diplomats and politicians mercifully under makeshift awnings but the villagers, school children, soldiers and public all out in the tropical sun. We sat there for four hours, waiting for something to happen, gossiping with whomever we could find. Around 12 noon a van drew up and small bottles of water were handed round to the dignitaries. Two hours later, the cortege slowly came into view down the dusty track, accompanied by the whole political elite of the country. To solemn music, the coffin was placed on a dais in front of the mausoleum. Inaudible and interminable orations and elegies were given. Schoolchildren sang, villagers danced and arms were presented by the military. We sat on. Around 5 pm, the Head of Protocol indicated to us that the heads of each delegation were to come forward and witness the interment inside the mausoleum. The interior was in fact quite small, big enough for maybe 50 of the 150 people being ushered inside. We all gallantly offered to make way for others, merely jamming the entrance till we were pushed inside by Protocol. The coffin was winched down and, amidst hymns and prayers, some labourers in hi-vis jackets and boots forced their way through the dignitaries to heave a massive marble slab directly over the grave. 'Just to make sure he doesn't get out again,' muttered the American ambassador. We emerged blinking to a glorious African sunset. Did we wish to join the villagers for their traditional feast in an hour or two, asked the man from Protocol? Having had nothing but half a litre of water since 7 am, we made our excuses and joined the convoy of flag cars crawling back to Blantyre and our hostel. Mercifully they had prepared a dinner. Never was roast lamb more welcome than that night. But never go to a funeral without sustenance in your pocket if you want to avoid joining the deceased.

The event had provided one useful opportunity. Arriving in Blantyre the evening before, we headed straight to the old colonial Governor's house to meet the Vice-President, Joyce Banda, now suddenly catapulted into the Presidency by Mutharika's unexpected demise. The modest house was little changed since colonial times, the furnishings dull and the old-fashioned electric lights dim. Down a dark corridor, we were ushered into what seemed in the flickering light to be a waiting room. I glanced round at the sofas, heavy with cushions, and headed for one against the far wall, to be interrupted by a loud cough. Looking round, I realised that the sofa behind me contained not cushions, but the President – in a voluminous brown dress that blended perfectly with the sofa covers.

'Your Excellency,' I exclaimed. 'How good of you to see us at such short notice . . .'

She was forgiving, and we had a useful conversation about how she would manage the transition and what support the EU could provide, particularly for her fight against corruption. When I saw her again six months later, in better light, she gave me a warm greeting.

One other thing I learnt in Ghana: sometimes the mere act of presence is enough. The Ghanaian Legal Year commences with a church service followed by a grand luncheon hosted by the Chief Justice and Attorney General and attended by every lawyer in the country dressed in full regalia of wigs and robes (despite the 35-degree heat). The lunch was a characteristic Ghanaian event: a vast buffet simmering in trays which no one touched until the speeches were finished, plastic chairs covered in classy covers, large round tables and music blasting so loud it defied any attempt to converse with your neighbour at the table. The lawyers just sat there, waiting patiently while our eardrums were battered. After the speeches, while food was taken, the music was turned up again, and all the louder when after the meal the (lady) Chief Justice took to the dance floor. The other justices followed suit, without their wigs at this stage. No conversation, let alone gossip, was possible throughout the event, but merely being present was enough; it built a sense of solidarity with the legal fraternity that would be rewarded at some future time. '*Subira huvuta heri*' as they say in Swahili: patience brings happiness.

Sometimes, as a British Ambassador to Algeria once remarked, it does feel as though one is being used as 'diplomatic wallpaper' for state events – decorating but not participating (Parris and Bryson, 2012, 103). But you never know what opportunity you might miss unless you are there.

Entertaining

Along with meetings, entertaining is 'the soul of diplomacy' (Marshall, 1997, 172). It is costly but vital, so depending on your level of resources you may have to improvise to make it happen.

Accepting as well as giving hospitality is important. In Washington DC I must have attended dozens of award or charity dinners, a peculiarly American form of entertainment that took place in vast identikit ballrooms in identikit hotels with identikit food, and pretty much identikit speeches, beginning with the first course and continuing through to coffee. But they were essential for connecting with the business community – my job – so I went.

There is something about offering hospitality that creates an environment conducive to sharing, whether personal experiences or political gossip, and creating the right atmosphere for that to happen is the art of entertaining. It is also bound up with reciprocal obligation: one cannot always receive without giving something in return, so finding an easy and affordable way to do that is important. Cultures vary enormously, and while in some countries locals are very happy to invite diplomats into their own homes, in others you can spend three to four years in a country without ever setting foot in someone's private home. Entertainment is undertaken in restaurants, hotels, bars, clubs, at sporting events, concerts, wherever – but not at home. It can be just as effective, as you want your guests to be comfortable and at ease. For working lunches with one or a few people, a nearby restaurant will be much more convenient in the middle of a working day.

Evening entertaining can more easily, cheaply and profitably be done at home. But even here there are regional variations. In Washington DC we found ourselves entertaining at home much less than in Tanzania not only because we had a young family, but because Washington is a morally serious town where people are often at work by 7 am and therefore like to leave evening events by 9 pm; this makes for either a very early or a very short dinner.

It goes with the role that an ambassador should have the wherewithal to entertain: a residence with space enough for receptions and dinners; a cook and a kitchen capable of preparing significant quantities of food; and a budget for entertainment. Where one or other is lacking, or you are non-resident and have none of these things in place, you can entertain, for the national day for example, in a convenient hotel – but it's not quite the same. Other than a deputy in a decent-sized post, more junior staff are nowadays rarely provided with the space or allowances for entertaining, but should be enrolled to support the ambassador's functions.

Receptions can come in all shapes and sizes, from a massive national day reception to a small drinks event for a visiting dignitary. There are some simple rules. Make the space feel comfortable: a few people in a vast ballroom feel uncomfortable and lost; too many people in too small a space, or one stuffed with furniture that impedes circulation, feels claustrophobic. So a few potted plants, screens or chairs can be deployed to create the right space for the numbers. People need places to put their drinks down, especially if you are going to ask them to applaud something, so scatter tables. If there are going to be speeches, make sure there is a clear and visible location for the speaker, and have a means of silencing the crowd to listen. If you are expecting eminent guests, make sure you have someone looking out for and looking after them when they arrive. Make clear when it is time for everyone to leave by withdrawing the drinks supply and closing the bar. And my habit was never to drink alcohol at my own receptions: a glass filled with ice, lemon and tonic looks just like a G&T but keeps you sober. Once everyone has gone, *then* you can break out the whisky. Remember the apocryphal story of a young diplomat on his first posting overseas in Peru who, attending his first big reception, was very much enjoying the unlimited free alcohol on offer. As the evening and the music warmed up, he spotted a vision of beauty in a long purple dress the other side of the room. As a particularly lively tune struck up, he took his courage in his hands and invited the person to dance. Turning to him, the vision replied: 'Sir, I will not dance with you for three reasons: firstly, you are drunk; secondly, this is not a dance, it is the national anthem; and thirdly, I am not a woman, I am the Archbishop of Lima.'

Dinners are more complicated. You need to ensure that the numbers, the menu and the *placement* are all correct to ensure a fruitful evening. The food in particular has to reflect your guests' cultural and dietary requirements, which it is now customary to ask for in advance. Pork is best avoided, and in some countries or company beef is also off the menu. Vegetarian and vegan options have become essential. You therefore need a versatile, as well as excellent, cook.

Seating depends on the numbers. An ideal number for dinner is around ten: small enough for a single round-table discussion if that is what you are looking for but big enough for people to break into individual conversations at other times. Once you get to twenty or more, it is very hard to have a single conversation which is both audible and of interest to all – though for a purely social occasion it can be fun. It is often easier to break larger groups up into a number of round tables. Less than eight and you can *only* have a single conversation round the table.

But large or small, where you put people to sit, the *placement*, is critical to success and requires a fine knowledge of protocol, culture and local politics. Some people can be most put out if they feel they have not been seated in the appropriate place. One ambassador was so offended at being placed too far from the centre of the table that, though he stayed at the table, he ostentatiously turned over his plate and refused to eat or drink anything all evening. So it is important that protocol seniority is respected wherever possible when sitting people around the table. The traditional habit of alternating men and women and separating husbands and wives is fading as diplomatic dinners become more diverse and single participants more common. In Accra, we hosted the Archbishop of York, John Sentamu, on a pastoral visit to the Anglican community in Ghana, and invited the heads of all local faiths to dinner. It was a matter of some theological sensitivity whether the Chief Imam outranked the Catholic Archbishop (the Cardinal couldn't come) and where to place the Moderator of the Evangelical Church of Christ. Miriam, however, was the only woman present. Traditionally host and hostess would sit at each end of a long table, but we found it much more congenial and effective to sit opposite each other at the centre with the principal guests on either side, who were then able to talk to each other as well as us, and who could more easily be heard by the whole table if we wanted everyone to listen.

More challenging is the uncertainty until the last minute over who will turn up. You need a seating plan based around replies received up until the day of the dinner, but have to be ready to rearrange it a few minutes before people sit down on the basis of who has turned up and who might still appear later. Some people clearly regarded a diplomatic invitation as something they could opt out of at the last minute without necessarily informing the host. For important dinners much chasing was done by the office beforehand to confirm attendance. In Ghana we occasionally faced the opposite problem of chiefs turning up with a retinue of followers, most of whom would camp in the front hall but one or two of the more senior among them might need to be seated at table – or a senior guest arriving with an unexpected 'niece' who needed to be found a seat. Ghanaians themselves get round the problem by having buffets and free seating, but that does not work for formal dinners with visiting ministers who want to have a serious conversation with carefully selected contacts. For that, serving plated meals to the table is much better, as it allows the conversation to flow, and for you to ensure who is sitting next to whom.

Speeches at dinners and receptions are best kept short and light, depending on the circumstances, and delivered without notes – at least, no more than you can jot on the back of a menu card. Always think in advance of what you will say, and link it to the guests present, so that they feel it is personal and their presence appreciated. Speaking at the beginning or middle of an event rather than the end enables people to relax and enjoy the rest of the meal. Most long-winded tended to be the valedictory speeches at farewell dinners marking the end of a posting. Everybody felt obliged to invite the departee for dinner and everyone insisted on saying something at each, so they could go on for hours. This is why it is best to give people as little notice of your departure as possible so that you can wrap everything up in one or two functions. Unless you like endless dinners, of course.

Networking

Diplomats network like fish swim in water. It's just what they do. Natural selection I suppose. So to suggest how to do it would be like teaching grandmothers to suck eggs. But for the sake of completeness, here, drawing on a lifetime of functions, I offer seven golden rules of networking:

1. Everyone is interesting: you just have to find out what about. That means talking to them directly, and listening to what they are saying. Bill Clinton apparently had a phenomenal ability to make people feel they were the most important and interesting person he'd ever met. The besetting sin of diplomats at functions is to keep their eyes looking just over your shoulder at everyone passing behind you in case one of them is more important, more interesting or just the person they're actually looking for. If you are talking to another diplomat, it doesn't matter – you're both surveying the field and know exactly what the other is doing. But normal people may feel you're not entirely paying them the attention they deserve.
2. It is good to say something about yourself, but not too much. Just enough to get people interested, then find out more about them. So have a handy,

succinct summary ready to deploy if asked, adapting it to the person you're speaking to. But you will learn more by listening to them.

3. If you are hosting, always check the invitation list in advance to find out who might be there that you particularly want or need to see. There is no one more offended than a celebrity or eminent minister who hasn't been recognised and who isn't introduced to the other eminent people there. Vanity, I suppose, but that seems to be human nature.

4. How you greet people is critical, especially if you don't recognise them. Always assume they are important, as they will either expect it, or be flattered that you think them so. If you are hosting, or on home turf, offer everyone a warm welcome and ensure they have a drink, or know where to leave their coat. If you are a guest, be sure to seek out the host and say how pleased you are to have been invited. Flattery goes a long way.

5. Find a means to circulate. Miriam and I had diametrically opposite approaches to receptions. She would find one or two interesting guests and spend the whole evening talking to them, building a great relationship. I preferred to make sure I'd met everyone there so as not to miss someone useful or important and therefore circulated ceaselessly. If you're in the latter category, it's useful to have a few manoeuvres to ensure you don't get stuck with a crashing bore, and can move on politely. 'Can I get you another drink?' enables you to break out of the group, slip back with a filled glass and move on before anyone tries to re-engage you. Carrying a plate of canapés likewise gives you a chance to move around, though can look a little odd if you've hired people to do that. Or you can offer to make an introduction, enabling you to take a guest over to the VIP, or to one of your team to have a conversation. And have some exit lines up your sleeve: 'Excuse me, but I just have to check if the meal is ready/ our guest has arrived/the PA system is working . . .', 'I'm sorry, I see my colleague needs to ask me something . . .', etc. Just don't make it too blatant. I once had to accompany Prince Philip around a reception of maybe 150 people we'd invited to the Residence to meet him. It was a masterclass. Although nearly 90 years old, in 45 minutes flat he circulated with little assistance from me (other than to tell him who he was talking to), spoke to almost everyone there personally, was witty, direct, engaged and made each feel he'd paid them attention. Practice makes perfect.

6. Be prepared to cope with disasters. These can range from the person who tips a drink down the front of a fellow guest, or themselves, to (in ascending order of gravity) a power cut, total PA failure, a torrential downpour of rain at a garden party, a guest of honour who never shows up, the uninvited guest who *does* turn up and for whom there is no place, the drunken guest who starts embarrassing everyone, two guests who get into a blazing row, or somebody dropping dead from a heart attack in mid-reception. Four things to remember if you are hosting: check the audio-visual equipment in advance; always know where the nearest cloth/toilet/water/First Aid kit is; be ready to re-arrange the placement at the drop of a hat; and always have a few words ready to calm everyone down and keep the show on the road.

7. Always follow-up new contacts immediately afterwards, even with just a quick text, WhatsApp or email to keep the contact warm and show them that you noticed and remember.

This list – Turner (2024, ch. 8) also contains useful examples – takes for granted the most crucial and (for me) most difficult networking skill of all: remembering people's names. It is another good reason for reading through the guest list in advance, and for checking through the business cards you've collected afterwards, annotating them with the date and place you met and any memorable character- istics. Some people can just remember. I envy them. For us less gifted, effort is needed.

Visits and summits

Organising visits, especially state visits and head of state or government level sum- mits, is as much about protocol as anything else.

The G8 summit in Birmingham in June 1998 required as much attention to the ceremonials as to the substance or the public relations with Jubilee 2000. Ensuring there was interpretation into German for Chancellor Kohl and Japanese for prime minister Hashimoto; agreeing the protocol line-up for the official photo with Her Majesty the Queen, and opportunities for the informal photos (like Figure 7.1); knowing how many stairs Chancellor Kohl could manage; selecting menus, wines and entertainments to suit all the leaders' tastes and offend none; deciding what gifts to give – something British, but not too extravagant, not too mean, with a goody bag for the rest of the entourage; agreeing the correct order for arrivals at the venue; and (one of the toughest jobs of all) agreeing the size of delegations accom- panying each participant, and how many could accompany the leader to the meeting venue itself; all these took up many hours and days and were integral to whether the leaders and their delegations were in the right mood to make the summit a success. The bigger the summit or event, the greater the logistical and protocol challenges, and the easier for someone to feel offended.

The European Council's protocol department is more used than most to handling large numbers of heads of state and government, but even they were challenged by an EU-Africa Summit with nearly 80 heads in attend- ance. Brussels traffic was brought to a standstill for two days as the convoys of presidential cars cruised back and forth between the conference venue and their hotels. Unwilling to cede top place in the protocol ranking, President Museveni never actually left his hotel for the duration of the summit, forcing anyone who wanted to meet to come to him, not he to them.

Figure 7.1 Leaders arriving at the G8 Summit in Birmingham, May 1998: (from left) Kohl, Yeltsin, Chirac, Blair, Prodi, Hashimoto, Clinton.

Source: author's photograph

The funeral of Queen Elizabeth II in 2022 and coronation of King Charles III in 2023 both posed immense challenges for the British protocol department given the number of heads who came. To have allowed each of the 18 monarchs, 55 presidents and 25 prime ministers who attended the funeral to drive up to Westminster Abbey in their own car with outriders and all would have required the first to arrive at 8 am for a funeral beginning at noon, and no head of state wants to spend four hours waiting for the others to arrive. So it was decided to bus them in by coach. Delegations were instructed to take their heads to the Royal Hospital Chelsea where their flag cars could park while the heads got on the bus. This was *not* popular with their respective chiefs of protocol, even if some of the heads in the end rather enjoyed the informality and chance to chat. But they had no choice. Only the US President was given exceptional permission on security grounds to drive up to the Abbey in 'The Beast' – his massive armoured car, flown in specially for the occasion.

Should you ever be involved in a fully fledged state visit, be prepared for the best part of a year's work. For anything involving the British royals, and similarly for other heads of state, a programme needs to be worked out to the exact number of steps required from one spot to another; timing has to be precise to the minute; photo and media opportunities have to be meticulously programmed in. Nothing, certainly not who is attending each event, can be left to chance or sorted on the day. *Placements* are set in stone weeks before. Security is a perpetual headache, not just the risk of terrorist attack but political protest. Some heads of state are particularly sensitive to protesters when visiting countries abroad where free speech is the norm: Xi Jinping's state visit to the UK in 2015 had to be carefully managed so that those protesting about the treatment of Uighurs or Falun Gong were not excluded, but did not embarrass the President. Major decisions on the programme or the ceremonies have to be referred to Buckingham Palace or the respective State House, so they take time, and the relevant head of mission will find themselves fully employed on just this task for weeks and months before. And yet it has real value. You never get better access to your host or the visiting head of state and their office. The contacts made in the course of preparations build an unparalleled network and a sense of solidarity (if all goes well) that will benefit the rest of a posting. And the publicity attending such visits is the golden opportunity to put across your messages to a wide public.

Mere ministerial visits seem straightforward by comparison, and again provide great opportunities to access senior politicians and officials to sort outstanding issues and drive forward the bilateral agenda. A head of mission's value, status and local reputation is often reflected in the level of access they can secure, and a visiting minister will note that. Your aim is to make the visit as productive and successful as possible.

I have experienced some disasters. At the inauguration of President Atta Mills in Ghana, we almost lost the British minister for Africa down a drain. The President's victory in the elections was so popular and the crowd come to celebrate so dense that the road to the VIP stand was completely blocked: not even the High Commissioner's flag car could get through. So we got out to walk. Lord Malloch Brown, the minister, is a tall man, and spotted a clear path through the mass of humanity that we could take. Forcing a way through the crowd towards it, we suddenly found ourselves teetering on the brink of a three metre-deep sheer-sided storm drain. We grabbed the minister before he toppled in, and fought our way on through the crowd, eventually gaining the VIP stand just before the ceremonies themselves began – though it was so overcrowded that I had to persuade a diplomatic colleague to give up his seat for the minister to avoid him having to stand for three hours. Sometimes, the scale of events can swamp even the most enthusiastic local protocol department, and you must always be prepared to improvise.

On the other hand, when the protocol works well, lives are enhanced, events run smoothly, and your ministers and fellow diplomats are enormously grateful. So it is always worth the effort. Making any visit work is a test of your ability to manage a mission so that all parts are working together effectively, and managing a mission overseas is an essential skill that all need to learn.

8 Leading a mission

The basic tenets of good management and good leadership are the same wherever you work, whatever your organisation, however big or small. There are thousands, even tens of thousands, of manuals on good management practice (e.g. James, 2022). But unlike managing domestic ministries or organisations, management of diplomatic or international missions involves dealing with staff who, when on a posting abroad, not only work together but often live together in close proximity, and work alongside staff recruited locally who often live completely different and separate lives. It is more like captaining a ship at sea where half the mariners live on the boat and the other half join for just one voyage, but bring their families with them. So you need particular sensitivities and specific skills if you are to keep the team together, happy, productive and successful.

During one of my postings, the mission was riven by accusations of racism, not as you might imagine between expatriate and local staff, but between two members of the UK-based staff themselves. On another, where I arrived shortly after the incident, the mission had divided into two rival camps when a senior member of staff suddenly abandoned his wife and took up with a new partner, while continuing to come into the office as if nothing had changed and his (soon-to-be former) wife continued to live in their official house. These things can happen at home too, but the impact on the working and living environment is less extreme.

This chapter explores how to provide effective leadership and manage such diverse teams, and how to handle the (usually unexpected) problems when they inevitably crop up.

Leadership

Leading any mission or a team within a mission, whether bilateral or (even more) multilateral, it is wise to bear in mind seven core principles:

1. Provide a strategic direction or broad vision, so that staff know where they are going, what the overall objective is and how their own role fits into that. An overarching strategic goal would normally be set by the minister, ministry or headquarters, so your role is to make it specific and relevant to the staff in your

DOI: 10.4324/9781003533436-8

mission. A local version that reduces the core messages to one page often helps, linking people's day-to-day work with the difference they are trying to make.

2. Ensure a clear division of labour so that each team member knows what their specific role is and has a clear set of specific objectives that enable them, and you, to measure how well they are achieving them. Clear guidance on cross-team working and how to co-operate with other parts of the mission and other diplomatic colleagues also helps.

3. Focus on the people in your team, motivating and guiding each individual. This helps maintain morale across the whole team and ensures that they see themselves as supporting each other. It is important that successes are celebrated and setbacks acknowledged with remedial action discussed and then taken. Success can often be elusive, but staff still need to know that what they are doing is worthwhile and appreciated. My experience is that you can never give too much praise, and that this makes it easier for people to accept tough messages or correction when they need to be given.

4. Be open to new ideas, to challenge and to innovation, even if not every idea will be feasible or sensible. Getting people to think constructively and be willing to express their views can often generate both enthusiasm and more effective delivery, as well as encouraging autonomy which can avoid every decision rising to the top. Explaining why some things won't work improves the level of understanding and can lead to more constructive suggestions. But also be clear which decisions *do* need to be referred up before action is taken.

5. Manage risks. While managing geostrategic risk is core diplomatic business, it is often more practical risks that trip you up: unexpected staff departures, sickness or vacancies; IT or communication failures; budget shortfalls; cancelled visits . . . It can be a host of things. So always maintain, even if only mentally, a risk matrix to help you think ahead about how you would handle such problems.

6. Delegate responsibility as far as it makes sense to do so and streamline working procedures. It is sadly common for managers to reach the top by working very hard, doing a brilliant job themselves, and therefore believing they know how to do every job better than those reporting to them. This creates a temptation to micro-manage, to ensure every job is done as well as they would do it themselves. This can be both frustrating for staff, impeding their ability to step up and take responsibility themselves, and create bottlenecks in decision-making. As a manager, though, you cannot allow the incompetence of one to imperil the work of the wider team. The aim of management as coaching is to raise the capability of all staff, and for each to do the maximum they are capable of. If, despite this, a member of staff proves incapable of the job they are doing, the whole team needs you as the manager to step in and deal with that. The final principle is therefore:

7. Ensure accountability. This is normally done through the staff reporting and financial accounting processes, but these are not always user-friendly. It is easy for them to become either excessively onerous or perfunctory. In the EU, it seemed almost impossible to include any, even well-intentioned, critical comment in a staff appraisal without the individual contesting it or the unions being

called in. A strange language of circumlocution emerged, where you had to read an appraisal for what it did *not* say – which revealed the weaknesses – rather than what it did. Similar pressures exist in other multilateral organisations where it is important to preserve the diversity of any team, leading to a wide variation in talent and the need to avoid criticism which might risk being attributed to some motive (national prejudice, gender preference, racism, etc.) other than the staff member's actual performance in the job.

Every organisation is a hierarchy. Almost every manager has another manager above them, and there is little more frustrating than working for a bad manager who interferes without helping, or fails to help when needed. Managing upwards – keeping a good and fruitful relationship with your own manager – can be as important as managing downwards, particularly if you are dealing with politicians who may have no management experience at all. In protecting your own staff from unreasonable demands from above, you may end up feeling rather like a buffer, battered from both above and below. It means being very clear, both upwards and downwards, that you are trying to achieve the organisation's objectives as effectively as possible.

Management

The peculiarity of managing a mission abroad is that you have no superior on the spot. There are, of course, managers back in the capital or at headquarters who send instructions and keep an eye on what you are doing, and the rise of remote working and regularity of video-conferencing makes this easier. But at post, you are still the boss: the buck stops with you. You have the overall responsibility for the conduct and management of the mission, and, as the visible representative of your government or organisation, you can be quite exposed if things go wrong either in bilateral relations or in internal management. So be prepared.

Things are changing in terms of staffing. Forty years ago, the assumption was still that if sent on a posting abroad, your family, if you had one, would come with you. Those with young children tended to bring them and find primary education at post. If the post had excellent secondary education, either at local or international schools, older children could also be educated there with the government covering the fees. But for some British families continuity of education in the British system was preferred, so they had the option of putting their children into private boarding schools which the government would pay for (on various conditions), providing in effect a significant enhancement of salary. Other countries have other traditions, most preferring to cover the cost of international education locally as long as it is available and the post deemed safe enough for families. It is far more common now, however, for diplomats to have partners with their own career, which may or may not be mobile, and children who want to stay at school in their home country.

The FCDO has therefore introduced the concept of 'commuter postings' in some places, where the family remain in the UK and the diplomat commutes to and from the post on a weekly, monthly or bi-monthly basis depending on the distance from

London. They may spend a week now and then, or regularly, working remotely from the UK, and receive a travel package that can be used flexibly for the diplomat to travel back to the UK or the family to travel out to post. Allowances and accommodation are adjusted accordingly. This option has advantages in retaining staff who might otherwise leave for other jobs which enable them to live with their family in the UK, and the ease of remote working makes it less disruptive than it would have been in earlier times. It also makes sense for posts that are insecure or not family-friendly. But there is a risk it diminishes the value added of having staff at post, where the great benefit (and key requirement) is building a knowledge of the country and a network of contacts, which is much harder to do remotely. The tendency of work in post to spill over into weekends, for social, sporting or cultural engagements or when dealing with the increasingly frequent political crises, means that work overseas doesn't have the strict 9–5 working pattern that is more normal at home (if you're lucky).

In managing teams where some live at post with their family, some live on their own, and others commute back and forth, it is all the more necessary to work on building the team spirit. Those permanently in place may feel either more fully involved or at a disadvantage compared to those commuting, and it is important to ensure that burdens, such as serving as duty officer over a weekend, fall equally.

I spent seven years commuting weekly between Brussels and London and found it had a great advantage and a great drawback. While in Brussels on my own I had complete flexibility to use my time most efficiently for official work and travel; and when in London at the weekend I could (mostly) focus on the family. My work involved Africa and the Middle East rather than Belgium, so my physical presence in Brussels was not essential at the weekend. On the other hand, Miriam became a *de facto* single parent all week, doing all the school-time parenting on top of her own job. As my son said, they saw me rather like a distant uncle who appeared every now and then and needed to be brought up to date on the family news, including things I'd been told before but had somehow forgotten. I wouldn't recommend it as a way of life. Living all together in Ghana for three years was a much richer, more rewarding and more enjoyable experience for all of us.

The trend towards 'localisation' in many posts has also accelerated. There being fewer diplomats from capitals and more local staff reduces costs, as no expatriation allowances are paid. In some places there were British nationals living locally or spouses of diplomatic staff with the necessary skills who could be employed in the mission, which reduced security risks. But where expatriate diplomats have become only a small percentage of the total staff, the burden of more sensitive work falls on fewer shoulders, and in a crisis this can be challenging.

For the diplomats, the social support that the community of diplomatic colleagues – national and non-national – provides can be important, and indeed a very enjoyable part of the job. More on this in the next chapter. As a rule, the larger the post and the more prosperous the country, the easier it is to lead an independent life and build your own social circle; the smaller and harder the mission, the more you see of each other, and the more important this mutual support becomes when facing difficulty or danger. This can mean the *esprit de corps* at a post is often in inverse proportion to the degree of comfort and safety – it's best where conditions are toughest. Some Foreign Office colleagues preferred going to hardship posts because the social life was better, the work more interesting, and the pay more generous. But it does make it all the more important for the ambassador to provide leadership going beyond the office to ensure that staff have social and personal support as well as professional support at work.

The management point here is that a head of mission cannot, and should not, avoid the social life of the mission. Though an ambassador's life is lived very much in the public eye, and the ability to retreat from it and have some private time is essential, you cannot live entirely independently of your team. You don't need to organise everything, but you do need to actively encourage and support those staff who are happy to organise social and sporting events that provide opportunities for staff to get together outside office hours and enjoy themselves.

The other side of this coin is that people may feel as though they are living in a goldfish bowl: everyone can see what everybody else is doing and, as in all small communities, that can cause claustrophobia and tension. In a confined space, that tension can occasionally erupt into conflict. It is therefore important that the head of post knows what is going on. It can be hard to ask people directly – as the figure of authority, the leader remains a rather distant and awesome person for many – so you need someone who is at home with the whole community of staff and can warn you in advance if there are problems brewing. This person might be your deputy, your PA, your consul, or your spouse – whoever is sufficiently informed, trustworthy and discreet that you can share fairly freely the challenges and frustrations of leading the mission. It is invaluable to have someone who knows the people, has your back, and is still able to point out weaknesses in your argument or approach which others may hesitate to mention.

Staffing

Picking the right staff to work in a team overseas is also more difficult than at home. These are people you have to live with as well as work with. How much choice you get depends on the willingness of the personnel administration to allow you input, but taking the initiative to keep in touch with headquarters on staffing is always worth it. If you are not formally part of the process, find a chance to express your views to the selection committee chair about the posting or the candidates in advance. Mild eccentrics can be a great asset overseas, but those who are too odd can cause problems: in a small post, one bad colleague can make life miserable for everyone. I referred earlier to dealing with an accusation of racism between staff working in the same mission. Clearly such behaviour, if proven, was contrary to the FCDO's values and rules of conduct and could not be tolerated. It threatened to undermine the credibility of the whole management at post. But the person concerned worked for a different government department, not directly under my authority. That department's investigation led merely to the mildest of reprimands, and it fell to me as head of post to rebuild morale while the individual remained there, requiring a mission-wide campaign to highlight the importance of those values and of showing mutual respect in all our dealings. It could not be left to fester. I also made very clear to the parent department of that staff member that they needed to take more care over whom they sent to posts abroad: some staff who may be fine at home were simply not suitable to work in a more diverse foreign environment, however much they might like the idea of an expatriate lifestyle.

Local staff play a crucial role in every mission. Some will work in a mission for 10–20 years at a stretch, providing invaluable continuity of experience and contacts. Others come to work for a few years and then move on, but some remain in touch. In Ghana, the Japanese were very pleased when their former locally employed information officer, John Mahama, became President in 2012. He continued every year to attend the Emperor's birthday party at the embassy, greatly enhancing the ambassador's prestige.

Local staff are recruited at post, usually by each team, so you have control over the process. But it can still be hard to get the skills you need. Senior positions in the mission are reserved for diplomatic staff, so promotion prospects are limited and ambitious and talented local staff therefore tend not to stay long – though not all go on to become president. Pay differentials can also be stark in poorer countries, with some local staff doing substantially the same work as diplomats (sometimes doing it better) for a fraction of the pay. It depends on local market conditions: graduate political analysts may be two-a-penny while skilled accounting or IT staff may command local salaries as high as those in HQ. Whichever way round it is, you want local staff to feel an integral part of the team. I found all-staff meetings including local staff, and occasional meetings with *only* local staff (plus the management officer), very useful. In Washington DC local staff had no hesitation speaking up in general meetings, whereas in Ghana or Tanzania they could be reluctant to take the floor when expat staff were present. But you need to know what they are thinking too. Including local staff in embassy social events is also important, even if it may not be easy for them to participate. In Ghana, many lived over two hours' commute from the High Commission as the only place affordable for them, so evening events were difficult; in Washington, local staff lived closer, but had a local network of friends and family and sometimes a reluctance to use their evenings for work; while in Brussels, local staff appeared to live not only in a different country but in a different universe.

That said, one of the best social events held during my time in Accra were the Inter-Embassy Olympic Games, organised almost entirely by the local staff liaising with their opposite numbers in other foreign missions. Ambassadors were invited to come and watch, though I rashly volunteered to join the 4 x 100m relay team (which came in second) and the chess competition, where I was thrashed by a Danish champion in the first round. Though competition was fierce, to be honest the results were secondary: it was an outstanding event enjoyed by all.

Security can be a particular issue in some countries, either because of political differences between your own and the host government, making it difficult for local staff to work for a foreign mission; or because all staff are targeted by the host intelligence service trying to recruit or implant moles within foreign diplomatic missions. Both diplomatic and local staff may be offered bribes or subject to threats to persuade them to hand over sensitive information – which can often seem relatively innocuous (organograms, travel movements, etc.), but can be both valuable and sensitive. This is a very real risk, but needs to be managed intelligently. On the one hand, to cut local staff out of all sensitive information may limit their usefulness, and a level of trust in local staff needs to be demonstrated to inspire their loyalty. But to risk compromising diplomatic secrets or the personal security of staff would be reckless and liable to severe criticism or disciplinary action. On such issues it is therefore always wise to consult headquarters on tricky issues, if only to cover your back in case things go wrong.

Managing money

As the leader of a mission, you also carry responsibility for the correct management of the budget. Ideally, this can be delegated to the administration officer and accountant, the head of consular or visas services or, where there is an aid programme, to the head of development. But the head of mission is normally required to sign off the accounts. This may be a once-a-year chore, or it may in some systems require more regular attention, signing off any contract or payment above a certain sum. In the EU this was a time-consuming task of unutterable tedium that heads of mission coming from member states' services could scarcely believe – all to ensure full accountability to the EU's many taxpayers. But the sums can be large and the risk of fraud real.

At one UK post I led, we discovered a fraud that had been perpetrated for nearly a decade, over-invoicing for fuel purchased for the High Commission's car fleet from a friendly supplier. It escaped detection by being a small discrepancy on a weekly basis in handwritten receipts which were simply filed, but over the decade amounted to thousands of pounds diverted to the pocket of the long-standing and otherwise respected member of local staff involved. He was sacked and the supplier changed, but the money could never be recovered. Though checking the budget takes time, you need to be sure someone has done it properly: do not take it for granted.

Development contracts have to pass through more rigorous financial processes, so in some ways the risk of fraud is less. But whether the money is then well used to the maximum benefit of communities concerned is a wider question that involves judgements going beyond strict audit. This happens less regularly, but is still important. The UK set up an Independent Commission for Aid Impact (ICAI) which produces regular reports on the effectiveness and value for money of British aid, pulling no punches where they thought it fell short (Lowcock and Dissanayake, 2024). Delivering humanitarian aid in a conflict zone can be particularly challenging because it may involve dealing with terrorist or rebel organisations which control the regions where people in most need are living. They may demand a 'facilitation fee' or the diversion of some of the food to their forces in return for providing access to those who might otherwise starve, as happened in Somalia; or it can mean being forced by governments to strip out medical or 'dual use' equipment like tent poles, before being allowed through to refugees or into rebel-held territory, as happened in Gaza and Syria. These are moral and political issues more than questions of financial propriety, and you would be wise to get a political steer at a higher level before agreeing the terms demanded. One head of UN humanitarian aid in Syria was considered by some donors to be too close to the Assad regime, but argued that this was the only way to get food to starving women and children. There is often no right answer (see the International Rescue Committee, 2021, for discussion of the dilemmas).

As a head, you are responsible for the mission's reputation and anything that may cause reputational damage is something you need to know about and make a judgement on. It is frustrating to find that someone has taken a stupid decision or made a careless mistake without you being aware, but which you then have to defend or take responsibility for, whether internally or in public. Nevertheless, that is your role. The art of good management is to have reliable systems and people in place to ensure this doesn't happen, without you having to micromanage every decision. Easier said than done, but it is what you should aim for.

Multilateral management

Managing multilateral missions requires all these skills, and more.

By 'multilateral' I mean any mission responsible to an international organisation rather than a national government, whether a UN peace-keeping mission, a World Bank office, an EU delegation, a humanitarian organisation or a charity. Such missions will often include expatriate staff of different nationalities and different statuses – permanent employees, temporary staff and contractors – as well as local staff from the country itself. They often operate in difficult circumstances where logistical challenges are added to the political and management ones; where there is no national solidarity to help bind the staff together; where additional complexities surround the need to keep a national and gender balance among staff and avoid divergent social attitudes causing friction (what may be acceptable in some cultures may be quite unacceptable in others); and where the choice of the staff you are given may be wholly outside your control.

Working for the EU in Brussels I was responsible for 40 EU delegations across Africa and subsequently 15 in the Middle East. As the jobs fell vacant, I was involved in picking and then managing suitable heads of mission. We submitted our recommendations to the HRVP, who had the final say on all such appointments and wanted to ensure a fair balance in the selection between skills, experience, member states and institutions. This led to a certain variable quality among heads of delegation: some were outstanding, most were competent and reliable, some weak but able to cope with sufficient support, and one or two were simply not up to the job. The last caused most of the work, requiring visits to post, reports and investigations, clearing up messes with the host governments, and dealing with the fallout when one of them irritated the local government so much he effectively became *persona non grata*.

But EU delegations were straightforward compared to UN missions, several of which I have observed from close quarters: UNOCI in Côte d'Ivoire, MINUSMA in Mali, UNSOM in Somalia, UNMISS in South Sudan, MONUSCO in the DRC and UNIFIL in Lebanon. I was also immensely impressed with the UN OCHA operations in Syria and Yemen, UNRWA's work with Palestinian refugees, Oxfam's support to Rwandan refugees in Tanzania in 1994 and the whole humanitarian operation in South Sudan. None of these missions were easy, and the dedication and hard work of the staff involved in each was outstanding. The heads were selected by the UN Secretary General, in consultation or with the approval of the Security Council, which applied rigorous (if sometimes rather political) scrutiny to the nominees, who had to have extensive experience, international stature, and strong political backing. The mandates of each mission are also drawn up and agreed by the Security Council itself, which has led to some that are less than crystal clear or very difficult to implement.

From what I have seen, there are three key lessons about managing such missions.

Firstly, these are mainly *mission-driven* operations. Keeping people focused on the mission therefore provides the overall strategic objective that will enable them to prioritise and deliver. It also helps to maintain morale. Where the mission is vague or obscure, the operation having been cooked up as a political compromise between diverging views, it causes problems. It is the leader's role to interpret it and communicate a clear mission to the staff in the field. MINUSMA and MONUSCO were both peace-keeping missions operating where there was little or no peace to keep; both were harried by rebel or terrorist groups for whom their presence was an inconvenience if not a provocation, and neither was consistently supported by the host government which felt ambiguous about their presence in the first place. Both did invaluable work protecting civilians, but their position became ultimately untenable when the two respective governments demanded their withdrawal, leading inevitably to higher civilian casualty rates in both places. Some, like UNIFIL, are constantly challenged by one or both parties they exist to separate and lead a precarious and rather dangerous existence. Others again, where a status quo has become entrenched on the ground and negotiations have stalled, run on for so long they become 'fat and happy', set in their ways, untroubled that any violence will actually break out.

Secondly, it is important to make a virtue of necessity and celebrate the diversity of the team you are working with. Such diversity has pros and cons, and every mission tends to develop its own unique culture. The leader needs to understand it but also shape it by their own actions. On the one hand, having staff or contingents from many different countries and cultures is a tremendous opportunity for everyone to expand their horizons, listen and learn. Most people who join such missions are likely to be open to others, are comfortable with diversity and will be willing to participate in joint activities that enable people to share. Though not all: some will want to lead a quiet life and should not be forced to participate. But most will be happy to contribute something to the common effort, even if more responsibility will sit with the head of mission to make things happen. On the other hand, such missions can develop cliques and 'mafias' within the team that you need to prevent undermining the effectiveness of the overall operation. Sound, honest and impartial advice is even more precious in these circumstances.

Thirdly, therefore, it requires even more effort than in a bilateral mission to build the team and to manage the stress on individuals that working in tough situations brings. This is particularly challenging in a military mission with a rapid turnover of contingents, who often appear for only 6, 9 or 12 months. Because appointments to your team may be driven by a variety of criteria besides pure talent or experience, every team will be a mixed bag. For some people, throwing themselves into difficult and demanding situations, particularly where they are helping others in extreme need, provides tremendous stimulation and great job satisfaction. Their stamina can be extraordinary, their morale unquenchable and their mental resilience seem impervious. But often there is a toll being taken, even if it is not visible. Even adrenalin-junkies need a break – especially, I would say – and they may need to be forced to take one before the strain becomes too much. So more regular checking in on staff to ensure they are bearing up is a good thing, and do not assume that everyone can manage the same level of stress that you can.

When people cannot cope (and this applies equally to any kind of overseas mission), they respond in different ways. Some overwork; some fall ill and go off sick; some take to drink or drugs; some seek relief in other ways; some become silent, some excessively voluble. As a head of mission you need to be aware enough of what is going on in people's lives to know when support or remedy is needed. Everybody gets sick from time to time, but in my experience unhappy people get sick more often than happy ones, and problems for one staff member have a bigger impact in a small mission overseas than in a big organisation at home. Forty years ago, people assumed there were two mental health issues that most frequently affected people at work: stress and depression. At a time when many were reluctant to admit to either, people would frequently try to work through the problem, or suffer from it until they seized up completely. This did not help the individual or the team's effectiveness or morale. There is now a kaleidoscope of recognised mental health conditions which people are encouraged to acknowledge, talk about and get treated. This helps, but can still be harder to do when you are overseas and away from family support networks and familiar health systems. So keeping an eye on where or when help may be needed is essential. This underlines the importance of calling on your HQ (if there is one) to help provide additional support after any major incident affecting staff; and where someone is plainly not coping it is often best for the individual and the mission for them to end their tour sooner rather than later.

Crisis management

It would be an unusual diplomatic career that did not involve managing a crisis at some point or other. In the light of recent developments, these are likely to become more frequent rather than less. But the world was ever thus, and as I explained at the beginning, besides avoiding crises, managing them is what diplomacy is all about. So it is best to be prepared. Quiet, peaceful and productive postings still exist, and crises of policy are commonplace (endemic to most jobs at some point). What I am talking about here are *physical* crises – wars, coups, rebellions, terrorist attacks and natural disasters, which require more than just sitting up all night writing reports and briefs, or working the phones to resolve a disagreement.

My own first encounter with a major crisis of this kind was the 9/11 attack in the US in 2001, while I was working in the British Embassy in Washington dealing with (among other things) air services. It illustrated well how people react to an unexpected crisis. The attacks came, wholly unsuspected, out of a clear blue sky. I remember my Treasury colleague Sue Owen coming into my office soon after we'd started work saying: 'Come and watch this – a plane has crashed into one of the Twin Towers!' And as we watched, we saw the second plane fly into the second tower. At that point it was clear this was a concerted attack. Half an hour later a third plane hit the Pentagon and we realised Washington itself was also under attack. Everyone was flummoxed: staff were standing in the corridor saying to each other, 'What do we do?' Normal work was pointless. In this situation, panic took the form of immobility rather than action. Many just wanted to go home as quickly as possible. All across DC it was announced that schools were closing and children should go home, so parents left to collect their children. Miriam collected our two and took them to the park. Another Treasury colleague was attending a conference in the Twin Towers that day, but was fortunately outside the building when the planes struck and was able to get away safely, though in a state of shock. The Ambassador summoned the senior team and we agreed to evacuate the Embassy except for a skeleton staff of those dealing with the crisis. The embassy building is located immediately next to the Vice President's house at National Observatory which was considered a potential target for the fourth plane, still in the air at that point. The skeleton team included the Ambassador and his deputy to liaise with the White House and NSC, two or three of the political team to keep in touch with Congress, State

Department and the FCO in London, the military attachés to contact the US military and the spooks to do the same with the intelligence agencies, myself to deal with air services as the whole of US air space was closing down, and a consular team to respond to the flood of enquiries already coming in from British nationals at home and in the US. (See the account in Meyer, 2005, 182–92.) In 2001, working from home was a much greater palaver than now, and only UK-based staff had laptops that could connect to the official system. So finding a way to message all staff at home was itself difficult, but we did get a daily update out to everyone to keep them informed. It was a week before anything like normal work resumed and staff returned to the office.

The most important lesson was that in any crisis it is essential to be prepared and have a plan. You cannot plan for every eventuality: we had plans for a fire or a bomb attack on the Embassy itself, prepared when the IRA was active in the 1970s, but not for the kind of terrorist attack that Al-Qaeda carried out. It was seeing staff paralysed, not knowing what on earth to do, which reinforced for me the need to have some plan that you can put into action to reassure people that the appropriate measures are being taken, what their role is, and who is taking the decisions. It is essential when you first arrive at a post, however peaceful and safe it may appear, to check the emergency plan, ensure it is up to date, that it covers the full range of potential crises, from bomb or war to pestilence or flood, and that it is practised on a regular basis. You also need to have a clear idea of the crisis management structures at HQ, whom to access and how to get decisions there made swiftly.

Secondly, the style of leadership often needs to change in such crises, from being a coach, facilitator or manager to a more directive command. It is essential to be visible, to show empathy and communicate frequently. External communications, to the public and the world, become even more important in these circumstances, and it is the leader's role to ensure they are clear, consistent and effectively distributed.

The third lesson is that you must look after the staff. You have a duty of care towards them that needs to be prioritised. This obviously cannot be to the detriment of the work that needs to be done in the crisis; but where normal work can longer be carried on, and staff are not needed for other duties linked to the crisis, or if such work can only be carried on at too great a personal risk to life and limb, then it is best to send them home, keep them somewhere safe or, if necessary, evacuate them. It needs to be clear to all of them that their health and safety are given due priority. Frightened and distracted staff are in any case unlikely to do much useful work. You may also be faced with the opposite problem: staff who are determined to continue doing their job despite the personal risk to themselves because other people are depending on it. You may need to judge when to tell them to stop and leave. This applies to you too. As one colleague who was involved in the final evacuation from Kabul in 2021 puts it:

> It is bad leadership to soldier on, or allow others to do so, beyond the point where exhaustion sets in. In a crisis, what you need above all is people who can think clearly and take good decisions.
>
> (Bristow, 2024, 115)

You have less ability to protect local staff, who are covered neither by diplomatic immunity nor foreign citizenship allowing for evacuation. This caused immense difficulty and trauma in Afghanistan. The heroism of humanitarian staff trying to support the civilian population of Gaza during Israel's all-out war with Hamas in 2023–5 is reflected in the appalling death toll they suffered – the highest in the world for UN staff doing their job, protected (in principle) under the laws of war from such harm, as specified in UN Security Council Resolution 2735 of June 2024. You have to be prepared for the fact that some governments simply ignore the rules.

The fourth lesson is to keep well plugged-in to your local networks, not just the foreign ministry, political leaders and fellow diplomats but journalists, academics, friends and contacts in the British community (in my case the airlines) who may have additional information on a complicated and rapidly evolving situation. You need to pool all available information in order to assess the likely developments, and be able to give an accurate picture of it to your ministers and headquarters.

The fifth lesson is to keep your headquarters informed at all times of what is going on. They need to know, and you need their support and their guidance on what to do. Occasionally, after a catastrophic hurricane or flood, all communications may be cut off and you have to make your own decisions. But most missions should be insured against this with back-up communications systems and satellite phones for use in just such emergencies. It is the head of mission's responsibility to ensure that these work before you need to use them. Internet and mobile phone connections are now pretty robust and have proven their resilience in many such crises. But where the problem is a coup, civil war or other conflict, you may find normal communication and internet access deliberately cut off and your back-up system becomes essential. Key decisions, such as what to say in public, whether to close the embassy or whether to evacuate staff, will normally require authorisation from HQ. Sometimes there can be differences of view: the man or woman on the spot may see consequences that are not understood in HQ, and the authorities at HQ may see political arguments that posts are unaware of. The more open and regular communications are between the two, the easier it is to iron out any differences.

Finally, if the situation demands it, you need to be ready to evacuate, both your national citizens and your staff. This definitely needs planning in advance; otherwise, you are putting people's lives at more rather than less risk.

In 2011, as the *Forces Nouvelles* (FN) marched on Abidjan to oust President Gbagbo after the elections, we had to evacuate our remaining staff from Abidjan. In my absence, only a political officer and the visiting military attaché from Accra were still based in the Ambassador's Residence in Cocody. In trying to fend off the FN advance, Gbagbo's troops set up a machine gun nest on the roof of the Residence. The staff locked themselves in the basement and spent hours trying to contact UNOCI to rescue them. Eventually the machine-gunners retreated and a UNOCI armoured car was able to take them to the French evacuation centre, whence they were eventually flown out with a few other remaining diplomats and French citizens. Both returned safely to Accra; but in other circumstances there may be no UN armoured cars to get you out.

Usually there is at least some early warning of possible conflict, and precautionary evacuation is better than leaving it too late. A natural disaster, like a tsunami, is inherently unpredictable, so you cannot always evacuate people in advance. But where you can, do so. The first step is to advise citizens to leave by commercial means while they are still available, and get non-essential staff and dependents out by the same means, as happened in Lebanon in 2024. It is remarkable the touching faith that many citizens overseas have that, if the worst comes to the worst, their government will rescue them at the taxpayer's expense. There is always pressure from the media to do so: 'Brits abandoned as diplomats fly out' is not a headline that any minister will welcome. But there is no pot of money waiting to pay for such eventualities. Caution is always the better part of valour.

As mentioned in Chapter 3, Sudan is a good example of the dilemmas. Political tension had been high since the military had ousted the civilian government in October 2021. But when fighting broke out unexpectedly in April 2023 between the Sudan Armed Forces (SAF) and the Rapid Support Forces (RSF) militia in Khartoum, both diplomats and the local community were unprepared for its severity. The airport was immediately put out of action, and fighting erupted right in the centre of town, not far from the British and other embassies. Existing evacuation plans were therefore immediately redundant. The significant population of Sudanese-British dual citizens appealed for evacuation to safety in the UK. The British Embassy was criticised for first getting the bulk of its own staff and their families to safety (with the help of British and American special forces and an RAF airlift to Cyprus), before helping other British nationals to get out. The government said there had been specific threats of violence against British diplomats, and most British nationals were subsequently evacuated successfully by air or road, though it was a nerve-wracking time for all (Radford and McGarvey, 2023). British diplomats are not, like the captain of a sinking ship, expected to stay on board until the last passenger and crew member is safe and then go down with the ship. The government has a duty to help them escape to live and negotiate another day.

One ambassador who did nearly go down with the ship was Sir Laurie Bristow in Kabul. Along with the US withdrawal from Saigon in 1975, the western flight from Afghanistan in 2022 as the Taliban swept back into power will stick in the diplomatic memory for many reasons: the failure to predict how swiftly the Ghani government would fall; the chaos and humiliation of the western departure; and the failure to provide refuge or transit for so many of the former Afghan employees who had worked for the western embassies and agencies trying to promote development and embed democracy in Afghanistan for the future. It was the last of these that did most damage to the West's reputation. Bristow's personal efforts to help as many as possible of Britain's former Afghan staff and their families to leave the country for their own safety will go on the record as an example of a head of mission who did his utmost in the circumstances. Even as he was evacuated to the airport to take the last flight out, he was signing off visas and issuing passports to enable Afghan staff to leave if they could. It was a heroic effort (Bristow, 2024).

One lesson has been that governments should in these circumstances accept some responsibility for not only their nationals but also for their local staff. To abandon them is no longer morally or politically acceptable.

God willing, most of us will not find ourselves in such extreme circumstances. But diplomatic life can be full of the unexpected, so it is wise to be prepared for that too. The next chapter therefore looks at the diplomatic way of life from a personal perspective – how to survive and how to flourish.

9   The diplomatic way of life

Diplomacy, and working in international organisations or companies, inevitably goes with a peripatetic way of life that can be challenging and difficult, whether or not you have a family or partner in tow. As we've seen in previous chapters, life and work are harder to separate abroad than at home. Learning how to manage it is as important as learning how to do the job.

Moving

If you don't like moving, don't become a diplomat. But most of us get used to it, and some even enjoy it.

Diplomatic life revolves around postings. They are often the most interesting, memorable and rewarding part of the job, and the bit other people are most interested in. The pattern of postings depends on many things, but rather less these days on the whim of the personnel department and rather more on the preference of the officer and the expertise they have accumulated, at least in some foreign ministries. The gifted amateur is giving way to the trained professional. In the 1960s postings were notoriously arbitrary. David Wilson, later Ambassador to China, was on his way to the airport for his first posting in Switzerland when he was informed he had been reallocated to Vietnam. He turned up in Saigon with skis and woolly hat in his baggage which languished, unused, for three years. When I joined in the 1980s, you could basically express a preference and exercise a veto, but otherwise went where you were sent. Staff are now able to submit bids for the posts they are interested in, though this has been adapted to require a minimum number of bids, including for a range of posts in easy and difficult countries, so you cannot insist on rotating between London, Paris, Rome and New York. It seems to work, though sometimes the more single and flexible feel that families get the pick of the comfortable posts with good schools – even if the 'commuter package' now, like boarding schools before, will help ensure that those with families can also go to tougher posts.

Being unable to plan your life more than four years ahead can be a challenge, one not faced by friends and relations who can happily stay in the same place for ten years or more. Others can move when they want or need to; for you it is baked in every three to four years, whether you like it or not. While waiting to find out

DOI: 10.4324/9781003533436-9

what your next job will be, you are also in a kind of limbo: will it be hot or cold, far or near, safe or insecure, familiar or alien, at home or abroad? Efforts have been made to plan a little further in advance than David Wilson experienced: many diplomatic services now try to give a year's advance notice of the next posting. But ministries, like people, never know what is going to happen next, so even the best-laid plans can be subject to last-minute change.

Britain is unusual in having its diplomatic staff move at any time of year. Most other European services, including the EEAS, manage postings around a single annual rotation in the summer months to make it easier for children to stay in education a full academic year wherever they are posted. In the Dutch diplomatic service, the personnel department used to manage a vast grid, with all staff down one side and all posts along the top, and simply fill in the blanks until everyone had a job and all posts were filled. You got what you are given, and lived with it.

The length of postings varies too. Given the cost of moving people round the world, the administration is often happy to leave people in situ as long as possible. Nevertheless, three to four years remains the norm, depending how debilitating or dangerous conditions at post are, with two- or even one-year postings for the toughest places. Extensions to five or even six years are occasionally granted if there are persuasive operational reasons for staying on, but many diplomats find they run out of steam after four years and look forward to the change. Gone are the days when the French Ambassador to the Court of St James, M. Paul Cambon, remained in post for twenty years, from 1894 to 1914, though it gave him extraordinary status and influence during his later years (Nicolson, 1939, 118). For career progression reasons, some high-flying diplomats will remain barely two years in a post before being hauled off to a higher-profile, higher-ranked or more demanding job. This broadens their experience, but doesn't always lead to operational effectiveness – or family happiness. For the US, ambassadors have to submit their resignation every time there is a change of President, which can be very disruptive given the time it takes to get Senate approval of each and every post. The Senate Foreign Relations Committee still insists on interviewing personally many of the Presidential nominees, and this can leave those nominated hanging around for three, six or nine months before they can finally proceed to post.

Each move, whether to another post or back to headquarters, involves packing up your life, lock, stock and barrel, and consigning it to 'heavy baggage' sent through a commercial mover who will ship it to your new destination over the period of a few months. In the meantime you (and the family) live out of a few suitcases. This can feel liberating. You realise how much simpler life is without all those possessions, tangling you up and weighing you down. A few clothes and a good book or two can keep you going for weeks or months. Perhaps it is the latent ascetic in me, but I rather enjoyed it. The British diplomatic service is unusual in providing furnished accommodation overseas, so you always had a bed to sleep in. The arrival of the heavy baggage in a new post or an old home, though, could come with both excitement and foreboding: how could there possibly be that much, would it all fit in, and what would be broken or missing?

Unpacking the boxes could take months. Occasionally a few boxes never actually got opened, but lived in the cellar for three years until the next packers came to take them away (insisting on re-packing them into their own brand of boxes). Still, for children and even for adults, there would be the joy of re-discovering some favourite possession, a book, rug or painting, photos, sports kit or toys. Absence can indeed make the heart grow fonder. If you are renting out a home while posted overseas, you may also have to put furniture or things you can't take with you into storage, where it sits for years until you finally return and reclaim it. Until I retired and finally scooped up all the scattered pieces, I was never quite sure where some things were, and whether they had got lost or were simply buried at the bottom of a long-forgotten box.

One benefit is that every three to four years you do an audit of your possessions and get rid of whatever you're never going to use again, or never really liked in the first place. Shedding things, often into the grateful hands of people staying on or to local staff who would never otherwise get access to them, is sensible and satisfying, and leaves you with a more rational and manageable collection of things.

Life can be brutal though. One colleague in Dar es Salaam found when she got home that her heavy baggage had been in a container that had clearly fallen in the sea at some port along the way. Everything – books, clothes, photos, the lot – was soaked in sea water and completely ruined. Another had just unpacked all his belongings on a new posting in Tehran when the house was stormed and ransacked by Iranian Revolutionary Guards during one of the periodic ruptures in relations – and all his worldly goods were trashed, including his treasured piano lovingly (and expensively) transported out. Insurance will cover you for the cost of the possessions, but nothing restores the lifetime of memories that they represented.

Often it is the diplomatic partner, the 'trailing spouse' as one described it, who carries the main burden of these moves, while the diplomatic officer swans from posting to post. It is to be honest a burden best shared, but if you are alone you have no choice but to do it all single-handed at the same time as preparing for or wrapping up a posting. This can be stressful. With children, it is added fun (see Keenan, 2005; 2014, for a vivid picture of diplomatic life from the partner's perspective).

If you have children, their education and welfare is a constant preoccupation, affecting the quality of family life and an officer's ability to concentrate on the job. There is no prescription. Every family is different and will find its own balance. Some children find the instability difficult and need extra support; others regard it as a great adventure and adapt to the new circumstances even more quickly and easily than their parents. Our own experience was that when the children were young, there are great advantages in keeping the family together, bringing them with us on postings. The spread of good-quality international schools across much of the world makes this more easily possible than forty years ago. Sending children away to boarding school from the age of six or eight is now rare. One advantage of international schools is that many of the children are in the same boat, and become good at making friends quickly, building a friendship group for support, and recognising that friends constantly come and go. The whole family, then, can share the experience of living abroad, exploring a new country and another culture, broadening the mind and learning adaptability. For other, and commonly for older children, there are advantages in staying at home, either at a boarding school, living with friends or relations, or with the rest of the family if the diplomat goes abroad alone. The continuity of school, friends and home can really help. But quite often there is no ideal solution, and you simply have to take the best possible decision in the circumstances you have. Foreign ministries have (had to) become more understanding of these dilemmas and are more flexible than they used to be – as long as it doesn't cost more money.

This constant moving makes it all the more important to have a home base that you can return to between postings, a place you and the family can feel is genuinely 'home'. While working, that often needs to be somewhere within reach of the ministry, but some prefer to pick a place early on that they will be happy to retire to, and use that as their retreat to rest and recuperate while on holidays from wherever they are posted at the time. Renting out homes while you are on a posting can be an invaluable source of extra income (despite the hassle), and you know it will always be there when you get back.

Exploring

Whether you have family in tow or not, exploring a new country is one of the joys of the job, and often an integral part of it. Time spent out of the office and – where it is allowed – out of the capital is never wasted.

The most important thing is to waste no time. Years pass quickly and though it is tempting to think you will have time to visit and re-visit favourite places, often you only get one bite at the cherry. We found the best guides about where to go were those already living there, not just the expats but more especially the locals. As well as asking what to read, it's always worth asking where to go.

On our first posting overseas together in Tanzania, we were introduced to the beautiful beaches and excellent bars by friends in the High Commission. But it was a couple of bird-watching friends, Neil and Liz, who'd lived there for 20 years, who showed us parts of the country we would never have dreamt of visiting but which became our most vivid and magical memories: the Kitulo plateau east of the main road to Mbeya, up an almost impassable track sketched on a napkin by Neil one evening in a bar, which appeared when we reached the top of the escarpment like a lost world of orchids, birds and stray cattle (one, which we mistook for a leopard, tried to eat our tent in the night – I have only been more terrified by Tanzanian bus driving); or the American mission station at Mumba, south of Sumbawanga on the border with Zambia, where they took us in and fed us mango pie when we arrived exhausted late one evening after a drive from hell. Later, with small children in tow during our posting in the US, nothing would stop Miriam's determination to explore wherever we went: picking ticks off each other in the forests of Chincoteague; losing our son on the beach at Rehobeth (we found him again, fortunately – hairy moment though); sampling fresh maple syrup in Vermont; taking our one-year-old into and rapidly out of certain bars in New Orleans ('Excuse me sir, your son is a minor. He's not allowed in this bar. We serve alcohol . . .'); cruising Yellowstone National Park in a monster RV; staying on board the old Queen Mary liner, moored at Long Beach, California, and so on. Actually, that last was my choice: I had sailed on the Queen Mary to the US at the age of two-and-a-half with my parents in 1958 and wanted to see if I recognised anything. I didn't, but it was worth the trip: it is an art deco gem.

In Ghana, where the Anglican church is growing rather than shrinking, we visited its newest diocese in Sefwi-Wiaso, a town in the far north-west on the border with Côte d'Ivoire. During the Lambeth Conference, which every ten years brings together representatives from the whole global Anglican communion, our local vicar in London, Giles, had invited Bishop Ackah of Sefwi-Wiaso to Putney parish church to give an African perspective on the tricky issues of women priests, gay marriage and the like. It was a lively debate. In return, Bishop Ackah invited Giles to become a Canon of Sefwi-Wiaso cathedral. The trip was arranged and with his wife and two friends we all set off together in the High Commission flag car for Sefwi Wiaso – about ten hours' drive from Accra. The roads became progressively worse, the forest thicker, and as we approached the town in the late afternoon we came to a ford across a small river where we were stopped by the welcome party: Bishop Ackah in full ceremonial regalia backed by four priests, the cathedral choir, a five-piece brass band, the mayor and what looked like a large part of his congregation. We got out of the car and I was formally invited to sit in a small dug-out canoe. I assured them we could ford the stream in the car, but they laughed:

'No, no, the canoe is not for the river. It is to carry you into the town.'

Six strapping young men stepped forward, ready for the task. I explained I was quite happy to walk, but this idea was not welcomed:

'No, you must take the canoe. It is our custom. The only visitor we have ever had from the British since you left Ghana was a Deputy High Commissioner. Now we have the Whole High Commissioner! You must take the canoe . . .'

I took the canoe. Respect for local custom took precedence. The canoe was hoisted shoulder high and carried through the town under a ceremonial palanquin – a vast embroidered umbrella – to the uncertain strains of old Anglican hymns played double tempo by the brass band. The people of Sefwi-Wiaso leant from their windows and variously laughed, waved, clapped and prayed. We climbed the main street and turned a corner at the top to finally catch a glimpse of the cathedral – and the whole purpose of our visit became suddenly clear. The cathedral had no roof. Fine walls, a lovely altar, but no roof. The arrival of the High Commissioner and Canon Giles was the answer to their prayers. Now there would be a roof. Improvising a diplomatic answer in response to the many speeches later that night was not easy, but at least it was Canon Giles who had to give the sermon at the three-hour roofless service the next day. When we returned to Accra, Bishop Ackah became one of my most regular correspondents. You don't get experiences like that in Putney.

Building friendships with local people in post is enormously rewarding, but not always easy. From their point of view, diplomats come and go with monotonous regularity and for many it is hardly worth putting much effort into getting to know someone you may never see again for the rest of your life. But for others, you are interesting, and many will want to meet or befriend you. If you have children at the same school, for example, you have things in common to talk about straight away. Others want to maintain their links with the embassy or your country because they do business there, have family there, or maybe just hope to get an invitation to your national day. Sometimes the most attentive are the ones you need to be most wary of, so make sure you know what their motive is. In other cases we just found we were on the same wavelength as some of the contacts we made through work, and became good friends for the duration of the posting or even longer.

In Washington, the President's aviation adviser and I found we shared a mutual interest in bluegrass music and would head to a bluegrass bar after a hard day's negotiating air services agreements. Finding areas of shared interest like music, sport, bird-watching or politics takes a friendship to a new level. I forget how many times I was asked in the US if I played golf: it was for many contacts the essential basis for both networking and friendship. They were always disappointed when I suggested tennis instead: exercise was not the purpose. In Tanzania we took up sailing for the duration of our posting, buying a small two-seater Wayfarer. It was a great antidote to office life to sail across Msasani bay to one of the small islands off the coast for a weekend picnic, or to join in the regular Saturday sailing races. We were much missed when we left, as somebody else now had to come last. Though many of the sailors were short-term expats like ourselves, others were permanent residents who knew the country inside out, and often had a better idea what was really happening than my political officer.

From each spell overseas, we kept maybe two or three friends for life. But they are precious, and lasting. If you are lucky enough to get a second posting in the same country, it is easy to pick up the contacts and the friendships again, and they will certainly last long after you've departed.

If your partner is able to work locally, that can also bring you into contact with a completely different set of people, very different from those you meet in the course of diplomatic duty. In Dar es Salaam, Miriam taught English as a foreign language at a pop-up language school in the basement disco of the Continental Hotel, a dark and sunless place during the day when they used it. She learnt more about the everyday life of Tanzanians in a week than I did in a year. In Accra, she taught at the Swiss-German school, finding out just how many Ghanaians have a German link of some kind. Her involvement with local charities also gave her a view far removed from the diplomatic circle, visiting city hostels for street children and a leper colony outside town, as well environmental projects far out in the villages. It took effort, application and time, but provided a fascinating insight into Ghanaian life and proved immensely rewarding.

Finding local work, however, is often difficult for spouses. As mentioned before, it is sometimes banned by the local government. In Tanzania, Miriam went to work while a non-diplomatic work permit was sought for her – it finally arrived a week after we left the country at the end of our posting. Elsewhere, we were dependent on kind local officials helping us find a way through the rules.

That is one reason it is often easier to make close friends within the diplomatic or expat community: fellow diplomats are very open to forming new friendships quickly; you are more likely to meet again somewhere else on the diplomatic circuit, in New York, Geneva, Brussels or their own capital; and they share and understand the way of life.

Some, like me, marry people they meet while on postings. If they are from the country where you are posted, it gives you additional insight into the local language and culture and sometimes excellent extra contacts, even if the diplomatic administration may worry that it brings conflicting loyalties or tricky business relationships. In some authoritarian countries it was also regarded as a security risk, and could be a reason why such a marriage could exclude you from a posting in the country in the future. But this is less commonly the case now. One recent British ambassador in the Middle East not only married a wife from the region but converted to Islam and took part in the Haj – the first, but probably not the last, British ambassador to do so.

Living

Most governments provide their diplomats with accommodation (furnished like the UK or unfurnished like most others) or with an allowance to rent a suitable property. This is undoubtedly a benefit, but comes with wrinkles.

Ambassadorial residences are traditionally grand affairs, but are not always comfortable to live in. Some are so resplendent that their governments publish coffee-table books about them (see *Ambassades de France: Les trésors du patri-moine diplomatique*, Fraudreau, 2003). The British government has not been so bold: a display of such opulence could send the tabloid press into paroxysms of envious outrage and the Treasury into lustful reveries of selling them off to reduce the national debt. But they remain invaluable assets. The British Ambassador's Residence in Paris, the Hotel de Charost just down the Faubourg de St Honoré from the Elysée, the Residence in Washington DC designed by Lutyens, the Villa Volkonsky in Rome and the residences in Tehran and Moscow (the latter formerly the Kharitonenko Mansion) are all architectural gems, even if they feel a little like the remnants of grander times, and are regularly in danger of crumbling (see Knox, 2011, Seldon and Collings, 2014, and Stourton, 2017). John Major, while Prime Minister and visiting the British High Commissioner's rather beautiful residence in Cape Town, was overheard to ask: 'You mean, we let you live here *and* pay you a salary as well?!'

Often, too, the magnificent public rooms in the Residence conceal family quarters that are small, pokey and tucked into some corner up the back stairs or down a dark corridor. In larger missions, the industrial-scale kitchen, designed to feed dozens for dinner and hundreds for receptions, is not somewhere easy to rustle up a quick omelette or sit around for a family dinner, nor is it particularly pleasant for two or three to sit down one end of a table for twenty in the dining room. Pressure from Residence residents has forced governments to make some adaptations, and most now have created more family-friendly quarters for the ambassadorial family in the building. The Paris Residence has a charming family flat in the former attic, well away from the public rooms below. Our Residence in Accra, however, was a concrete Modernist block from the late 1950s, purpose built by the Public Works Department after independence, which would win no architectural prizes. The terrace and garden were nice, but the indoor living spaces were more functional than homely.

The British government provide furnished accommodation overseas on the assumption that it is cheaper than paying to transport people's furniture round the world every few years. The furniture is certainly bought in bulk, with the result that wherever you are posted, you will end up in an embassy property with the same coffee tables, same sofas, same bookshelves, same beds, same bed-covers, same curtains and same knife, fork and spoon – all as chosen about 30 years earlier by some long-retired functionary in the Estates Department whose taste was for dark faux-mahogany olde English furniture. It's ghastly, and yet somehow you get used to it. Every now and again a proposal is made to buy local, but there always turns out to be some health and safety, fire-retardant requirement that scuppers the idea. To make home feel slightly more personal, many colleagues accumulated portable possessions that don't take up too much space and are permissible under the heavy baggage rules, such as rugs, family photos, paintings or sculptures, textiles to hang or spread over the awful sofa covers, even weird and wonderful cushions to cast around.

If you receive only a housing allowance, you have the challenge of finding a suitable and convenient rental property in a foreign and all-too-often expensive capital. These days in most capitals you can search online before you set foot in the place. But it is still wise to see in person before you rent, and ensure your government will cover the cost, especially if rent is required in advance. Some unlucky diplomats have ended up spending months in a hotel while a suitable property is located and made ready for habitation.

Once you have a place to live, you can start living.

As an ambassador you are a public person and it becomes hard to do anything privately. You are followed either by the press, the public or the local secret service. So you get used to living your life in the public eye. Even junior staff are representing their country, and therefore need to preserve a degree of decorum. But this does not prevent you leading a fairly normal life and seeking your recreation where you want.

The British have a reputation for setting up clubs – sporting, dramatic, dining, bird-watching, games-playing – wherever they go. Without a shadow of doubt, wherever you pitch up someone will have founded a club for something, and if no-one has done so in an area of interest to you, you can always set up your own. The Hash House Harriers, initiated in Malaya in 1938 but now almost universal, are a running and social club. They like to describe themselves as a drinking club with a running problem, but were always friendly and welcoming, so offered a good way to both exercise and socialise. Besides some form of sport, personally I found amateur dramatics a good way to let off steam outside the office, whether through Shakespeare in Brussels or pantomime in Dar es Salaam and Accra. For all their eccentricity, such clubs can be an invaluable way to preserve sanity in difficult places and tough times. When the Red Guards broke into the British Embassy in Beijing, the members of chancery were reportedly engrossed in a game of bridge – but still managed to escape.

In tough places it was also recommended to make friends with the US marines: they give the best parties, and in Dar es Salaam in the 1990s theirs was the only place you could get a decent burger.

Loving

For some reason, sex and diplomacy have had a long relationship. I don't know why. Maybe it is the constant displacement, detachment and opportunity; maybe that diplomats are just naturally charming. Who knows? But it happens.

The abduction of Helen of Troy, as we saw at the outset, was one of the first recorded 'diplomatic incidents'. Dynastic marriages and the affairs of monarchs are recorded throughout history as influencing their foreign alliances. Henry VIII's break with Rome over his divorce from Katherine of Aragon and marriage to Anne Boleyn, followed by Thomas Cromwell's attempt to consolidate a Protestant alliance for England by bringing over Anne of Cleves to be Henry VIII's fourth wife, did not end well for any of them – though Anne of Cleves at least kept her head (MacCulloch, 2018). The negotiations at the Congress of Vienna in 1815 were certainly helped along by the fact that the mistresses of both Metternich and Tsar Alexander lived in the same building, on the same floor, and both knew the other's lover surprisingly well it seems. To add to the mix, Metternich's mistress's younger sister became the lover of Talleyrand, the French negotiator. Only the British foreign secretary, Lord Castlereagh, remained aloof, accompanied as he was by his devoted wife Emily (Meyer, 2009, 60). During the Second World War, the extraordinary diplomatic and amorous activities of Pamela Churchill, later Harriman, were of such consequence that she was recently the subject of an extensive and revealing biography (Purnell, 2024): she became effectively a British secret weapon in the wartime transatlantic alliance. In my own time, some of the best information we received about the intentions of one international organisation came from a colleague whose girlfriend worked there.

Some of the most reliable and useful intelligence can come from such informal contacts rather than official intelligence channels. But this is why diplomats, young and old, will still be targeted by the 'honey trap', laid by those keen to find out more than they should. The Soviets made a speciality of it, and when I was recruited we were regularly warned by our security department to be wary of those we met who were too charming, too attentive, or too readily available. Such 'sexpionage' was once so prevalent that it became a serious subject of academic study (West, 2009; see also Turner, 2024).

There is a popular belief that the peripatetic and stressful way of life leads to a higher divorce rate among diplomats, but my own observation is that it is no greater or less than among the population as a whole. Certainly, diplomatic life can be stressful for partners and families, but in many cases this can strengthen rather than weaken relationships. When you have been cocktail-partied to exhaustion, survived death by diplomatic dinner, escaped a coup and camped out together in the back of beyond of some distant country, you have plenty to talk about in your old age. And you need someone who, once the guests have left, the staff gone and the doors are closed, you can laugh with about the absurdities of diplomatic life and the eccentricities of those you meet. Of my contemporaries, 40 years on from when we first joined, most remain firmly wedded to their original spouse, though it certainly helps if both partners understand the kind of life you're going to lead before you get hitched.

Of those who move from one humanitarian crisis to another, the isolation and stress of dealing with these situations can leave people in even more need of company during the mission, to share the troubles and find ways to forget them. The 'mission spouse' is perhaps the antithesis of the 'trailing spouse', a temporary understanding among people flung together in adversity; but both are unkind terms for relationships that often work very well for those concerned.

Dying

The British Consulate-General in Istanbul is one of the treasures of the diplomatic estate. The Pera House, in effect a palace, was built in the 1840s to house the British representative to the Sublime Porte, as the court of the Ottoman Sultan was known. It is a vast and magnificent building, surrounded by gardens and with a stunning view over the Golden Horn, a dream posting for any British diplomat. In 2003 a major renovation project was undertaken to restore it to its 19th-century glory and adapt it for 21st-century needs. The Consul-General, Roger Short, and his staff moved temporarily into the gatehouse while the work was going on.

At 11 am on 20 November 2003, an Al-Qaeda suicide bomber drove a truck loaded with explosives through the security gate of the Consulate and detonated it. The explosion was massive. The gatehouse was completely demolished, the garden wall collapsed onto the road, crushing passing cars, and a fire raged in the garden. Twenty-seven people were killed. Roger Short was one of them. I knew him slightly, an experienced and popular diplomat much admired for his knowledge and love of Turkey. His personal assistant, Lisa Hallworth, was also killed. Three years before, she had been my PA while working in the Economic Relations Department of the Foreign Office. She was only 38, charming, quiet, dedicated, modest, someone who simply loved the life of working in missions overseas. She had joined the Foreign Office for a life of travel and adventure. Being blown up by terrorists had never been on the agenda.

There is now a memorial in the FCDO to all those killed in the line of diplomatic duty. Most died at the hands of terrorists, like Britain's Ambassador to Ireland, Sir Richard Sykes, blown up by the IRA in 1979. The current count is around ten. It doesn't happen often, thank God. But the elaborate security arrangements that now make it such a slow process getting into the FCDO or a British embassy abroad – indeed any country's embassy – are not just to keep the information in, but to keep the terrorists out. US embassies are now built, and many look, like fortresses and are guarded by a contingent of marines. Diplomacy is not a risk-free occupation.

And yet we love it. And despite the places you go, the food you have to eat, the hours you work, the protocol and tedium you have to bear, diplomacy is not an unhealthy profession. The variety and activity involved kept many of us alive and well, fit and healthy. The numbers who go on long-term sick leave are generally very small.

It was not always so healthy, however. When I first went to work in Brussels in the 1980s, the all-day meetings of the Budget Committee involved sitting alongside the Italian delegation who were perpetually wreathed in a cloud of cigarette smoke, cheerfully joined by the Greek further along, and occasionally by the French delegate. I have only ever been a passive smoker myself, but this concentration of airborne nicotine was an ordeal. Along with late-night doses of Gamel Dansk, I cannot say the Budget Committee improved my health. These were the days too when drinking a bottle of wine or a few pints of beer at lunchtime was still common. I was told informally when I joined the FCO that the *average* length of time former British diplomats drew their pension was three years. It has improved since.

While I was working in Accra, we recruited the redoubtable Sue Hogwood to be the new political officer in Abidjan. Sue was an FCO survivor: apart from the occasional stint in London she had served almost continuously over a 25-year career in hardship posts, and was famed throughout the Office for her skill at baking cakes for her team wherever she went. Her 'Oh-My-God Cake', about the richest, most wonderful chocolate cake you have ever eaten, was the stuff of legend. And yet, thin as a rake, she seemed to survive on a diet of nothing but caffeine and nicotine, plus the odd glass of wine. She had survived single-handed a number of African posts, and was just the safe pair of hands we needed for an unstable place like Côte d'Ivoire. A few months after she arrived, she went down with what she told me was flu. 'Are you sure it's not malaria?' I asked her over the phone. 'I doubt it,' she said, 'and anyway, I've had it before so I'll just go to bed till it passes.' Two days later, still in bed, her driver finally persuaded her to go to the hospital. The doctor rang me to say they'd never seen such a high malaria count, but had put her on quinine and a drip and she was doing fine. The next day she died of a heart attack.

The problem was finding any relatives in the UK. We eventually tracked down a cousin, who came out for the funeral, conducted on the spot by the only Anglican priest in Abidjan. The relative asked us to bury her locally, took a few mementos and told us to give everything else to charity.

I often think of Sue, partly because I still have her hand-typed cookbook of cake recipes. Her case illustrated the point that, though your ministry may look after you pretty well, as a diplomat you have a responsibility to look after yourself wherever you are, especially if you are on your own.

Assuming you survive, however, every diplomatic career eventually comes to an end and the time arrives to come home.

10 Coming home

A former colleague who had been ambassador in a number of major posts once commented: 'You know when you've retired, Nick, because you sit in the back of the car . . . and it doesn't move.' But retirement need not be the end of the diplomatic road, unless you want it to be.

Whether employed by a government or for some other organisation, diplomacy is a career in which skill and knowledge are cumulative. As in all walks of life, some people eventually wear out, lose energy, lose interest or lose touch, or simply decide it's time for a change. Diplomacy equally needs the energy and ideas of youth. But diplomacy is a vocation as much as a career and the best diplomats, like great musicians or academics, keep getting better. The importance of experience, knowledge, networks and judgement means that someone who has been through a few crises, has lived long in a particular region and may know personally many of the political actors there can provide invaluable insights and offer well-judged solutions to otherwise intractable problems. The advice of such experts was recognised as critical in avoiding nuclear war during the Cuban missile crisis in 1962 (Cooper, 2021, 319–41). Kofi Annan was still actively involved in negotiating peace agreements when he died in 2018 at the age of 80, and Henry Kissinger continued advising and publishing on foreign policy issues into his 100th year (Kissinger, 2015 and 2024).

Nevertheless, the time may come when you want to call it a day – or your organisation decides to call it for you – or you want a change. You may become weary of the peripatetic life, the wait for promotion, or going where you're told rather than where you want. You may even cross one or two colleagues who seem more devoted to their personal promotion than to public service. When I joined the Diplomatic Service, retirement was compulsory and automatic on your 60th birthday. This has now been extended to 65 or even later, so if you're enjoying it, you can often carry on. However, a growing number of former colleagues have been leaving early to take up other career opportunities outside the diplomatic service. It can also be a mistake to go on too long: knowing the right time to step down is an essential life skill and good for others as well as yourself (as President Joe Biden found in 2024).

For the diplomat, sooner or later, there's a time to come home.

Some organisations provide 'retirement courses' on how to adjust from frenetic activity to infinite leisure. This can include useful advice on managing your

DOI: 10.4324/9781003533436-10

money, your time, and keeping healthy. One EU course included a health expert who reminded the participants that the process of ageing invariably involves a few aches and pains: 'if you wake up in the morning without any pain anywhere, it means you're dead' he announced. He also advised them to live each day as if you might die tomorrow – 'because you might' (Keenan, 2014). But you will probably have a few years left. Some are entirely happy with a quiet life of leisure, recreation, travel and family, though the last may be not so quiet if you are blessed with grandchildren. But for many it is hard not to remain interested in international affairs, and to want to be engaged in doing something about it. For others there may be a desire, or a need, to continue earning money, and find that in the right job you can earn far more for less work than you ever did in public service.

So this chapter is about what happens then: what will you do? Where will you live? How will you cope?

Skills

For a start, a life in diplomacy gives you some very transferable skills that can be a real asset in the diplomatic afterlife. All have value, but the ability to build a consensus and negotiate acceptable outcomes, to establish networks of contacts and know how to use them, to manage diverse teams, and to assess geopolitical risk are all particularly attractive or marketable to other organisations or employers.

It is a sad fact of life that many people don't seem to regard reaching agreement as a priority. Some just like to have an argument; some want to win at all costs; and some simply want to make their case and have their say, without regard to any eventual outcome. Understanding and, where necessary, accommodating the other side's point of view is an essential part of diplomacy but, as we saw earlier, can be a positive hindrance in commercial deal-making. Nevertheless, as a member of boards and councils, in chairing meetings and inquiries, and in managing disagreements in almost any sphere, diplomatic skills are a tremendous asset and can be widely deployed. The ability to listen, understand and navigate different points of view, as well as identify common objectives, build common ground, diffuse disagreements, avoid blind alleys and guide the discussion in a more fruitful direction even in the absence of agreement, are all skills that you can bring and which will be (or at least ought to be) appreciated by others.

The instinct to network, to build connections and use contacts to move things forward is another skill you can bring to almost any new role. You will start the afterlife with an enviable range of international and government contacts, but you already know how quickly they decay unless you maintain them actively. So you need to find ways to keep them fresh if you want to use them. Attending conferences, participating in think tank discussions, seeing former contacts when they pass through town, looking up old friends and contacts when you travel are all useful ways to maintain connections and sustain the value of your network if you are looking to capitalise on it. If you're not, no need to bother – unless you simply want to keep in touch as friends.

Not all diplomats are good managers. In fact (without naming names), there have been some spectacularly bad ones. But the good ones have an innate ability to get the best from teams that are extremely diverse in terms of their backgrounds, ideas and abilities. If you thrive on this kind of work, you will be in high demand. Many diplomats I know, however, leave the trials and tribulations of everyday management behind with a sigh of relief, however good they have been at it – it is one of the unalloyed pleasures of leaving a senior management post that you no longer have to complete the annual appraisals, approve the budgets or fill in the forms that seems to be the lot of even the most senior manager in public service; and no longer have those difficult conversations with colleagues who are not coming up to scratch. Even so, the knowledge of how to manage well can make it a painful and frustrating experience working in an organisation that is badly managed. Sometimes you have to bite your tongue, sometimes make it better, sometimes just leave.

Geopolitical risk assessment is normally second nature to any diplomat, but you need to be able to adapt how to present it for new and different audiences. Ministers and fellow diplomats share a set of assumptions and an objective for the outcome that dictates how you present the risks and opportunities of world events and crises as they emerge. Businesses, which are the main market for this kind if analysis and are increasingly willing to pay for it given the serious financial consequences of miscalculated risk, have different interests and different perspective that you need to adjust to.

The same applies to the media, which is overwhelmingly focussed on the immediate news story: what governments should do now and what happens next. They work on very tight deadlines – 24 hours' notice is generous, and if you want to get yourself on air, on social networks or in the papers you need to get your views out swiftly and monitor emails, texts and messages hourly not to miss the requests for comment or the opportunity to put your point. Think tanks usually have a longer term perspective, and are willing to take longer pieces with a wider analysis of the issues, but even they often have an audience that wants instant and concise assessments.

Jobs

With these skills, a wide range of jobs are open to a former diplomat, if you want to work. But unless you have been a very prominent ambassador, the job offers tend not come rushing in unbidden. You need to work at it, to create your own opportunities. You may notice that as retirement looms, some senior colleagues devote more attention than usual to visiting business leaders, academic institutions building local partnerships, or senior UN officials. You need to be conscious that most businesses, like governments and international organisations, have a commitment to diversify their senior management and ensure more equal and diverse representation. The days of white male dominance are gone, which may of course work to your advantage or disadvantage, depending. You may need to calibrate your expectations, or look in new areas for future roles. One recruiter despaired to me of the surfeit of middle-aged white males he had on his books who all expected to walk into plum jobs but for whom there were no openings, and how desperately short he was of black, female and non-western candidates for whom his clients were clamouring. Either way, there is no harm familiarising yourself with the many recruitment agencies that now operate in the field and who are increasingly used by companies and charities alike, even if your best chance of a job may still come through personal friends or contacts rather than through formal applications and processes. Putting feelers out in all directions is essential, as is knowing where you have realistic chances. Watch out for and follow up on jobs advertised: even for the most senior, talented and experienced applicants, only one in ten opportunities may end up in a potential job offer.

For a very few, there may be jobs in international organisations. This, however, requires the right combination of skills and experience, the right regional expertise, the right nationality, strong political backing from your government, and plenty of good luck. So don't bank on it.

Working with the private sector offers more opportunities. Major international companies often recruit former diplomats to support or run their government affairs offices. But it is increasingly common for companies to hire in expertise from 'strategic advisory' services when they need it to deal with particular countries or specific issues. Providing geo-strategic analysis and political advice has become a fast-growing industry in recent years. Firms that specialise in lobbying the US Administration and Congress have always been a feature of political life in Washington DC, but the business has now spread worldwide. As well as permanent employees, such firms often have an extensive panel of expert advisers who are brought in (and only paid) when their expertise is required for a specific piece of business. As with the media, there can be a symbiotic relationship between these strategic advisers and serving diplomats: they may have inside political contacts that the diplomats don't, but the diplomats have information that the others need. So, as long as you handle with care and do suitable due diligence (some of the advisory firms serve particular political or national interests), cultivating a relationship with these companies over the years can reap rewards when you are eventually thrown onto the free market.

The other area where there is wide range of opportunities is in the not-for-profit 'third sector': charities, artistic and cultural organisations, academic institutions, think tanks and non-governmental organisations of every stripe. They are less lucrative, and often your skills will be sought *pro bono*, for no financial return at all; but they can be even more rewarding in other ways. Your experience of dealing with governments, donors and development organisations can make an invaluable contribution to fund-raising, and experience of dealing with the media can also help an organisation tell its story and position itself publicly in a way that raises its profile. Not all want a high public profile, and those that work in the peace-building and conciliation business often deliberately try to avoid it in order to build trust and relationships with groups who may be anathema to governments or business. So for them, your experience of working behind the scenes, out of the public eye, and building trusted relationships with difficult people can be equally valuable. Given their good intentions, it is also surprising how scarce good management skills can be in the non-governmental sector. Perhaps because they are working for a cause, people assume everyone will get on. Often that solidarity and cooperation does exist; but human nature is such that even here (and in some cases especially here) problems will arise, as in any workforce, and knowing how to motivate and manage the team and bringing some professional management skills to an organisation can be a major contribution to its success.

After leaving the FCO in 2018, I worked for six years as director of a not-for-profit, the Royal African Society. It was a small but many-splendoured organisation, dedicated to promoting Africa in the UK and Africans in the world. It had a tiny budget and a small but diverse and dedicated team. Together we made a difference, running a top-rated academic journal for African studies (*African Affairs*), and an African news website (*African Arguments*) that promoted the work of African journalists who often enough could not get published in their own country; we supported the British All-Party Parliamentary Group for Africa, preparing their reports; organised a regular events programme for African speakers, politicians, businessmen, journalists and academics, and ran two biennial festivals: *Africa Writes* promoting the latest and best writing out of Africa and its diaspora, and *Film Africa* which did the same for African film-making. It was a wonderful and inspiring place to work, with great colleagues and intense debates, not least during the Black Lives Matter movement when 'decolonising' institutions and businesses rose to the top of the agenda. But it became increasingly full time, up to 50 or 60 hours a week, which ruled out other things I wanted to do. Having put it on a sound footing, after six years it was time to move from fund-raising and event organising to focus on teaching and writing.

Academia can offer a more tranquil resting place, though only in the US or Oxbridge are you likely to find it well-remunerated. The much sought-after opportunity to head a college in Oxford or Cambridge comes to a very favoured few, but is great if you can get it. Others have been recruited as Chancellors or Presidents for universities which, though primarily honorific and representational roles, can provide the chance to engage with the student body, and bring chairmanship skills to sometimes rather anarchic management cultures. Britain's most prominent foreign policy think tanks – Chatham House, the International Institute for Strategic Studies, the Royal United Services Institute and others – also have a roster of honorary advisors that enable many former diplomats to keep abreast of international events and contribute actively to policy discussions.

Elsewhere, opportunities vary greatly from country to country. In the US, there is a regular flow of diplomats into universities and think tanks, partly as a result of the stronger tradition of interchange between academia and government, and partly because of the more generous funding of institutes dealing with government and global affairs. Other countries in Europe, Asia and Africa, are also expanding the role of higher education institutions and free-standing institutes to contribute to the training of officials and discussion and research into global affairs. A number of African diplomats I know have set up think tanks on their retirement (sometimes with donor funding) which help develop foreign policy thinking and debate on the continent. Gulf countries have also actively promoted foreign policy institutes to support the work of their foreign ministries, and India is beginning to expand its intellectual investment in international affairs. Chinese think tanks, often linked to the Communist Party, play an important role in having licence to engage with foreigners and explore new areas of thinking that are forbidden to the foreign ministry itself. But they remain a shop closed to outsiders.

The chance to work with other experts in a particular field and write freely in public, after years of the self-restraint imposed by government employment, is often a relief: at last you can say and publish what you like, giving your thoughts and opinions free-rein in public. As we've seen, ideas matter in public policy debates, and getting new ideas out into the intellectual and international bloodstream is a contribution that former diplomats are particularly well-equipped to make.

Whatever employment you may find, paid or unpaid, your skills and experience will be a lasting asset.

Home

When you have led such a peripatetic international life, and may have a partner from another country, it is not always a simple question where you call home. It is good to have one – for you, your family and your retirement. But where it should be is something to think about in advance.

For most, it means returning to your home country and living somewhere you have had for a while, or have found specifically for the later years of life – maybe near children, maybe out in the country, wherever. Some prefer to live overseas, perhaps somewhere sunnier, warmer, more beautiful, where they feel at home and can enjoy a better quality of life. Others, particularly those who have worked most of their lives in international institutions, find they have spent so long living in New York, Geneva, Washington or Brussels that they are more at home there than in their country of origin, and prefer to settle where they live, especially if that is where their children remain. Home is ultimately where you make it.

After our last posting as a family in Ghana, when I moved to a new job in the EEAS in Brussels, we agreed it best for our children to have their secondary education in the UK, and Miriam was also keen to have the chance to build a more solid teaching career for the last 15 years of her working life. So the family moved back to our home in Putney, the children went to local schools, and Miriam found a job teaching German and Italian at a new school nearby in Kew. I commuted to and from Brussels every weekend, when not travelling to Africa or elsewhere for work. It was not ideal, but the Foreign Office had little of interest to offer, and the role of Managing Director for Africa in the EEAS was new, stimulating, engaging, and sufficiently well-paid to support us all. In the end we kept up this way of life for seven years, as I moved in 2015 from the Africa job to be the EEAS's Managing Director for Middle East. In 2017, however, my wife unexpectedly developed a heart condition. An operation revealed that the problem was more serious than we thought, being caused not by a faulty valve but by amyloidosis, an incurable condition. So at the end of October that year I resigned, packed all my Brussels belongings into a car and drove home.

My son was in his last year at school, my daughter away at university, and my work required only a cycle ride to Bloomsbury where the Royal African Society had its modest offices at the back of SOAS. So we lived together as a family once more while my wife carried on her work and underwent chemotherapy treatment. The chemo helped for a while, but only a while. In July 2018, after watching our daughter successfully graduate from university and our son from school, she passed away.

Any bereavement is tough. But without those last nine months together as a family, the re-adjustment to single life would have been even more difficult. It brought home to me that the cost of working apart is often something you don't realise until afterwards. Despite the conveniences of modern technology, enabling constant communication by video as well as text and voice, relationships can drift, things go unsaid, people can change, and you are less able to deal with the unexpected. So be aware in your diplomatic life of the need to stay connected to those you love, prioritise being with them for important moments, and hope that when the work is done, you will have the chance to look back together on a life well-lived, on adventures, challenges and travel undertaken side-by-side, arm-in-arm, hand-in-hand. I have a loft (and computer) full of photographs from around the world to look back on, a house full of souvenirs, paintings, sculptures, furniture, each with its story from our life and travels together. I can see them, remember and reflect, but alone.

Future

You never know what will happen next. I have been lucky as well as unlucky – and met later another single diplomat with whom to share life, work and the future. So never give up hope.

Diplomacy is not for the faint-hearted. It is a worthy calling, and an essential one. Without it none of us would be able to live in peace. And for the diplomat it provides opportunities to visit places, to meet people and to influence the course of world affairs that no other career can do. Not every diplomat brokers a peace deal or stops a war. But all of them, great and small, make a difference.

Looking back, I ask myself what difference I have made? I have no glorious treaty to triumph (except perhaps a small part in the Maastricht Treaty), no war stopped (though we successfully prevented the Syrian war spreading to neighbouring countries in 2015), no individual lives saved (though the G8 Summit initiatives in 1998 on malaria and debt brought a significant reduction in mortality over the years, and many of the millions of refugees from Syria and Iraq were sheltered and fed from the funds raised at the conferences we organised). It is the lot of most diplomats to play a small part in big events. But that is not insignificant. Every diplomat must play a constructive part for the world to move forward more peacefully rather than less.

There will always be people for whom power, status and personal gain are more important than peace, prosperity and the common good. Sadly, that is human nature. Freedom, democracy, human rights and decent livelihoods wither and are destroyed without a constant effort to defend them, internationally as well as nationally. Having come close to global destruction in the middle of the 20th century, our predecessors constructed a multilateral system to try and contain and address those destructive urges and reduce the poverty that drove them. It worked, for a while. My career has been, in almost every job in different ways, a contribution to making that system work. It was a constant struggle: conflicts continued, but not ones that devastated the whole world, and the world's population grew both more numerous and richer, if unequally so. The system is now fraying, and the risks of climatic and political destruction are growing. The task for the next generation, for anyone reading this book, is to manage the tensions in international relations in new ways, ways that persuade leaders, and leaders to persuade people, that there is more to be gained from the peaceful rather than violent settlement of disputes.

If I draw a lesson from the past 40 years, it is that diplomats must not neglect domestic politics. As we understand how the world works, it is essential to explain to our fellow citizens that to turn inwards, to shut up the gates and hope that the threats simply go away, will not solve the problems or make them vanish. The world will come to your gates and break them down if you simply ignore the problems. Antagonists can too easily trap themselves, politically and mentally, into believing that only the destruction of the other will solve their problem, as we have seen so tragically in the Middle East in recent years. It never does. The purpose of this book is to prevent that kind of zero-sum calculation and give the next generation the tools to engage with the world and solve these ever-changing but eternally familiar problems.

If humanity still exists a few hundred years hence, so too will diplomats. In fact it may still exist *because* of its diplomats, helping persuade the world to tackle climate change more urgently and head off the self-destructive competition that could so easily wreak havoc.

At the time of going to press, international relations are looking more uncertain than at any time since the 1930s – a decade that did not end well. If international structures weaken, so will their ability to manage conflicts and find peaceful settlements for them. This is already apparent in countries where other pressures, from population growth and climate change to ideological or ethnic differences, are making it harder for governments to meet the needs and aspirations of their people. Resolving such conflicts, or at least preventing them spreading, will increasingly depend on international cooperation within an unstable 'balance of power', where every player is constantly trying to tilt the balance in their own favour. This will create more, and more challenging work for the world's diplomats. So, paradoxically, as the prospects for the world darken, the opportunities for diplomats multiply. We need more of them, and better trained in the ways of diplomacy, to carry forward the labour of Sisyphus and keep pushing the boulder up the hill towards the summit.

I hope this book has contributed to that effort.

Bibliography

Aggestam, Karin (2012), *Ways Out of War: Peacemakers in the Middle East and Balkans* (London, Macmillan)

Amoako, K.Y. (2020), *Know the Beginning Well: An inside Journey through Five Decades of Development* (Trenton, Africa World Press)

Annan, Kofi (2012), *Interventions: A Life in War and Peace* (London, Allen Lane)

Ashcroft, Sean (2024), 'Rio Tinto Brings Simandou Guinea Iron Ore Saga to End', *Mining Digital*, 22 July 2024, https://miningdigital.com/operations/rio-tinto-brings-simandou-guinea-iron-ore-saga-to-end (accessed 5 July 2024)

Ashton, Catherine (2023), *And Then What: Inside Stories of 21st-Century Diplomacy* (London, Elliott and Thompson)

Axworthy, Michael (2013), *Revolutionary Iran: A History of the Islamic Republic* (London, Penguin)

Badawi, Zeinab (2024), *An African History of Africa: From the Dawn of Humanity to Independence* (London, Penguin Random House)

Bagehot, Walter (1867), *The English Constitution* (London, Chapman & Hall)

Bailey, F.G. (1969), *Stratagems and Spoils: A Social Anthropology of Politics* (Oxford, Blackwell)

Bajoghli, Narges and others (2024), *How Sanctions Work: Iran and the Impact of Economic Warfare* (Redwood City, CA, Stanford University Press)

Bayly, Christopher (2004), *The Birth of the Modern World, 1780–1914* (Oxford, Blackwell)

BBC World, 'Jamal Kashoggi: All You Need to Know about Saudi Journalist's Death', BBC, 24 Feb 2021, https://www.bbc.co.uk/news/world-europe-45812399 (accessed 5 July 2024)

Bennett, Anne (2020), *Dining with Diplomats, Praying with Gunmen: Experience of International Conciliation for a New Generation of Peacemakers* (London, Quaker Books)

Berridge, G.R. (2015), *Diplomacy: Theory and Practice* (5th ed.; Basingstoke, Palgrave Macmillan)

Bjola, Corneliu and Manor, Ilan, eds. (2024), *The Oxford Handbook of Digital Diplomacy* (Oxford, Oxford University Press)

Blanning, Tim (2007), *The Pursuit of Glory: Europe 1648–1815* (London, Penguin)

Bonnafont, Jérôme (2022), *Diplomate: Pour Quoi Faire?* (Paris, Odile Jacob)

Boot, Max (2024), *Reagan: His Life and Legend* (New York, Liveright Publishing)

Bregman, Ahron (2014), *Cursed Victory: A History of Israel and the Occupied Territories* (London, Allen Lane/Penguin)

Brenton, Anthony (1994), *The Greening of Machiavelli: The Evolution of International Environmental Politics* (London, Routledge)

Bristow, Laurie (2024), *Kabul: Final Call: The Inside Story of the Withdrawal from Afghanistan, August 2021* (London, Whittles Publishing)

Brown, David (2010), *Palmerston: A Biography* (New Haven and London, Yale University Press)

Brown, Will (2024a), 'Deserted: Europe's Dilemma in the Sahel', European Council on Foreign Relations, 24 July 2024, https://ecfr.eu/article/deserted-europes-dilemma-in-the-sahel/ (accessed 24 Oct. 2024)

Brown, Will (2024b), 'The Sweating Bear: Why Russia's Influence in the Sahel is under Threat', European Council on Foreign Relations, 9 October 2024, https://ecfr.eu/article/the-sweating-bear-why-russias-influence-in-africa-is-under-threat/ (accessed 24 Oct. 2024)

Brownlie, Ian (1998), *Principles of Public International Law* (5th ed.; Oxford, Oxford University Press)

Brownlie, Ian (2009), *The Peaceful Settlement of International Disputes* (Oxford, Oxford University Press)

Bulkeley, Harriet and Newell, Peter (2023), *Governing Climate Change* (3rd ed.; Abingdon, Routledge)

Bull, Hedley (1977), *The Anarchical Society* (London, Macmillan)

Bunde, Tobias and Franke, Benedikt, eds. (2022), *The Art of Diplomacy: 75+ Views behind the Scenes of World Politics* (Berlin, Econ)

Burns, William J. (2019), *The Back Channel: American Diplomacy in a Disordered World* (London, Hurst)

Buzan, Barry and Lawson, George (2015), *The Global Transformation: History, Modernity and the Making of International Relations* (Cambridge, Cambridge University Press)

Calvocoressi, Peter (1982), *World Politics since 1945* (4th ed.; Harlow, Longman)

Cambridge Dictionary (2024), Cambridge University Press, https://dictionary.cambridge.org/dictionary/english/diplomat (accessed 1 July 2024)

Carter, James (2021), 'Burning the British Mission in Beijing', The China Project, 21 April 2021, https://thechinaproject.com/2021/08/18/burning-the-british-mission-in-beijing/ (accessed 4 Oct. 2024)

Chesterman, Simon (2007), *Secretary or General: The UN Secretary-General in World Politics* (Cambridge, Cambridge University Press)

Chollet, Derek (2013), *The Road to the Dayton Accords: A Study in American Statecraft* (London, Macmillan)

Clark, Alan (1993), *Diaries* (London, Weidenfeld and Nicolson)

Clarke, Peter (2004), *Hope and Glory: Britain 1900–2000* (2nd ed.; London, Penguin)

Cohen, Raymond and Westbrook, Raymond, eds. (2002), *Amarna Diplomacy: The Beginnings of International Relations* (Baltimore, John Hopkins University Press)

Cooper, Andrew (2008), *Celebrity Diplomacy* (New York, Routledge)

Cooper, Andrew, Heine, Jorge and Thakur, Ramesh, eds. (2013), *The Oxford Handbook of Modern Diplomacy* (Oxford, Oxford University Press)

Cooper, Pete (2024), 'Harry Dunn: Justice for Family Three Years after Crash Death', BBC, 21 March 2024, https://www.bbc.co.uk/news/uk-england-northamptonshire-63328171 (accessed 15 Oct. 2024)

Cooper, Robert (2003), *The Breaking of Nations: Order and Chaos in the Twenty-first Century* (London, Atlantic Books)

Cooper, Robert (2021), *The Ambassadors: Thinking about Diplomacy from Machiavelli to Modern Times* (London, Weidenfeld & Nicolson)

Cormac, Rory (2021), *Disrupt and Deny: Spies, Special Forces and the Secret Pursuit of British Foreign Policy* (Oxford, Oxford University Press)

Crawford, Neta and Klotz, Audie, eds. (1999), *How Sanctions Work: Lessons from South Africa* (London, Macmillan)

Croxton, Derek (2013), *Westphalia: The Last Christian Peace* (London, Macmillan)

Cull, Nicholas J. (2019), *Public Diplomacy: Foundations for Global Engagement in the Digital Age* (Cambridge, Polity Press)

Dercon, Stefan (2022), *Gambling on Development: Why Some Countries Win and Others Lose* (London, Hurst)

Doyle, Leonard (2008), 'Obama Is 'Uninspiring' Says British Ambassador to America', *The Independent*, 3 Oct. 2008, https://www.independent.co.uk/news/world/americas/obama-is-uninspiring-says-british-ambassador-to-america-949853.html (accessed 22 March 2025)

Durrell, Lawrence (1957), *Esprit de Corps: Sketches from Diplomatic Life* (London, Faber & Faber)

Edwards, Ruth Dudley (1994), *True Brits: Inside the Foreign Office* (London, BBC)

Embassy Pages (2024), https://www.embassypages.com/ (accessed 3 July 2024)

Engelke, Matthew (2017), *Think like an Anthropologist* (London, Pelican Books)

Feltham, R.G. (1982), *Diplomatic Handbook* (4th ed; Harlow, Longman)

Ferrero-Rocher (2007), advertisement, YouTube, 25 May 2007. https://www.google.com/search?q=youtube+ferrero+rocher+diplomat+ad (accessed 3 July 2024)

Fletcher, Tom (2016), *Naked Diplomacy: Power and Statecraft in the Digital Age* (London, Collins)

FCDO (Foreign, Commonwealth and Development Office) (2023), *Annual Report and Accounts for 2022–2023*, HMSO, 17 July 2023, https://www.gov.uk/government/publications/fcdo-annual-report-and-accounts-2022-to-2023 (accessed 14 Oct. 2024)

FCO (Foreign and Commonwealth Office) (2020), *Annual Report and Accounts for 2019–2020*, HC553, HMSO, 16 July 2020, https://www.gov.uk/government/publications/foreign-and-commonwealth-office-annual-report-and-accounts-2019-to-2020 (accessed 14 Oct. 2024)

Frankopan, Peter (2015), *The Silk Roads: A New History of the World* (London, Bloomsbury)

Fraudreau, Martin (2003), *Ambassades de France: Les trésors du patrimoine diplomatique* (Paris, Éditions Perrin)

Gallagher, John (1982), *The Decline, Rise and Fall of the British Empire* (Cambridge, Cambridge University Press)

Geldenhuys, Deon (2009), *Contested States in World Politics* (Basingstoke, Palgrave Macmillan)

Ghattas, Kim (2020), *Black Wave: Saudi Arabia, Iran and the Rivalry that Unravelled the Middle East* (London, Headline)

Graham, Thomas (2016), 'Paul Nitze and a Walk in the Woods: A Failed Attempt at Arms Control', Association for Diplomatic Studies and Training, https://adst.org/2016/03/paul-nitze-and-a-walk-in-the-woods-a-failed-attempt-at-arms-control/ (accessed 2 July 2024)

Greene, Graham (1973), *The Honorary Consul* (London, Bodley Head)

Greenstock, Jeremy (2016), *Iraq: The Cost of War* (London, Heinemann)

Hall Hall, Alexandra (2021), 'Should I Stay or Should I Go? The Dilemma of a Conflicted Civil Servant', *Texas National Security Review*, 4:4, pp. 91–114

Hamilton, Keith and Langhorn, Richard (2011), *The Practice of Diplomacy: Its Evolution, History and Administration* (2nd ed.; London, Routledge)

Hannay, David (2013), *Britain's Quest for a Role: A Diplomatic Memoir from Europe to the UN* (London, I.B. Taurus)

Harding, Luke (2002), 'Tea and MBEs for Two Kabul Heroes who Kept the Flag Flying for Britain', *The Guardian*, 28 August 2002, https://www.theguardian.com/world/2002/aug/28/afghanistan.lukeharding (accessed 14 Oct. 2024)

Harding, Rebecca and Landsman, David (2023), *Sanctions and Patient Diplomacy: Having it all or just a Diversion?* (London, British Foreign Policy Group).

Harrison, Thomas, ed. (2009), *Empires of the Ancient World* (London, Thames and Hudson)

Henderson, Nicholas (1984), *The Private Office* (London, Weidenfeld and Nicolson)

Henderson, Nicholas (1994), *Mandarin: The Diaries of Nicholas Henderson* (London, Weidenfeld and Nicolson)

Herodotus (1954), *The Histories*, trans. A. de Selincourt (Harmondsworth, Penguin)

Hinsley, F.H. (1963), *Power and the Pursuit of Peace: Theory and Practice in the History of Relations between States* (Cambridge, Cambridge University Press)

Hopkirk, Peter (1992), *The Great Game: On Secret Service in High Asia* (London, John Murray)

International Rescue Committee (2021), 'Counterterrorism and Humanitarian Impartiality', September 2021, New York, https://www.rescue.org/sites/default/files/document/6284/counterterrorismandhumanitarianimpartiality.pdf (accessed 6 Nov. 2024)

James, Obi (2022), *Let Go Leadership: How inclusive leaders Share Power to Drive High Performance* (London, Rethink)

James, William D. (2024), *British Grand Strategy in the Age of American Hegemony* (Oxford, Oxford University Press)

Jenkins, Simon and Sloman, Anne (1985), *With Respect, Ambassador* (London, BBC)

Jönsson, Christer and Hall, Martin (2005), *Essence of Diplomacy* (Basingstoke, Palgrave Macmillan)

Keenan, Brigid (2005), *Diplomatic Baggage: The Adventures of a Trailing Spouse* (London, John Murray)

Keenan, Brigid (2014), *Packing Up: Further Adventures of a Trailing Spouse* (London, Bloomsbury)

Kissinger, Henry (1994), *Diplomacy* (London, Simon & Shuster)

Kissinger, Henry (2015), *World Order: Reflections on the Character of Nations and the Course of History* (London, Penguin)

Kissinger, Henry (2024), *Leadership: Six Studies in World Strategy* (London, Penguin)

Knox, Tim (2011), *The British Ambassador's Residence in Paris* (Paris, Flammarion)

Krasner, Stephen D. (1988), 'Sovereignty: An institutional Perspective', *Comparative Political Studies*, 21:1

Kyle, Keith (2011), *Suez: Britain's End of Empire in the Middle East* (London, I.B. Tauris)

Landale, James (2022), 'Nazanin Zaghari-Ratcliffe: Why Has She Been Released Now?', BBC, 17 March 2022, https://www.bbc.co.uk/news/uk-60768437 (accessed 10 Oct. 2024)

Larson, Erik (2011), *In the Garden of Beasts: Love and Terror in Hitler's Berlin* (New York, Crown)

Le Carré, John (2001), *The Constant Gardener* (London, Hodder & Stoughton)

Lichtheim, George (1964), 'The Second Oldest Profession', *New York Review of Books*, 19 March 1964, https://www.nybooks.com/articles/1964/03/19/the-second-oldest-profession/ (accessed 24 Oct. 2024)

Lowcock, Mark, and Dissanayake, Ranil (2024), *The Rise and Fall of the Department for International Development* (London, Center for Global Development)

MacCulloch, Diarmaid (2018), *Thomas Cromwell* (London, Allen Lane/Penguin)

MacDonald, Alistair (2018), 'Soft Power Superpowers', London, British Council, Nov. 2018, https://www.britishcouncil.org/research-insight/soft-power-superpowers (accessed 14 Oct. 2024)

Mackay, Lauren (2015), *Inside the Tudor Court: Henry VIII and his Six Wives through the Eyes of the Spanish Ambassador* (Stroud, Amberley)

MacMillan, Margaret (2001), *The Peacemakers: Six Months that Changed the World* (London, John Murray)

Malloch-Brown, Mark (2011), *The Unfinished Global Revolution: The Limits of Nations and the Pursuit of New Politics* (London, Allen Lane)

Marks, Olivia (2021), 'Tact and Tactics: Meet the Leading Women Diplomats Representing Britain Abroad', *British Vogue*, June 2021 (London), https://www.vogue.co.uk/arts-and-lifestyle/article/female-diplomats (accessed 17 March 2025)

Marshall, Peter (1997), *Positive Diplomacy* (Basingstoke, Macmillan)

McDonald, Simon (2022), *Leadership: Lessons from a Life in Diplomacy* (London, Haus)

Melzer, Nils (2023), *The Trial of Julian Assange: A Tale of Persecution* (London, Verso)

Meyer, Christopher (2005), *DC Confidential* (London, Weidenfeld and Nicolson)

Meyer, Christopher (2009), *Getting our Way: 500 Years of Adventure and Intrigue: The Inside Story of British Diplomacy* (London, Weidenfeld and Nicolson)

Migration Watch UK (2016), 'The British in Europe – and Vice-versa', Briefing Paper 354, 23 March 2016, https://www.migrationwatchuk.org/briefing-paper/354 (accessed 14 Oct. 2024)

Mills, Greg (2021), *Expensive Poverty: Why Aid Fails and How It Can Work* (Johannesburg, Pan MacMillan)

Moore, Christopher (2014), *The Mediation Process: Practical Strategies for Resolving Conflict* (4th ed.; New York, Wiley)

Moorhouse, Geoffrey (1977), *The Diplomats: The Foreign Office Today* (London, Cape)

Moyo, Dambisa (2009), *Dead Aid: How Aid Makes Things Worse and How There Is Another Way for Africa* (London, Penguin)

Muller, Benito and Gomez-Echeverri, Luis (2024), 'Good COP? Bad COP? Time to Reform COP!', Oxford Climate Policy Blog, 10 Feb. 2024, https://blog.oxfordclimatepolicy.org/author/benito/ (accessed 14 Oct. 2024)

NAO (National Audit Office) (2024), *Progress with the Merger of the FCO and DFID*, London, 25 March 2024, https://www.nao.org.uk/reports/progress-with-the-merger-of-the-fco-and-dfid/ (accessed 10 Oct. 2024)

Neumann, Iver B. (2012), *At Home with the Diplomats: Inside a European Foreign Ministry* (Oxford, Oxford University Press)

Niblett, Robin (2024), *The New Cold War: How the Contest between the US and China will Shape our Century* (London, Atlantic Books)

Nicolson, Harold (1939), *Diplomacy* (London, Thornton Butterworth)

Nicolson, Harold (1961), 'Diplomacy Then and Now,' *Foreign Affairs*, 40:1 (October 1961), pp. 39–49.

Nye, Joseph S. (1990), 'Soft Power', *Foreign Policy*, no. 80, pp.153–71

Nye, Joseph S. (2005), *Soft Power: The Means to Success in World Politics* (New York, Public Affairs)

Otte, T.G. (2001), 'Nicolson,' in G.R. Berridge, M. Keens-Soper and T.G. Otte, *Diplomatic Theory from Machiavelli to Kissinger* (Basingstoke, Palgrave)

Parris, Matthew and Bryson, Andrew (2012), *The Spanish Ambassador's Suitcase: Stories from the Diplomatic Bag* (London, Viking)

Patten, Chris (2005), *Not Quite the Diplomat: Home Truths about World Affairs* (London, Allen Lane)

Pepys, Samuel (1995), *The Diary of Samuel Pepys*, vol. 2: *1661* (London, Harper Collins)

Perlo-Freeman, Samuel (2017), 'The Al Yamamah Arms Deal', World Peace Foundation, Tufts University, https://sites.tufts.edu/corruptarmsdeals/the-al-yamamah-arms-deals/ (accessed 10 Oct. 2024)

Pew Research Center (2024), 'Global Attitudes and Trends', https://www.pewresearch.org/expertise/international-attitudes/ (accessed 8 Oct. 2024)

Peyrefitte, Alain (2013), *The Immobile Empire* (New York, Knopf Doubleday)

Phillips, Christopher (2020), *The Battle for Syria: International Rivalry in the New Middle East* (2nd ed.; New Haven, Yale University Press)

Powell, Jonathan (2008), *Great Hatred, Little Room: Making Peace in Northern Ireland* (London, Bodley Head)

Powell, Jonathan (2015), *Terrorists at the Table: Why Negotiating is the Only Way to Peace* (London, St Martin's Press)

Purnell, Sonia (2024), *Kingmaker: Pamela Churchill Harriman's Astonishing Life of Seduction, Intrigue and Power* (London, Virago)

Quote Investigator (2018), https://quoteinvestigator.com/2018/04/03/diplomat/ (accessed 5 Oct. 2024)

Radford, Antoinette, and McGarvey, Emily (2023), 'Sudan Violence: UK Diplomats Evacuated from Khartoum', BBC News report, 24 April 2023, https://www.bbc.co.uk/news/uk-65367019 (accessed 6 Nov. 2024)

Reus-Smit, Christian and Snidal, Duncan, eds. (2008), *The Oxford Handbook of International Relations* (Oxford, Oxford University Press)

Ricketts, Peter (2021), *Hard Choices: What Britain Does Next* (London, Atlantic Books)

Roberts, Ivor, ed. (2017), *Satow's Diplomatic Practice* (7th ed.; Oxford, Oxford University Press)

Rolland-Piegue, Etienne (2018), 'Jokes about the Second Oldest Profession', LinkedIn, 18 November 2018, https://www.linkedin.com/pulse/jokes-second-oldest-profession-etienne-rolland-piegue-1e/ (accessed 5 Oct. 2024)

Ross, Carne (2017), *Independent Diplomat: Despatches from an Unaccountable Elite* (2nd ed.; London, Hurst)

Satow, Ernest (1917), *A Guide to Diplomatic Practice* (Cambridge, Cambridge University Press)

Schama, Simon (2001), *A History of Britain*, vol. 2: *1603–1776* (London, BBC)

Seib, Philip (2016), *The Future of #Diplomacy* (Cambridge, Polity Press)

Seldon, Anthony, and Collings, Daniel (2014), *The Architecture of Diplomacy: The British Ambassador's Residence in Washington* (Paris, Flamarrion)

Smith, Lisa (2020), 'Where Do British Expats Live?, iExpats.com, 26 May 2020, https://iexpats.com/where-do-british-expats-live/#h-the-25-most-popular-countries-for-brits-abroad (accessed 5 Oct. 2024)

Sparrow, Andrew (2019), 'What Kim Darroch Is Reported to Have Said about Trump – and What It Means', *The Guardian*, 7 July 2019, https://www.theguardian.com/politics/2019/jul/07/what-kim-darroch-is-reported-to-have-said-about-trump (accessed 22 March 2025)

Stearns, M. (1996), *Talking to Strangers: Improving American Diplomacy at Home and Abroad* (Princeton NJ, Princeton University Press)

Stewart, Rory (2023), *Politics on the Edge: A Memoir from Within* (London, Cape)

Stourton, James (2017), *British Embassies, Their Diplomatic and Architectural History* (London, Frances Lincoln, Quarto)

Taylor, A.J.P. (1954), *The Struggle for Mastery in Europe, 1848–1918* (Oxford, Clarendon Press)

The Herald (1991), 'Game Set and Match Says Prime Minister. Major Masterstroke Clinches an EC Eeal,' 11 Dec. 1991, https://www.heraldscotland.com/news/12651951.game-set-and-match-to-britain-says-prime-minister-major-master-stroke-clinches-an-ec-deal/ (accessed 4 Dec. 2024)

Thucydides (1954), *History of the Peloponnesian War*, trans. Rex Warner (Harmondsworth, Penguin)

Turner, Leigh (2024), *Lessons in Diplomacy: Politics, Power and Parties* (Bristol, Polity Press)

United Nations (2024), 'Growth in UN Membership', https://www.un.org/en/about-us/growth-in-un-membership (accessed 20 Oct. 2024)

Van Middelaar, Luuk (2013), *The Passage to Europe: How a Continent Became a Union* (New Haven, Yale University Press)

Weiss, Thomas G. and Dawes, Sam (2020), *The Oxford Handbook of the United Nations* (2nd ed.; Oxford, Oxford University Press)

West, Nigel (2009), *Historical Dictionary of Sexpionage* (Lanham, MD, Scarecrow Press)

Westcott, Nicholas (2008), *Digital Diplomacy: the Impact of the Internet on International Relations*, Oxford Internet Institute, Research Report 16, https://www.oii.ox.ac.uk/wp-content/uploads/old-docs/RR16.pdf (accessed 1 Oct. 2024)

Westmacott, Peter (2021), *They Call it Diplomacy: Forty Years of Representing Britain Abroad* (New York, Apollo)

Widyono, Benny (2007), *Dancing in Shadow: Sihanouk, the Khmer Rouge and the United Nations in Cambodia* (New York, Rowman & Littlefield), https://www.un.org/en/chronicle/article/spectre-khmer-rouge-over-cambodia (accessed 3 July 2024)

Wilson, Godfrey and Wilson, Monica (1945), *The Analysis of Social Change* (Cambridge, Cambridge University Press)

Wintour, Patrick (2020), 'Man Arrested over Leak of Kim Darroch Cables Criticising Trump', *The Guardian*, 18 Oct. 2020, https://www.theguardian.com/politics/2020/oct/18/man-arrested-over-leak-of-kim-darroch-cables-criticising-trump (accessed 22 March 2025)

Xiaolin, Duan and Yitong, Liu (2023), 'The Rise and Fall of China's Wolf Warrior Diplomacy,' *The Diplomat*, 22 Sept. 2023, https://thediplomat.com/2023/09/the-rise-and-fall-of-chinas-wolf-warrior-diplomacy/ (accessed 14 Oct. 2024)

Zarakol, Ayse (2022), *Before the West: The Rise and Fall of Eastern World Orders* (Cambridge, Cambridge University Press)

Index

For Product Safety Concerns and Information please contact our EU
representative GPSR@taylorandfrancis.com
Taylor & Francis Verlag GmbH, Kaufingerstraße 24, 80331 München, Germany

www.ingramcontent.com/pod-product-compliance
Lightning Source LLC
Chambersburg PA
CBHW070331270326
41926CB00017B/3837